FINE DINING MADNESS

FINE DINING MADNESS

The rules & realities of fine dining

◆

BY JOHN GALLOWAY

IUNIVERSE, INC.

NEW YORK   LINCOLN   SHANGHAI

FINE DINING MADNESS
The rules & realities of fine dining

Copyright © 2005, 2006 by John Galloway

iUniverse books may be ordered through booksellers or by contacting:

iUniverse
2021 Pine Lake Road, Suite 100
Lincoln, NE 68512
www.iuniverse.com
1-800-Authors (1-800-288-4677)

ISBN-13: 978-0-595-33777-4 (pbk)
ISBN-13: 978-0-595-67006-2 (cloth)
ISBN-13: 978-0-595-78568-1 (ebk)
ISBN-10: 0-595-33777-5 (pbk)
ISBN-10: 0-595-67006-7 (cloth)
ISBN-10: 0-595-78568-9 (ebk)

Printed in the United States of America

All of the 2005 royalties for
this book were donated to
Hurricane Katrina relief efforts.

Much Acclaim for FINE DINING MADNESS:

"Hilarious, fascinating, and above all, realistic!"
Pierre Wolfe, host of "America's Dining Guide" (national)
and "The Good Life" (regional) KCRN, Denver

"A fire hose jolt of furious humor!"
Bob Lape, WCBS 880, New York

"One of the best books I've read in years."
Pat Whitley, WRKO, Boston

"Galloway's humor, wit and experiences are a shining light to great meals. FDM is much more than just sound restaurant advice, it's a fabulous read!"
Celebrity Chef Jamie Gwen, host of "The Chef Jamie Radio Show"
Talk Radio 790 KABC, Los Angeles
www.chefjamie.com

"MADNESS is The indispensable dining guide."
BookViews

"Humorous and scandalous at the same time. FDM is a definite read for anyone who eats out."
Prudence Sloane, TV and radio food show host

"Savagely Funny!"
The Louisville Courier Journal

"FINE DINING MADNESS is a triumph in nonfiction!"
The Anchor

"Pure Gold!"
Call Back Magazine

"FINE DINING MADNESS leaves you fighting mad but well-informed. Here's a chance to redeem ourselves for our culinary sins, and walk away laughing."
Rachel & David Cane, hosts of "A Matter of Taste"
Talk 910, KNEW, San Francisco

"Galloway's MADNESS is a literary work of art."
The Ivy League Review

More Accolades for **FINE DINING MADNESS:**

*"An absolutely brilliant window into the
other side of the dining experience."*
Kristi Ahlers
Amazon Top 150 Reviewer and Contributing Author
of *'No Laws Against Love'* Anthology

"Fine Dining Madness is Divine Dining Comedy."
Tanya Kieron, Rhode Island Review

*"John Galloway is not only a gifted writer,
but a great American patriot as well."*
Helen von Erck, author of *"The Warmth of a Song"*

"Galloway Scores with MADNESS!"
ESPN Hollywood

"Very funny, and yet at times, deeply moving."
Charles Ashbacher
Amazon Top 50 Reviewer

*"In Fine Dining Madness, John Galloway opens every window
and door to worlds long hidden from the sun."*
Jack O'Neill, Author of
"ECHELON, Somebody's Listening"

"FDM is always amusing, and often unsettling."
The Staten Island Informer

*"A delightful perspective into, not only the life behind fine dining,
but also the life through the eyes of every hard working American."*
Vosta Michele, Author of
"Tangled Webs of Desire"

*"FINE DINING MADNESS is a very funny book,
and thank God for that, or we'd all be in tears."*
Laura McClendon, Author of
"Too Many Secrets"

2005 Reader's Choice Award Winner

The Tribute Flight is coming.
A flight for 77 days, to all 50 states
Flying to every city and town
Where our lost soldiers come from
In a specially modified aircraft
With the names of the fallen
Painted on the wings and fuselage
Those killed in Afghanistan and Iraq
Both Coalition and American
With proceeds going to a survivor's fund
And to those disabled defending America.
Call Sign: TANGO FOXTROT SEVEN SEVEN

When the troop ship sails its compass to war
The sum that returns will be less than before
And many who come home will not be whole
But it's not a question of if we should fight
Still it's hard to press on when they're gone from our sight
So look to the sky where the Tribute flies
Enshrine with your heart, and know they're close by
And call to your soldier from that sea of despair
"I'll see you in time, I'll see you upstairs"
There's a table waiting, and for all there are chairs
I can hardly wait, 'til I see you upstairs.

From the Song *"See You Upstairs"*
Written by John Galloway
Tribute Flight President
A Flight to Remember.
TF77

www.TributeFlight.com

Dedication

This book is dedicated to the following five very special and extraordinary people:

My father, John Allison Galloway, M.D., a brilliant doctor, Korean War combat veteran, scholar, mentor, my best friend, and finest of honorable gentlemen.

My mother, Shirlee Delpiaz Galloway, artist, architect, nurse, school founder, and most loving mother. All you did was give. You are the reason why there is compassion in my heart and creative thought in my mind.

My older sister, Elizabeth Galloway Burris, who always gave more than she took, or had. You were everyone's rock to lean on, the heart and soul of two families.

To Elizabeth Robertson Delpiaz, my maternal grandmother, who proved that the most frail can often be the strongest. You endured more heartache and adversity than anyone should ever have to, and still pressed on with a kind heart and gentle soul. I think of you every day and miss our times together in Delaware.

And to Joni Johnson, whose artwork and poetry will not let us forget the people we loved.

"There is no great genius without some touch of **MADNESS**."

Lucius Annaeus Seneca

(4BC—65AD)

The Chapter Menu:

www.finediningmadness.com

SHOUT

SHOUT

LET IT ALL OUT

THESE ARE THE THINGS I CAN DO WITHOUT

COME ON

I'M TALKING TO YOU

COME ON

Tears For Fears, "Shout," *Songs From The Big Chair*,
Mercury Records Ltd. (London), 1984

A —ALPHA	N —NOVEMBER
B —BRAVO	O —OSCAR
C —CHARLIE	P —PAPA
D —DELTA	Q —QUEBEC
E —ECHO	R —ROMEO
F —FOXTROT	S —SIERRA
G —GOLF[†]	T —TANGO
H —HOTEL	U —UNIFORM
I —INDIA	V —VICTOR
J —JULIET[†]	W—WHISKEY
K —KILO	X —X-RAY
L —LEEMA	Y —YANKEE
M —MIKE[†]	Z —ZULU

[†]The author of this book recommends the FAA officially change the phonetic alphabet for the following 3 letters: *Golf* to **GEORGIA** (in homage to Ray Charles), *Juliet* to **JAVELIN**, and *Mike* to **MARLIN**.

Chapter 1

These Are the Soul Cages[†]
(invisible sharks)

"In winter 1963
It felt like the world would freeze
With John F. Kennedy
And the Beatles."

Dream Academy, "Life in a Northern Town,"
The Dream Academy, Warner Bros., 1985

Exile, not aspiration, is the force that pulls an individual into fine dining service. Something went wrong along the way, a bump in the road that flipped the apple cart, leaving all those study hall dreams and notebook doodles unrealized. People, however misguided, aspire to be chefs, sommeliers, or restaurant owners, but in today's society, young men and women don't grow up wanting to be food servers and bartenders. The bump could have been any of a million different scenarios that left you holding the spoon—a chaotic home life and tumultuous adolescence, a lack of money to finish college, compulsive and/or chemical addictions, a terminally ill parent or relative, or maybe a midlife divorce and a deadbeat ex who would take jail time over making child support payments. Like a snowflake, every bump is unique, but when the thaw hits, all the snowflakes melt into a nameless puddle, the collective drops that are the people of the service industry. As for this writer's exile, it was the failure to become a naval aviator, a restless, gregarious personality, and a youth spent working in private club kitchens.

[†]A quote from the title track of *The Soul Cages*, by Sting, arguably one of the greatest albums of all time. Produced by Hugh Padgham and Gordon Matthew Sumner, A&M Records, Inc. 1991.

The initial hand dealt to me was a fine one. Born the year Kennedy was assassinated, on the same winter day as George Washington, I was a purebred WASP with a strong Scottish pedigree, the third ragamuffin of four. My father was a successful physician who monitored the treatment of diabetes for a major pharmaceutical company. My mother was an architect and founder of a private school. Together we were the stereotypical upper-middle-class family, traveling whenever possible and living in an enormous house in Carmel, the elite bedroom community of Indianapolis, that my mother had designed. We even had the German shepherd (Queenie) and annoyed cat (Bitty, the inner-city kitty) to make the picture complete. But the sea never stays calm for long and happiness turned to anguish in 1975 when my mother died at the age of thirty-seven, a sucker punch from God. I was twelve and devastated, overwrought with pain and emotional emptiness. Though he was grieving himself, Dad stayed strong, and with the help of my older sister Elizabeth, the Galloway clan pressed on as best we could despite having lost someone so vital to us.

In 1977, at the age of fourteen, I took my first job as a kitchen apprentice at Cedar Forest Country Club, thinking a career as a restaurateur might suit me somewhere up the line. With the exception of two European chefs, I was the only Caucasian on an otherwise all African-American staff. Despite no common ground in socialization or demographic profile, I was accepted by my coworkers and began learning the ropes of a commercial fine dining kitchen. The common fibers of all the ropes were grueling hard work, and the new white boy on the staff whose daddy was a doctor would not be spared from the hardest travail the kitchen had to offer. On the contrary, I was first pick for all the unpleasant, labor-intensive tasks. Whether it was scrubbing thousands of pots and pans, dragging tons of garbage to the dumpsters, deveining shrimp for hours on end, or whipping gallons of Hollandaise sauce over a sweltering steam table until my arm muscles ached, the cracker kid always got the call. Though exhausting, my education was achieved in

the culinary trenches, majoring in Gourmet Food with minors
in Practical Sociology and R&B Music.

At seventeen I moved away from home to Ohio, working
and living at the Uptown Club in Cincinnati to continue
my hospitality education. The Uptown Club was a private
hotel and I finished my senior year at a local inner city high
school while working nights as a sauté cook, bunking in one
of the club's less desirable rooms. The job and board were
offered to me by a management acquaintance made at Cedar
Forest. The work was arduous and my mother's death still
lay heavy on my heart, but such were the trials of life. During
my tenure at the Uptown, it became very clear that fine
dining was a world I wanted no part of. My new dream was
to be a naval aviator, catapulting off carriers and shooting
down Soviet hardware. Such visions had honor and self-
respect, concepts unrecognized in places where alcoholism,
drug abuse, and gluttony reigned supreme.

Purdue University was next. In order to be a military
flyer, one needed a college education, but the odds of
becoming a naval aviator weren't in my favor. I didn't have
the scholastic profile the Navy wanted, in high school or in
college. The Navy desired a high academic standing, athletic
team player, with social and political campus involvement—
the "picket fence," as it was referred to, with ratings of "1"
in every recruitment category. I didn't have any of that, not
even close. I was a fair student at best and worked nights
waiting tables to help pay for school. Predictably, my application to Naval AOCS was shot down like an intrusive MIG
Foxbat in rapid fashion.

After graduating from Purdue, I moved to Washington,
D.C. and continued trying to get into any military flight
program, with no success. Having descended from a long line
of successful men and distinguished war heroes, the dejection
and sense of dishonor felt in not becoming a valiant military
officer was overwhelming. My spirits ran aground on the
ocean floor when my sister Elizabeth died of leukemia in
October of 1987. She was just twenty-seven and had given

birth to a son only seven months earlier. She was gone ten weeks after diagnosis. Liz was everyone's best friend, especially mine, and had always looked out for me. Now she was gone, just like Mom. I withdrew into a dark world of despair, feeling as though an invisible shark had taken a bite out of my side and swum away.

Nothing was right in my life and the two people most important to me were gone. I thought if God needed to snatch people up before they'd had an opportunity to live, he should have taken me, not my mother or sister. But the Almighty doesn't take suggestions, answer phone calls, invite criticism, or rewrite fate because someone is hurting. Pain is pain, and my emotional pain brought me to the edge of suicide, rejected only by the fear of causing my father more grief than he had already endured. Also, I could best honor the memory of my sister by being there for her son.

Often people end up in jobs that seem devoid of integrity. This was my unwavering opinion about upscale clubs and restaurants in general. Most fine dining restaurants have several common and decidedly negative characteristics—alcoholism, drug consumption, and nicotine addiction topping the list. Infidelity is rampant, a precursor to the alarming divorce rate if not already spawned by the grueling, unorthodox work hours. Employee theft is prevalent as are criminal amounts of waste, be it time, potential, or tangible assets. You will always find some degree of nepotism, most often in the alien ranks.

Every restaurant has the same employees, only with different names and faces. Old crows who abandoned their white collar hopes, struggling teachers working nights to make ends meet, tattooed line cooks with cracked moral compasses, and managers trying to keep order amidst the pandemonium. There are the dishwashers who work so hard for so little yet are the most contented of the staff, and the drug purveyors who sold their souls three decades ago. There are agitated bookkeepers that haven't smiled in years and owners whose passion or apathy will determine if they succeed or go bankrupt and die penniless. Finally are the chefs who are repellent and clinically insane from stress.

Fine dining wasn't a world I wanted a part of, but like Big Unit throwing left-side heat or Phil Collins singing about heartache, restaurant work was something I did well. But I didn't want to believe that a life of serving food was my raison d'être. Earning my wings at the expense of the Navy wouldn't happen, but my wings could still be earned. Money was the key to getting into flight school and because I had a great need for cash and only debts from college, I continued waiting tables. This time I worked at Charles Street Chop House in Alexandria. CSCH was a casual eatery and tavern in Old Town with a predictable flock of loyal regulars who would dine there a few times a week.

After two years of fine-tuning my service skills at CSCH, I set my sights a little higher and went for the big money, dashing north across the Potomac to the Coventry on Pennsylvania Avenue. At the time, it was the best restaurant in D.C. A stone's throw from the White House, the Coventry was extravagant, expensive, and overwhelming, boasting one of the most talented executive chefs in America, Zach Cavanaugh. Zach was an eccentric perfectionist, more intense than a firestorm on Venus and obsessive-compulsive about restaurant sanitation, a rare and fine quality in a chef.

Serving at the Coventry required simultaneous mental organization and physical quickness as well as a tolerance for the tremendous homosexual undertow that was pervasive at both staff and management levels. The queens, two-thirds of the waitstaff and three-thirds of the maître d's, ruled the roost while earning the top money, prancing about as if their place of employment was some Greenwich Village fraternity. Sadly that frat lost its charter when nine of its members died of AIDS between 1988 and 1996. The Coventry also lost a heterosexual female to AIDS, acquired from her heroin-addicted husband.

Though waiting tables at the Coventry meant perpetual fatigue, the educational process was also incessant. I served celebrities and political powerhouses of all kinds while learning more about fine wine and food than I ever imagined. But with my knees aching from working double shifts on marble floors and my psyche tormented by the rear echelon swashbucklers, a change of venue seemed due. After three years of high-strung service at the Coventry, I defected with seven other Coventry tribesmen, heading a mile west to King Lear on J street.

Whether you were a customer or waiter, King Lear was the hottest ticket in D.C., the best place to serve and be served. There were more perks, more business, more money. King Lear was different from the Coventry in every way. The Coventry was Democratic, Victorian, quiet, bright, and delicate with artful food arranged like puzzles served by a dainty gang of effeminate runway model rejects. King Lear was Republican, Manhattanish, powerful, and loud with gargantuan drinks, lobsters the size of kindergartners, and servings of beef large enough to feed East Timor with a single slab. King Lear was owned by Clay and Constantine Papandreas, two of the most talented restaurateurs in hospitality history. Like capturing lightning in a bottle, they had built and perfected D.C.'s premier power steak house, fine-tuning the magic that cast its spell on Washington's parched and famished. Being hired by the Papandreas brothers wasn't easy, requiring five interviews over a six-month stretch. Getting the nod was like being called up from Triple A to pitch in the Majors. King Lear was the top contender in the elite world of the eastern seaboard's exclusive restaurants, and I was excited just to make the team.

My tenure at King Lear lasted almost seven years until I had enough money to begin commercial flight school in Vero Beach, Florida. To combat the endless expenses of flight training, I used my waiting talents and joined up with another fine dining restaurant, Augustine's in West Palm Beach. I had no intention of waiting tables at Augustine's for any extended period of time, but the job helped fulfill my immediate monetary needs. This time the approach was different. Unlike going in wide-eyed, hoping for a job as I did at the Coventry and King Lear, I knew immediately I could get a position serving at Augustine's.

After reviewing my curriculum vitae, Augustine's owner hired me without an interview. He often said that he felt lucky to have me on his waitstaff, fine praise from a man who lived in southern Florida's finer eateries when not running his own. The commute from Vero Beach to West Palm four days a week was exhausting; however, the income justified the travel. The ops manager at Augustine's was Silas Fontenot, a tremendous academician and marathon runner. Silas was the kind of person you would want in any organization, working harder than an Iraqi coffin maker and cooler under fire than Robert Duvall in *Apocalypse Now*. Silas was one of the best managers I had ever worked with, staunch in his insistence that I write this book. My father, who by no coincidence answers to my name, was the primary catalyst.

In the summer of 1999, I left Florida and moved to Las Vegas to work as a flight instructor and to compile this book. In doing so, I took my final waiting position with power-house and King Lear competitor Romeo Charlie's Steak House. Romeo Charlie's was a tried and true professional restaurant in every respect, yet still affected by the difficulties inherent in any modern upscale eatery. From a waiter's standpoint, Romeo Charlie's was much like King Lear, offering outstanding products in an exclusive atmosphere. As a server, with a little luck, you could stay ahead of the curve, making good money without too much pain when push came to shove. At the Coventry and Augustine's, chaos ruled. If you wanted to make any respectable cash, you would be hurting after the battle, drunk or worse before the cease-fire. I will qualify this statement as it relates to Augustine's. Since I was deemed one of the more capable waiters, I was responsible for a higher percentage of the customer count during the evening rush. Service at the Coventry left me pondering arson and hungry for a fistful of barbiturates.

In Las Vegas, the cost of living may appear to be low, but that's only from a detached economic perspective. For many hospitality workers, residing in the Silver State adds yet another vile toxin to the overly-potent hypodermic needle of lifestyle dysfunction. If the trick bag of long hours, physical trauma, mental duress, infidelity, alcohol/drug addiction weren't already enough to leave you discontented and licenseless, the sweet beckon to gamble waits ready to divide and conquer your life. Pick a side and double your money—it's that easy. And once bitten by the gambling bug, devastation's rusty wrecking ball (the pendulum of pandemonium) forever swings outside your window, that is, if eviction or foreclosure even allows you to have a window. And like all addictions and peripheral damage, the family members of bettors are the ones who pay the hard toll for a compulsive gambler's sins. The sons and daughters of incessant gamblers won't ever attend college, receive a slightly-used economy car for high school graduation, or recall a lavish wedding, lest they pay for the aforementioned themselves. Pathological gambling is the grinch that will steal *every* Christmas. Lies and a severe lack of personal accountability are the cornerstones of a loose cannon wagerwhore's existence, and the repudiated truth is that it's all just whiskey tango (wasted time). So listen, Pathy Gambi, when they say, the best throw of the dice, is to throw them away. In Las Vegas, the cost of living can be astronomical. Sometimes even fatal.

And let us not forget that wonderful phrase, *"What happens in Vegas stays in Vegas."* Never have a mere seven words conveyed so much fumacious bullshit. What happens in Sinatra City stays in Elvisville, but only until the frat-braggings, email gossip, and cell phone pictures make the rounds. Then the sub-zero bank statement arrives, along with the hotel room damage charges and threat letter. Your tox screen comes back kaleidoscope positive, and the itching won't stop from your afternoons at Areola 51 (between Raw Heidi {a German-Western bar, home of the livestock-free rodeo} and the China Vagina Massage Parlor, behind Club Man Date, on Clap Street). Your speeding ticket and illegal u-turn citation never had a chance of staying in Vegas and the back-home bookmaker is eager to collect the entire of your retirement savings, a sure-lock lost when Duke choked against LSU. You tried to double-or-nothing the deficit with UConn on the money line versus tiny team George Mason, but Denham Brown's OT three didn't sink, which meant Jon Pawn Jovi's would be keeping your pawnbrokered wedding band. Your heartbroken wife believed the "ring was lost at the wave pool" lie, but doubts that the club you frequented, The Cock Pit, was indeed a pole-less aviation-themed bar, devoid of naked, aggressive, contortionistic, jungle-sex-hungry women for hire. You were impersonating Gene Simmons when you chipped that bicuspid at the karaoke bar, pretending the Corona bottle was a microphone, and you've been walking real funny ever since you passed out in Siegfried & Roy's Secret Garden. Those chino-tearing extra 15 pounds of gutmush will only stay in Vegas so long as you do, and what were you thinking flipping-off that Asian gang? Of course there's the bent-framed rental car return drama, an unfortunate consequence from your off-roading shenanigans. And finally, there was that Boeing 737 mess that had the folks at Southwest (Hee-Haw Airlines) up in arms and fellow exit rowers screaming. How were you supposed to know there's a bag for such things? And damn it, that didn't even happen here in Dice Town, you were flying over Utah somewhere. If what happens in Vegas stays in Vegas, it's only for a nanosecond, though still, a fine time was had by all.

This book is the sum of my more memorable restaurant experiences, recollections of people, and a few indispensable rules to dine by. This is the tale of a journey, and a hard look at modern day commerce, chemical addiction, and human behavior. In recalling the people and recounting the stories, I mean no injury or slander against anyone. I also harbor no ill will against anyone of any racial, ethnic, or political group and any comments, observations, or conclusions made should in no way be construed as a lack of respect. Some of the names of people and places have been changed to provide anonymity. Characteristics of a few of the participants in the events described in this book have been embellished, mixed and mismatched as to not represent any actual people. However, the events, crimes, and quantities consumed are all true. Please note that the use of the word "waiter" in this book is not intended to indicate gender, nor should it ever.

THE TOP NIGHTCLUBS IN LAS VEGAS:

THE VATICAN *("Honey, I'm going to The Vatican")*

THE PEPPERMINT HIPPO

INFECTION *(Order the lobster and still get crabs)*

THE BLUE PACKAGE

HO' TELL *(Formerly Whoreshack's)*

ETABRUTSAM

MANHUNT *(Home of the Liberace Experience)*

BITCHNUTS

UGLY STICK *(Next to Good Vibrations: toys for single women)*

BUSH COUNTRY

THE POWDER ROOM *(Tell' em Kate Moss sent you)*

THE POLLUTED WOMB

HOT SPOONS *(Where Colombians drink free)*

GUY SAVVY *(Not affliated with Guy "Gi!" Savoy)*

THE WET SPOT

TANG *(Behind Joy Stick Vibrator Warehouse)*

PENIS DI MILO

BLUE DEVILS *(Try the Kidney Punch)*

VAGINA CITY *(The future name of Pahrump)*

Chapter 2

The Phone Call

(Amateur Night)

"...that's what I'd say
I'd tell you everything
If you'd pick up that telephone."

Electric Light Orchestra, "Telephone Line"
A New World Record, Sony, 1976

Deciding to dine at a fine restaurant is the first move, making a reservation is the second. At most upscale restaurants, reservations are recommended if not required. If this is your initial contact with a restaurant, it is a sterling opportunity to display your stupidity and utter lack of common sense. For those taking the call, brace yourself to be angered. Maybe pound a double George Dickel neat behind a trio of diazepam. You'll need it.

Since I spent my afternoons sober and wasn't a wide-eyed strip club devotee, I was often relegated to phone duty at King Lear, an obligatory function for captains, maître d's, and managers. At King Lear, the phone lackey was known as the "answerbitch." Included in this book are the proper rules of restaurant engagement, starting with the telephone call, so take heed.

Rule number one when calling a restaurant is never call during crunch times, noon to 2 p.m. and 7 to 9 p.m. The restaurant doesn't care about how many meetings you have or the fact that you made partner at your law firm when you were eleven. If you were that smart, you would know when to call a restaurant, which is 10 a.m. to noon and 2 to 5 p.m. That gives you five hours to make a ninety-second phone call.

The worst offenders of crunch time calling are senior citizens who have been up since 4 a.m. and planned their day around calling a power restaurant during critical mass. To them we'll grant a pardon—but you should know better. Calling a restaurant very late or very early is also a bad idea. Should you call at reveille, the cooks are groggy, hungover, disoriented, and trying to get the kitchen set up for lunch. The kitchen is jammed with delivery personnel and their wares. Odds are that the cooks have no idea where the reservation book is in the unlikely event they speak enough English to allow for an exchange. The accountant is inundated with error-riddled waiters' checks and credit card slips from the previous night, a mound of nonsensical numbers and scribblings that will take her half the day and two packs of Virginia Slims to correct. When calling a restaurant late at night, the phone may not be picked up right away because the staff knows the call is unrelated to that night's service and personal profit, making your call even less of a priority. The staff is already buzzed and the maître d' is fending off a dozen impatient waiters, eager to check out and rendezvous with a woman, a bottle, or ideally, a woman with a bottle. Just be one of the smart ones and be a non-crunch caller.

I hate to quote the Rolling Stones, but I must. *"You can't always get what you want."* Profound lyrics as they pertain to the hopeful restaurant patron/answerbitch relationship. When prospective clientele don't get the specific reservation they desire, those rejected follow a pattern similar to that of someone suffering from a terminal illness. First there is anger when the news is broken.

Maître d': "I'm sorry, Mr. Crunchberry, we have nothing available for you then."

The crushed caller then barks in desperation, hoping the

energy of his pleading might overturn the verdict. The top ten retorts with sarcastic mental garnish going:

1. "You're kidding." *No, I'm not.*
2. "Are you sure?" *Don't I sound sure?*
3. "Do you know who I am?" *Is this the guy who made love to Seattle Slew?*
4. "Aww-Damn it!" *Don't cuss in my ear!*
5. "Look harder." *I'm squinting and I still see nothing.*
6. "I can't believe it." *Take it like a man.*
7. "There must be something." *Try methadone.*
8. "Who is this?" *The guy who knocked up your daughter, twice.*
9. "What will it take to get me in there?" *Any scenario involving Eva Longoria will do it.*
10. (My favorite) "But it's my anniversary tonight!" *Yes, I know how these things creep up with no warning whatsoever.*

Denial then follows. This happens despite there being a greater likelihood of Howard Stern being elected president of the National Organization of Women than the epicurean wannabe getting a table that evening. During the denial phase, the pleading intensity increases from that of angered caller to the rantings similar to those of a baseball manager displeased with the umpire's final judgment on a suicide squeeze. And gentlemen, how do you forget your anniversary? Though it may be difficult to believe, every day thousands of men call restaurants in frantic desperation hours before dinner because they've forgotten their wedding anniversaries. Even if you're a polygamist, there is no excuse for not recalling the dates you were shackled. If you can't remember dates well, get a tattoo or do what a lot of uncreative trash does and get married on Valentine's Day. You can even go one further and hunt down a bride (or groom) who was born on February 14th, killing three birds with one stone.

Boys, take your pride up a notch. On the rare occasions you do harbor foresight, plan earlier. As a rule, book at least a month ahead when making reservations for New Year's, Valentine's, proms for the high schoolers, and GED dinners for Mississippians. Any restaurant worth going to will be booked solid several weeks ahead.

But there are always last minute pleaders, blabbing away, yakking and wasting time. Your time may be free but the clock is ticking for the restaurant. Benjamin Franklin's second virtue is *"Silence, speak not but what may benefit others or yourself. Avoid trifling conversation."* Listen to Frankie, he knew, even before telephones were invented. When speaking to a restaurant, use an economy of words. The maître d' is juggling at least three phone lines and hasn't a second to spare. If you want to get disconnected, try putting the maître d' on hold. This is a common maneuver executed by executive secretaries that do the dialing for their corpulent puff daddies in the next room. Putting the house on hold kills any chance you had of getting a decent table once you've redialed the restaurant. Equal in transgression is putting the maître d' on speaker phone. Hold the receiver to your face or don't make the call. Putting the house on the speaker of your car phone is the bottom of the chum bucket. It is the absolute worst move you can make. It doesn't take two hands to drive your never-been-off-road Hummer and the maître d' will not listen to the static as you fade in and out while driving under bridges and past airports. Just park the car and make the call or stay home and spare the restaurant the agony of your presence. Echoing back to a third party is also a telephone felony. The maître d' doesn't want to hear you repeat what he just said to someone else.

Name-dropping is another chump move in restaurant phone negotiation. While people think that saying they know the owners, blurting out the name of a star regular, or insisting they're tight with Joey Buttafuoco will earn them preferential treatment when the inn is full, it does just the opposite. Name-droppers tend to be lying, cheap bastards, always in need of extra attention, and dragging down the level of service for the entire restaurant. Their names are circled in red hot, indelible ink. Don't drop names, claim fame, or make future tense promises to restaurant veterans. A bird can cough up a word, but a bird also never shuts up, and fills its cage full of shit. Restaurant people view name-droppers the very same way. We know who's important, who's not, and who the problem children will be. The quiet ones are the champions. Trust me.

The only prayer of getting a table in a thundering power restaurant without notice requires two things. First, that you are a regular customer. This means you dine there at least four or five times a year and your visage is remembered by some of the staff. Second, that on your previous visits you treated the house well. This is more than blue ribbon tipping. Were you punctual? Did you leave your table after a reasonable amount of time? Were you courteous to the staff? And finally, did you ever not show up for a reservation and fail to call and cancel? If so, your name is Dr. Samuel Mudd and you're destined for Jack in the Box.[†]

Last are the multiple bookers. Unlike the man who doesn't know how to plan ahead, the multiple bookers make reservations everywhere for the same evening, then dine at the establishment their guests most prefer. They often use false names, give wrong numbers for confirmation, then call to confirm the reservations before the restaurants call them. The culprits are, for the most part, desperate housewives with no regard for a restaurant's revenue, only the need to be perceived as a perfect hostess. The closest thing they've ever done to restaurant work was placing the room service breakfast tray outside the hotel room door. You can thank such people for reservation deposit fees, increased prices, and restaurants intentionally over-booking to compensate for no-shows. Maître d's have several effective countermeasures to combat multiple bookers. Caller ID, a black list, a blackjack, networking with other maître d's, and a good memory top the list. King Lear often caught repeat multiple bookers who had elected to honor a reservation, though we maintained our poker faces. We just kept the party waiting at the bar, on and on, until in a fit of rage they would storm out and drive away, gastronomically unfulfilled.

[†] On April 15th, 1865, Dr. Samuel Mudd set the broken leg of President Lincoln's assassin, John Wilkes Booth. Dr. Mudd was found guilty of complicity and sentenced to hard labor for life. His actions were the origin of the expression "...or your name is Mudd."

The Rules Reiterated
Subjects: Getting a preferred table, calling protocol, and reservations.

1. **Case The Joint**, or call it a scout trip. Forget about calling, actually go to your desired restaurant. Have a drink or a solo meal and look around. And since everyone has a different idea of what a great table is, first you must determine your own criteria for an optimum table and take it from there. Once in the restaurant, ask a staff member what he or she feels is a good table. Then find out the number of the table that works best for you. But let us not overrate table selection. You dine out for the food, the service, the ambiance, and hopefully, to savor the company of those with whom you dine. *Note: If you think a restaurant might be too pricey for your budget, case the place online or at the very least, ask them to fax you their wine list and menus.*

2. **Don't Call During The Crunch!** Don't even think it. Call 10 a.m. to noon, 2 to 5 p.m. Remember, if you nag the surgical team during peak operational hours, don't cry when you get stabbed in the face with a hemostat.

3. **Don't Name Drop.** Remember the story about a bird, a word, and a whole lotta shit. That's you when you name drop. No one cares who you know. Remember, to the staff it's just whiskey tango.

At one infamous D.C. restaurant, the owner had died and even years after his passing, people would still come in and drop his name. "Hi, we're the Geranium party. We don't have a reservation but we're dear friends of Rolo. Is he here tonight? "Well, possibly in a metaphysical way, yes. He died in 1998." "What! Are you sure?" "Well, we poked him with a stick and the coroner seemed convinced, but I suppose it's possible we buried the poor guy alive."

4. **Plan Ahead.** New Year's, Valentine's, anniversaries, and

birthdays tend to hold stationary positions on the calendar. Do you follow? Is all that sarcasm wasted on you? At the very least, book those reservations as if you were buying an airline ticket. Also, it's okay to celebrate a special occasion a few days before or a few days after the exact date. If someone's birthday or Valentine's day falls mid-week, go plus or minus a few days on that special dinner so you can really celebrate properly.

Ask any service vet and they'll tell you that New Year's Eve and Valentine's are extremely bad value times at restaurants, known as **amateur nights** in hospitality vernacular. Over-cologned customers are Haitianed into dining rooms like lettuce pickers piled on a Clampett jalopy. It's murder by numbers, when your restaurant dollar is at its very weakest. You'd do far better by spending that money on room service at a scenic resort, getting exfoliated and massaged at a luxury spa, or sending the kids to pappaw's and having a gourmet feast and wine tasting at home.

5. **Remember The Call Taker's Name.** When they do you proud, forward them a five spot and you'll be square in the middle of the fairway for your next swing on another evening.

6. **Save Those Minutes And Book Your Rezzies Online.** Or simply use that **OnStar** technology.

7. **Having A Reservation Is A Guarantee Of Nothing.** Just ask the Nez Perce Tribal Nation about that.†

8. **NEVER Make A Reservation At Closing Time.** You'll be both despised and rushed by the staff. *"Ready to order? Ready to Order? How's your meal? Are you finished? Are you finished? Are you finished? No dessert or coffee oh too bad here's your check!"*

---

† The United States' failure to honor the 7.5 million acres of reservation lands guaranteed to the Nez Perce Indians in the Treaty of 1855 led to the 1877 Nez Perce War. The U.S. Army pursued the Nez Perce over 1,500 miles to northern Montana at the Canadian border. It was there the exasperated leader of the Nez Perce Tribe, Chief Joseph, surrendered, saying *"I am tired; my heart is sick and sad. From where the sun now stands, I will fight no more forever."* The Treaty of 1863 reduced the Nez Perce lands to one-tenth its original size. The Dawes Act of 1893 made even further land reductions, leaving the Nez Perce with a sum of noncontiguous lots totaling only less than 10,000 acres.

NOTE: THE AUTHOR OF THIS BOOK HAS PATENTED THE PHRASE <u>NOWAR ZONE</u>, WHICH IS AN ACRONYM FOR NO WIRELESS ACCESS OR RECEPTION. <u>NOWAR ZONE</u> IS ALSO A DOUBLE HOMONYM. IT SOUNDS LIKE NO WAR, AND IS PRONOUNCED LIKE "NOIR" THE FRENCH WORD FOR BLACK.

A <u>NOWAR ZONE</u> IS ANY PLACE THAT HAS INSTALLED A SIGNAL SCRAMBLER TO JAM WIRELESS RECEPTION, SUCH AS MOVIE THEATERS, CHURCHES, MORTUARIES, CONCERT HALLS AND THEATERS, AND OF COURSE, RESTAURANTS. SO WHEN LOOKING TO BOOK AN IMPORTANT RESERVATION, SEE IF THAT RESTAURANT IS A <u>NOWAR ZONE</u>.

Chapter 3

Sins of the Service Wreckers
(Step away from the bread)

"Who's gonna tell you when it's too late?
Who's gonna tell you things aren't so great?
You can't go on thinking nothing's wrong.
Who's gonna drive you home, tonight?"

The Cars, "Drive," *Heartbeat City*,
Elektra/Asylum, 1984
(Benjamin Orzechowski, 1947-2000)

From the root to the fruit, dining out avails you countless ways to infuriate the staff of the restaurant at which you are eating. Why would you want to do such a thing? Do you really want your image burned in effigy by the waiters? Surely not, so listen well. Contrary to common lore, the customer is not always right; we just say you're right to get you to shut up. In some cases, the customer is the enemy whose abhorrent rantings are why he was just served an entree that fell on the kitchen floor. But the ephemeral relationship of the customer and restaurant can best be likened to that of a tree and an arborist. We'd love to see you grow and flourish given the proper care, but some trees just have to be chopped down and ground into mulch. This doesn't have to be you.

This chapter is a short course in etiquette and proper restaurant behavior as deemed proper by those who serve you. It is an imaginary night on the town. Also included are a few consumer hints to maximize the bang of your buck. Presuming you've made reservations at some place not endorsed by a sports figure, not proximate to a mall, and that doesn't sell advertising space on their menus, you're on your way.

Punctual Arrival

Get there on time. Perhaps you think this is an obvious point, but it's the simple things in life that trip people up. A restaurant, like an airline, runs on a set schedule. When your flight departure is delayed or cancelled, you simply grunt and swagger over to Starbucks. But when a restaurant is late in getting you seated, you are incensed and feel betrayed. Why are restaurants held to a higher standard than the airlines?

The primary reason a restaurant runs late in honoring reservations is due to other patrons who were late for their reservations on earlier tables, if they posted at all. Slow moving diners also delay the crusade. So be punctual. And any person living in any city with more than three area codes knows that traffic delays can slow even the most determined driver, so factor that into your equation as well. Pad your time and if you're late, chuck the maître d' a ten and trot to the bar. Don't waste time (whiskey tango) crying to the maître d' with your excuses. Never say to a maître d' that you were promised an immediate table or guaranteed no waiting. He knows you're a lying sack of gravel. There is only one promise in fine dining: that is the promise of no promises. The only guarantee is for pain and doubt. For those who never want to wait for a table, dine early. You'll be home in time for *Celebrity Justice*. Note: Celebrity Justice is an oxymoron. It's like saying "Latin Grammy," "delicious haggis" or "wholesome Vegas girl."

Coat Check

Check your coat. Waiters and busmen loathe those who try to save a dollar or two by not checking their coats and umbrellas. It is also a crystal clear sign of frugality-to-come and immediately takes you out of contention for decent service. Your coat, draped around your chair, is an obstacle and service personnel will go out of their way to step on it if its owner was too cheap to check it. Plus it makes the dining room look like a Salvation Army

showroom. Women who drape their furs over their chairs give
the dining room a Yukon theme the owner never intended. Just
check your coat, or don't wear one.

And for that specific group of California and Florida golden
girls, why are you wearing that fur coat when it's 75 degrees
outside? Yes, the entire restaurant noticed you, but you're also the
joke of the dining room.

Check in with the Maître d'

This seems easy, but can also be quite ugly. The maître d'
refuses to seat your incomplete group and you start to go into
spasms. Don't get that way and don't ever blame a restaurant for
not seating an incomplete party. Many couples book a spacious
four-top and then get a fictitious last minute call from their dining
mates who had to cancel because their wombat had angina. And
then there is the four that might be six. Might means nothing in
the restaurant world. Either your party is complete and there on
time, or not. "Yeah, Jonah said he's calling from inside a whale's
stomach three oceans over, but he might make it." He won't
make it; he never does. If he were going to make it, he'd be there
right now. Invite him over to your house on a later occasion when
you have Tandoori delivered. And when a slow float does show
up late for the parade and the rest of the party is halfway through
the meal, the service of everyone suffers. The waiter will have to
recite the specials again, make an additional trip to the bar, take
a second order, rush it out, and possibly lose a turn on the table
because of the one laggard who's never mastered time
management. Just be there on time or don't make it at all. And
when you're up there pestering the maître d', don't read his notes
on the reservation list. That's personal scripture and you just may
read something you won't like.

Trip to Your Table

You can do this, I know you can. This is when you follow the
maître d' or host to your assigned table. But it's never so simple.
When endeavoring to seat regulars at King Lear, often the patrons
would stop and talk to every chemical-peeled mug they knew,

turning a twenty-second walk into a fifty-meter march through the Iroquois gauntlet of pain. Mercy, please. The maître d' is busier than an Oshkosh air traffic controller and does not have time to stop on your whim and listen to you gush about your trip to Bali. Respect his time constraints, and if you must talk to everyone in the dining room, double-back once you know where your table is, or better yet, have your blabathon in the parking lot.

When you get to your table, spare us the runaway bride eyes and Howard Dean yelp. Your table is your table. The maître d' has evaluated your value to the restaurant and the table you receive is commensurate with your worth. Preferred customers get preferred tables, so use deductive reasoning when questioning why the maître d' just seated you at a grease drum next to the dumpsters. A frequent protest to a table is that it is too loud. What the hell is wrong with you? Asking for a quiet table in a power restaurant that's about to feed three hundred people is like asking for sobriety during spring break in Daytona; it's not going to happen. If you have important business to discuss, do it at the office, and if you and your lover want a quiet meal together, have a picnic on Yucca Mountain.

Sitting Down

Ladies get the view of the room. Gentlemen, if you want the view of the room, don't invite any women, or better yet, dine alone. That's the way it is. If the party is all men, the oldest man gets the view of the room. It's a matter of respect, though it shouldn't matter who sits where anyway, you're there to enjoy the company of your guests, not restlessly look about the dining room all evening. When dining with your mother, grandmother, or aunt, be gallant and pull the woman's chair out. Though if you can't even send your mother or grandmother flowers once a year, pulling a woman's chair out or opening a door will seem analogous to solving differential equations with a rusted abacus.

Once seated, boys, leave your dress coats on. In many upscale restaurants, it's the rule. If you're too hot, the blame is yours. What were you thinking wearing a tweed coat in July? Even the staff at Old Navy is making fun of you right now. When you take your dress coat off in a power restaurant, it's a signal to everyone in the room that you don't belong there, you may still live with your parents, and your car is likely some shade of grape.

Enter the Waiter

When the waiter approaches, shut your cake hole and acknowledge the person. The best way to ensure apathy in service is to ignore your waiter or treat him with the smallest degree of contempt. If you want attentive service, a smile and a salutation to the person about to serve you is a fine start.

King Lear was renowned for its baked, almond-crusted Brie served as an appetizer. Every night, a posse of spoiled patrons would plop down at a table and before one cordial word could be spoken, one or all would bark out "Brie!" Not "Hello, John," or "We would like an order of Brie." Just "Brie!" in the same tone that one might say "fetch" or "mush, dog." Only one word spoken, yet plenty enough negative karma to derail the train for the entire night. Don't play nasty with a professional waiter. He has a black belt in atonement and was pushed to the edge long before he ever walked up to your table.

There are other things you can say to start your evening out on a bad note. The first is "We're in a hurry." Fine dining and haste run in parallel lines; there is no intersection. Either find the time, eat after the show, or skip the meal altogether. The dude ranch rental horses run when they see you, take the hint. Whatever you do, don't rush us. Find time or don't dine.

Another horrible thing to say is, "We want separate checks," a phrase that is pure pancake house lingo. Unless an upside down coffee cup is part of the table setting, no dice on separate checks.

But perhaps the worst thing to say to begin your meal is to ask the waiter's name and then blurt it out all night long like an infant who just learned how to say "da-da." "John, how ya doin'? John's a tall fella. John, get me this. John, do that. John, this is my wife. John's a white boy. John's probably an out-of-work actor. John, bring me some more of this. John-john-jay, John, and john and on and on." Enough! You disgrace your waiter's name when you speak it in that manner. He's not your friend and he's not your stooge and you constantly blurting out his name is the reason why he's crouched in the fetal position in the corner of the bar popping Tramadol and sucking down a flask of Jameson. This isn't a game show. Decorum exists until you destroy it with your junior high school behavior. If you ask your waiter's name, use it but once, at the conclusion of your meal, after you've tipped a hard twenty percent and are thanking him or her for outstanding service. Also, never touch your waiter outside of a grateful handshake, never snap your fingers, and never refer to him as garçon.

Drinks

This is no time to hesitate. You're in the big leagues now.
Server: "May I offer something from the bar?"

Customer (The following, well-enunciated, torturous soliloquy told at a tooth-growth pace):

"Would I care to have a drink? Hmmm. Well, the seductive thought of liquid pacification does carry a certain lure of hedonistic outlandishness. A drink? Yes, perhaps. Some distinctive form of thirst quenching beverage. Indeed. A glassed libation whose consumption would ferry some mesmonic level of intoxication. That might well prove most enjoyable. A liquid refreshment prior to the meal. Yes. Of course. Bravo, young lad! Such a wonderful idea. You are to be commended for possessing the aggressive guile to suggest the very idea of engaging in something that assuredly would prove to be so utterly satisfying. With the permission of my dining companions, I believe that I would very much like you to bring me a.......humm, oh say...a...cocktail."

Server, just prior to the aneurysmal embolism (Imagine the following screamed by Sam Kinison, in five seconds, maximum volume, maximum inflection):

"Baaaahhhh! What the fuck is wrong with you? You want a "cocktail?" A "cocktail!" That tells me absolutely god-damned nothing! I've just been slammed with ten tables in the last two minutes, everyone's starving and in a rush, the kitchen's a month behind in order production, half of the menu is eighty-sixed, and the health inspectors are here. We're in the middle of an audit, the computers just crashed, my busser's on lithium, the linen delivery never arrived, the ice machine is busted, and NOW I have to spend winter and half of spring listening to you trying to order a god-damned drink? Fuck you! You get nothing!!!!!"

First and foremost, never use the following phrases within the confines of a restaurant when attempting to order: "bring me," "fetch me," "get me," "hurry up and get," "chop-chop you damn dog," or "bringittomenowdammit!" There are only two appropriate phrases to use with mild variations. They are "may I have" and "I would like to have." Say them, use them, write them down. You can even take matters to an Ivy League level and add "please" and "thank you" whenever possible.

The second issue is putzing around with your drink order. If you desire a drink, speak clearly and concisely, stating what you want in the fewest possible syllables. A few fine examples are Ketel and tonic, Crown and water, perfect CC Manhattan up, dry Merlot, Grey Goose gibson, Glenlivet 18 neat, and the penguin's favorite—Jack rocks. Don't waste your life telling waiters and barmen things they already know. We know Chardonnay is served cold, that mist means crushed ice, gibson means pearl onions, that dry means no vermouth, Sambuca gets three coffee beans, dry Rob Roys get twists. We know that Charbay, Vomitroth, and Krylon are vodkas, that Cardu, Talisker, and Madwife are scotches, that Coyopa, Skidrow, and Pinkslip are rums, that gin and vodka tonics get limes, and with the exception of cosmopolitans and martinis, if you don't say "up," it will be on the rocks. Never say "dry" more than once and for the love of Moses, **there is no such thing as a twist of lime in barland**, only wedges of lime; lemons can be either.

What are the worst drinks to order? First is anything in a blender. Blender concoctions may taste magical on the sun-drenched shores of Martinique, but are homeless in big city power restaurants. To order them leads to suspicion that you own a bowling ball. Next is any fine Cognac mixed with ice and a soft drink. Not that such a drink is so difficult to make, but it does brand you as a person out of their element in fine dining, though it is fun to infuriate the French. The Old Fashioned is another bad drink to order. Perhaps it was the favorite drink of your grammie, but you had indoor plumbing when you were born and should know better. But, the absolute worst drink to order is the dreaded Champagne cocktail. It is to fine drinks what pork & beans is to haute cuisine, ordered only by the sluttiest Chattanooga trailer park trashettes. A Champagne cocktail is a pain to make and will never be ordered by anyone with the tiniest amount of refinement, and what you drink says everything about you. Are you a cheap, bubbling, sweet, time-consuming, nuclear pink-colored pain in the ass? Or are you a smooth, earthy, polished, bronzish, respected, twenty-four-year-old single malt, lowland scotch? Your waiter will know the answer to this question the instant you've placed your drink order.

Your Daily Bread

Fetch your pencil and paper again. One of the uglier sides of human behavior rears its head when people get their bread. You would think they hadn't eaten in a month. First the patrons plead for it as if they were seconds away from slipping into a diabetic coma. Next is the actual consumption of the bread, eating like Tony Siragusa at White Castle. Good god man, you eat like a ranch hand. Is the herd due in Cheyenne tomorrow? People have no idea what pigs they are. Stop it now, I beg you. First, bread is not a right, it is a privilege, just ask anyone in Somalia. Second, don't touch the breadbasket until you've ordered, and even then, take it easy. Bread is an accompaniment, not an appetizer. Allow your server to tell you the specials and take the order before you start stuffing your face.

For a waiter, it is maddening to watch people devouring bread while he's trying to recite the specials. Even an uneducated dog will not eat when being spoken to. The only customer action more disgusting is a customer eating and ordering simultaneously. Stop chewing, start listening. Don't even sip your drink when listening to the specials. Still, we're not out of the proverbial

Note: Never order a drink that requires electricity to make.

woods yet. The next few sentences apply exclusively to women. Stop talking while the specials are recited. Must you comment on every item mentioned? No wonder your husband left you. Nothing is more annoying than hearing you interrupt or talk concurrently while trying to recite the specials. If you talk concurrently with a mouth full of bread, I'm going to my car and getting my gun.

Ordering

Ladies first, whether it's a lifeboat seat or ordering dinner. Just like ordering drinks, use an economy of words, as if every syllable spoken is a painful lash from a cat of nine tails and you've been a mutinous Limey on the HMS *Bounty*. By being efficient and not wasting your waiter's time, the level of service you receive will skyrocket. On the other hand, if you nag the pilot for too long, the plane is certain to crash.

How do you know what to eat? First, read the menu from top to bottom. Most menus in fine dining read like collegiate football polls or baseball line-ups; the best teams and players are listed on top. It's the same way on a menu; restaurateurs put their finest entrees at the top of the menu. Entrees listed on the bottom half of the menu will not be one of the better items the chef has to offer. Second, beware of specials. Oftentimes, the chef is trying to sell certain fish and meats before they become spoiled. He bought a discount dump truck of rockfishes, but now they're getting so sticky that even the starving alley cats lost interest. Third, ask the waiter what he likes. If he says everything, either he's not credible or thinks you're a dirtbag, or you tipped him poorly on a previous visit and you are a dirtbag. All honest, upscale waiters will tell you that on any menu, some items are better than others. If you gratuitously failed to curry his favor on previous visits or it took you two minutes just to place your drink order, then he will have no inside information for you.

You can figure out a lot just by putting the facts together. Do you really believe that "fresh Norwegian salmon" you ate in Phoenix on Tuesday was flopping on the floor of a Sandefjord dory on Monday? Think about it. No way. That unlucky salmon has been dead for a month and it owes its bright orange color to reactor core HAZMAT leakage from unmaintenanced Russian submarines. Should you want to know about fresh fish myths, read a book on commercial fishing and if you want the best meal a restaurant has to offer, let the waiter order for you. Finally, when you are unable to properly pronounce the French title of an item on the menu, point to the item on the menu or refer to it by its English description. No French is better than bad French.

Wine Time

Do you think taking a wine class or subscribing to a wine periodical are wastes of time and money? Think again, mon amie. The knowledge gained will pay for the course or subscription a thousand-fold.

The worst values in most upscale restaurants can specifically be found on the wine list. The restaurant purchases a bottle for $22 and sells it to you for $89. Also little known is the fact that often it is less expensive to order a bottle of something rather than four individual glasses of the same. Knowledge is the best way to cope with runaway wine list prices. High-end, well-recognized Champagnes also tend to be bad values on wine lists. People usually order flash name Champagnes for status, not because of their superior quality. They will be missing those poorly spent deutsche marks at retirement. There are also several buzz-name red wines that are horrible values at restaurants. Conversely, there are countless lesser-known wines, both red and white, that are exceptional values, but finding these gems takes some research and perhaps, a few pleasant weekends in wine country. The fresh air will make you wonder why you live in the city.

As for ordering wine, remember, it's "I would like" or "may I have." This is another opportunity to go with the pro by asking what the server thinks is good wine; you won't regret it. After you've chosen, tell the waiter the bin number when you are unable to correctly pronounce the desired wine. When the wine arrives, check the label and year before the waiter or sommelier removes the seal. Don't expect the cork to be given to you when ordering a white and when it is given to you when ordering a red,

don't sniff the cork. Feel the cork for moisture and look at it for seepage or signs of improper storage.[†] When tasting the wine, swirl it for aeration and to inspect the wine's properties, holding the glass by the stem, not the bulb. Your hand around the bulb will warm the wine, which you do not want.

Don't be one of the ignorant customers who want the giant crystal Bordeaux glasses for their bargain basement Sauvignon Blanc. Also note that the days of matching wine and food by color are gone. Grilled sea bass might best go with a gripping red Zinfandel and a precocious Chardonnay could match well with Beef Wellington depending on the sauce. But the most important rule is to drink (and eat) what you enjoy best and forget all else. If Beringer White Zinfandel and well-done steaks with ketchup (code named "house red") are your thing, then drink, gnaw, and be merry.

Last, please know that every wine list has a skid row of welfare swill that should be served in an aluminum can or from a cardboard box, unfit even for Gitmo detainees. Don't ever order the cheapest wine on the list and then ask the waiter if it's good or be disappointed when you taste it. The cheapest wine on any wine list is just that—cheap wine. It belongs in a horse trough, concealed in a paper bag, or used as a desperation pour at a Lambeau tailgate party. Never bring your own wine to a restaurant. It's a fool's move and the corkage fee will cost you an Andrew Jackson or better. And it's a smart move to tell your server or sommelier your financial ceiling as for wine. No shame here. On the contrary, your candor will be appreciated, sparing us all that whiskey tango. *Note: Let your waiter taste the wine for you. It's a champion class move and you just might learn something.*

Salads Arrive

What is the difference between an elephant chewing grass and the average man wolfing down his salad? The answer is the elephant is more dignified, eats slower, and doesn't speak with a mouth full of greens. You need three things to happen before you start inhaling your salad. First, everyone must be served. Second, you must wait for everyone to be peppered. Third, you must wait for

[†] Though defiant of tradition and not synonymous with elegance, the screw-top cap is an extremely effective method for sealing wine bottles. Several quality vineyards now use screw-tops exclusively.

all the women to begin eating their salads before you even touch your fork. If any of these three conditions are not met and you've already started your chewfest, then you're an uncouth, bucolic, Ozark Mountain yahoo who had to wear braces on his teeth for ten years to correct his inbred overbite. Slow down the pace. Use the smaller fork on the left.

And the pepper dance is definitive evidence that evolution never occurred. The jumpy jimmies are first to wail. "I need pepper, don't forget the pepper!" Your waiter will not forget your pepper; he's still serving everyone his or her salads. When he does start peppering, the women get cracked first. And please, don't make that blasted pepper gesture. If you do, call AA, I'm going off the wagon right now. Often, when pepper is offered, many patrons have already eaten half of their salads. If the first half was fine without pepper, why do you want it now? And are you going to force the waiter to interrupt the table again? He's clearly standing there with a pepper mill, cut the man a break. Shut up and notice him. "Harold, I think the waiter wants something." Yes, the waiter wants a meteor to crash through the ceiling and incinerate this table and its occupants. What do you think the waiter wants, standing there with a pepper mill? And ladies, don't turn the pepper service into some kind of sexual Freudian nonsense, "Oooh, yes. Bring your big didgeridoo over here young man, start grinding me, yes, that's where, faster, keep it coming, use both hands, hurt me you bastard! Now get that thing out of my face. Is this a smoking section?"

Please know the following. The chef has already seasoned your salad the way he feels is appropriate. You should just eat the salad as it was served. Also, your "dressing on the side" requests, as per your latest diet, ruins everything sacred to a chef and slows up service. You've been dieting for four decades now and haven't lost any weight, so either develop a drug habit, start running three miles a day, or get your ass over to Curves. Finally, a note to restaurateurs: End the pepper crackathon madness and set each table with a small pewter pepper mill, allowing the patrons to self-crack.

There was one salad incident in 2003 at Romeo Charlie's I'll never forget. I was teaming with quick-wit waiter Elliott Lazarus, who had given his two weeks notice, leaving his server post to manage a sausage bar, The Male Box, between Milfs and Club Relapse on Fandango Avenue.[†] His last table was a group of five mean Koreans (I'm guessing North), one of whom had stacked all of his party's empty, soiled, salad plates and piled them on the floor beside the table. Curious, furious Elliott walked up and noisily kicked the stack, drawing attention to the dog eater who put them there. The angry Korean said, "You make everyone rook at me! Why you so stupid? You want fight me? I make big trouble for you!" Calmly, Elliot responded, "Me sorry, sir. I didn't mean to make everyone *rook* at you when I made that dink noise with your salad plates. But you got gook on the carpet. See there, it's all yellow. In this restaurant, we respect China."

Entree Vous

In upscale dining, every room, table, and seat position has a number, and when food is ordered it is assigned to that table and seat, like a zip code or a Global Positioning Satellite for food. Furthermore, women are given special designations in order that they may be served first. This means that the jackass who thinks he's George S. Patton directing traffic on the muddy roads of Sicily in 1943 should shut the hell up and stop pointing. Your food will arrive, and in front of the appropriate person. Boys, wait. Just like the salad course, the women must be served and have begun eating before you start gorging. Try to keep pace with your guests. As for the slow movers, if your entree is cold by the time you eat the last bite, you've taken too long to dine and monopolized the table's conversation. Two hours for an entire meal is good advice.

When you've finished, lay your knife and fork across your plate. Don't stack your plates, and for God's sake, don't ask the busman or waiter to clear your plates when others at your table are still eating. It is one of the rudest gestures there are. The only thing worse is openly picking your teeth, regardless

---

[†]The Male Box is known for its low-budget replica of the Aussie man troupe *Thunder From Down Under*. TMB's version is called *Genitalia From Australia*. When at The Male Box, ask for their specialty drink, a delicious, minty Homojito. 2nd Note: Homojitos (and Mojitos) are a pain in the ass to make, no pun intended.

of whether or not women are present at your table. Demanding a server clear a plate before others are finished is insulting to your guests and makes them feel rushed. I refused to do it, though this was not received well by many of my customers. When everyone is finished, lean back so the staff can clear and crumb the table. A soft-voiced "thank you" says a lot and is appreciated more than you know.

Dessert Storm

If you are intent on not having dessert, speak up before dessert is offered. Women are usually the guilty ones when it comes to dessert window-shopping. They make the waiter recite dessert options when they have no intention of actually ordering dessert. No less than a hundred times I've heard the request, "We're not going to have dessert, but tell us what you have anyway." Then there is the enraging older woman who orders one dessert for eight people, demanding forks and spoons for all, thinking she's sporting a new shade of clever as the restaurant loses money on the washing of silverware alone. The point is, get your own dessert and if you must share, share with only one other person. If you request a dessert menu, remember, like the entree menu, the best items are listed on top. Don't ever get ice cream in a restaurant. You're dining out to try items not commonly found or easily reproduced in your own kitchen.

Coffee

Like the pepper nonsense, the decaf pleas have gotten far out of hand. In any upscale restaurant, club, or hotel, ask for decaffeinated coffee one time, and rest assured you will be given decaffeinated coffee, including refills, for the duration of your meal. If you ask for decaf more than one time, jokingly threaten the waiter, have overstayed your welcome, have wasted your waiter's time, or have already paid the check and the tip is even one cent shy of twenty percent, all bets are off. If you just can't refrain from saying "if this isn't decaf I'm going to call you in the middle of the night!" then you will get such an enormous dose of caffeine that your heart will think you're a hummingbird and you'll need duct tape and PCP just to close your eyelids that evening. It's a code of honor among waiters to inflict malevolence and suffering on those who inflict the same upon us. This code goes far beyond the coffee cup. If you don't want venereal disease then don't buy satisfaction in a Bangkok brothel, and if you desire sleep in the forthcoming week, don't throw sass at your waiter or insult his intelligence. He'll screw you every time with a giant grin you'll never see. I have even had people tell me that they would die if they had caffeine. How convenient. I wanted them dead and was standing in front of them with a piping hot pot of caffeine-rich coffee. The Coventry never even purchased caffeinated coffee, only decaf, served as both regular and decaf, and yet still people would call the restaurant and complain, insisting that their waiter had served them regular coffee. Just give it a rest. If you were up last night, it was your conscience hindering your slumber, not caffeine.

Espressos and cappuccinos are also bad values in fine dining. High-end restaurants get anywhere from $6 to $10 dollars for a double espresso, almost pure profit. Hot tea is pure profit, too, and it's a pain in azimuth to make and those who drink it are usually table campers. For all your java needs, I recommend relocation. Get up and take a romantic walk to a coffee shop to finish your evening out. The quality of coffee in a coffee specialty shop is often better than that served in the restaurant. The stroll will do your heart good, you won't feel rushed, and you'll save a few farthings.

As for cigars, listen up, listen hard. If you want to fire up a cheroot, take your stogie and hightail it to a cigar bar or, better yet, a remote corner of an abandoned housing project, preferably in a policeless neighborhood somewhere in East St. Louis. Most dining rooms are now smoke free, but fast-traveling cigar stench from the bar is sickening and offends everyone. You look ridiculous standing there with your lips wrapped around that burning tobacco dildo and everyone's clothing stinks because of your selfish exhibitionism. Why not go to a psychiatrist and discover the psychological impulses that drive you to suck on that Cuban phallus? I'll save you the lira. It's feelings of inadequacy, and a desperate plea for attention where breeding, education, and achievement in the workplace have failed to provide it.

In the same vein of pain are the sheep and their cellular phones. Inflicting annoyance on other patrons with the incessant ringing of cell phones, they sabotage service by making the waiter wait while they try to find out who won on *Survivor Chechnya*. The sight or sound of a cell phone is another red flag on your table resume and immediately takes you out of contention for any decent level of service.

Check Mate

Never fight over the check. If someone wants to treat, allow them to, and you can grab the tab next time. When it comes to a challenge, the check always goes to the name on the reservation. This is another time when patrons with death wishes like to threaten their servers. Don't even think it. If you wanted the check and didn't get it, it's your fault, not the waiter's. You can even slip him a credit card prior to the meal, but if contested, the name of the reservation wins every time. Also, tread cautiously when you and your dining companions throw multiple credit cards at the server to pay for one meal. You're still bitter about not getting separate checks so you try to punish your waiter with five credit cards to pay for one check. It's a bush league move, slows down service, and you can wager hard that your check will be numerically swelled. Antagonism never works well on a waiter. Never.

The Rules Reiterated

Subject: The ideal dining experience.

1. **Be There On Time**, not one second late, not one person shy. If you don't care about the restaurant, don't expect the restaurant to sincerely care about you. Do *you* understand the words that are coming out of my mouth?

2. Check Your Coat And/Or Umbrella, Fella.

3. Women Always Get The View Of The Room When Seated. The eldest woman gets the view when there is more than one she. The eldest man when there are no women. If all men of the same age, the most effeminate guy gets the view. If all women of the same age, the one who didn't play collegiate field hockey gets the view.

4. Acknowledge And Listen To Your Server. Heed their advice on every aspect of the meal. No one knows the restaurant better than the front housers.

5. Know How To Order Your Drink in the fewest possible syllables. Imagine that you're a pilot flying into a jamming busy airport, and your preferred drink is your airplane's tail number. You only have 2 seconds to tell it to the tower or be denied clearance and vectored off to Fresno. And remember, it's a crime to twist a lime. Only lemon, orange, and fate can be twists.

   If you are only drinking water, you are obligated to order bottled water. There are no exceptions to this rule. And why are you drinking that Fiji water on ice? Those ice cubes were made from the same slimacious industrial park swamp swill you were trying to avoid by getting bottled water.

   And if you're drinking iced tea, you're allowed a maximum of two refills. No exceptions here, either. Your waiter has more important things to do than be your Frisbee dog iced tea refiller. And what's with the thirty packets of sugar? Crimony, man. Diabetes has you on its short list.

6. Front The Busman (Server Assistant/Table Captain). Such vital information is explained in the next chapter. Bus personnel are the offensive linemen of restaurant service execution.

7. Don't Be A Bread Bastard. You know better. Your signal flare to taste the bread is **After** the server has taken your order. Even then, moderation is advised. That breadbasket isn't a UNICEF food parcel and you're not a starving citizen of the Congo.

8. Don't Linger, And Most Certainly, Don't Rush. Haste is to fine dining what hair coloring is to the band members of The Moody Blues. *"Cold-hearted orb that rules the night, why's my mop and beard so white?"*

9. Beware Of Specials. That kumquat-stuffed yard bird is one day away from becoming the employee meal, two days away from becoming the feature meal on *Fear Factor.*

10. No Cell Phones, Blackberrys, iPods, Lap Tops, Game Boyz, ABI's (Alien Brain Implants), TREO's, Palm Pilots, Earbuds, Blue Teeth or any other such concraptions.

    And A Note To Servers: If on initial approach to a table, any of however many guests are using cell phones, check back in ten minutes or more. If the transgressors are unrepentant, dig deep into your repertoire of atonement and let the lessons begin.

11. Learn About Wine. It's an education that can pay for itself. You'll learn how to find great wine values in countries like Spain, Italy, Argentina, Chile, New Zealand, Australia, and most especially, here in America. Foremost, drink what you like and damn the snooty judgments of the boorish oenophiles. No one likes those guys anyway. **The two most important aspects of any wine are VALUE and FLAVOR. If some wine fairy tries to tell you otherwise, tell him to take that star on a stick and shove it up his...**

12. Don't Sniff That Cork, Mister! Yes, 007 did it, but Sean Connery didn't know what the hell he was doing. Sniffing is for coke addicts and French truffle hogs. Cork sniffers wear the dining room dunce cap. Now go sit by those Boca Raton women in their fur coats.

A cork, made of cork, smells like cork. A synthetic cork smells like synthesis, and synthesis smells exactly the same as a cirrus cloud, the rings of Saturn, the rudder of the *Flying Dutchman*, a lone valence electron, Aphrodite's morning breath, and Barry Bond's integrity.

13. **Don't Be A Plate Stacker.** It labels you as a restless loser.

14. **Have Coffee Off Campus,** or skip the cup of joe entirely. Let that Oyeliwop Super Tuscan or 1998 Chateau Haut-Brion Pessac-Leognan be the last thing on your palate. Yeah Baby.

15. **One Check, One Credit Card.** And swing righteously on the grat. Ask any server, those dollars are hard earned. And don't blame the waiter when your card is declined. It's all those Jäger (*yeager*) Bombs, lap dances and cyber tang that ate up your liver tissue and credit limit.

Note: In menu vernacular, **Surf & Turf** *is any steak and seafood combination entree. A steak prepared "blue" is served with a cold center. Surf & Turf with the steak ordered* **blue** *is called* **Smurf & Turf.**

The most accurate description of a **blue** *cooked steak was a customer who said "Don't cook it, just interrogate it." The term for an extremely well-done steak is* **Oblivión** *(say it like Pepé Le Pew). "Oblivión, uh! Puh, I spit on you stupide Americuns! No, that's not a napkine, it's a surrender flag!"*

Historical Note: 30,426 Americans killed in World War II are buried in 6 French cemeteries.

TEST YOUR CUSTOMER IQ:

QUESTION: YOU ORDER A DRINK, IT'S SERVED, BUT THERE'S LIPSTICK ON THE RIM AND A LIVE SPIDER IN THE GLASS. WHAT IS YOUR BEST COURSE OF ACTION?

A. DEMAND A FREE MEAL

B. HOLD THE DRINK HOSTAGE

C. LEAVE THE RESTAURANT

D. SAY NOTHING AND DRINK AS IS

E. COMPLAIN TO THE WAITER

Answer A is incorrect because you will not be getting a free meal for such a minor infraction. If there are spiders in your appetizer and lipstick on your salad fork, you may have a shot at free hossenfeffer. Answer C is incorrect because you're not going to leave the restaurant because of a cocktail spider. Answer D is incorrect because at $14 a pop, a spider-free, Lancomeless glass is a reasonable expectation. Answer E is incorrect because of the word "complain." If the pharmacy loses your insulin, then complain, but for a hoochbug and a schmear of face paint, aht. Answer B is correct. **Inform** the waiter (remember your approach is everything) and hold the drink hostage until a fresh cocktail is made and served. If you give the waiter the flawed drink before seeing a new one, odds are the bartender will simply pour the old contents into a new glass, minus the spider and lipstick. This is usually not the waiter's fault. Bartenders will demand servers recycle drinks to lower liquor costs. *Note to the staff: Walk that arachnid outside and spare its life for good karma.*

Chapter 4

Parsimonious Obduracy

(*Tipping A Hard Fifth*)

"This is a war of the unwilling
Led by the unqualified
Dying for the ungrateful."

Vietnam G.I. Latrine Graffiti, 1969

Larceny is the crime, a felony against those who sought to tame the famishings raging within your mortal coil. You betrayed the people who had spent the last few hours exerting themselves against the limits of sobriety to pamper you and your assemblage of pixies. We toiled, and in mute fashion, tolerated your hideous idiosyncrasies, nurturing faith in the unwritten promise that, at the conclusion of our ballet of efforts performed to please your epicurean monarchy, we would be duly rewarded, not with generosity, but with a reasonable sum commensurate to the service just received.

But no. The pigeon within you prevailed. Like a magnificent bridge that gave silent assurance to support the train as it chugged across the River Kwai, you collapsed in mid-choo. The little engine could, and was about to, when you and your frugal-assed personality caused calamity. Race, age, religion, arrogance, country of origin and most of all ignorance, are not acceptable excuses to tip short of the mark, that mark being one fifth. The gavel has fallen. Larceny is the crime and you are the felon.

Gratuity ground zero is twenty percent of the entire cost of the meal. One fifth given, one fifth taken. Either you're a part of the antidote or the poison itself. Those who want star status have to act the part, remembering that a waiter's pie gets cut many ways. The busman gets a sizable percentage, as do the bartenders, the food runners, and the sommeliers. Even the maître d' expects a little grease. Noble waiters even pitch a few dollars to the cooks and dishwashers. A hard twenty percent is the rule on any check received in any restaurant, upscale or not. An early five or ten to the busman is a very smart way to start an elegant meal. Shrewd regulars who tip the busmen instead of the maître d' are never in need.

People show their true colors when they tip, just as when they drive. The verbal gushers are the stenchiest layer of customer cesspool sewage, tipping in polysyllabic flattery and tiny percentages. Throttle back on the platitudes if you have no spine when it comes to tipping a fifth. Like smoke in the cockpit, hearing you rant on about how great the meal was tells us something bad is about to happen. Tipping the maître d' for a prime table and then docking that amount from the waiter's take is also sedition. The maître d' is going to lean on the waiter to give the palmer extra attention and may have even held a table in that waiter's station. This means lost revenue due to an idle table and perhaps losing a turn. But without question, **the most egregious tipping transgression is not tipping on the value amounts of gift certificates and credit vouchers.** It is the Murder One charge of gratuity felonies.

The finest tippers are mobsters. These well-dressed men of the criminal underworld recognize loyalty, dedication, and hard work. It took an entire chapter of this book just to give props to Mob and union heads. Regular customers get the silver medal for hard gratuities. Regulars who tip poorly find that service falters and foreign matter becomes garnish in the food of their favorite eatery. Soon they're not regulars anymore. Other waiters as customers are third on the fine-tipping depth chart. Our only flaw as customers is our thirsty nature, which requires the one serving us to make many trips to the bar.

Japanese businessmen place fourth. A pleasure to serve, these men are the embodiment of efficiency, etiquette, and civility, kicking American keister in every category, not to mention grammar and diction. Japanese fine diners also tend to have tremendous wine knowledge and always tip well because they know how the system works. Last on the list of fine tippers are prom couples. Fine dining is a rare occasion for prom parties, making them a pleasure to serve. It is amazing how a group of bankrupt teenagers can tip twenty percent at the same time a crusty business codger frets over nickels.

Holy rollers are the lowliest of sinful sinners in the matter of tipping. If your customers are speaking in tongues when you try to take a cocktail order, thine ass is screwed. Rollers won't order alcohol and will complain that Satan himself has inflated the menu prices. You'll never see much of a gratuity; they've pre-tithed your tip for you and already given it to Jesus. What they will leave is a righteously-worded religious pamphlet with an address to a Louisiana post office box so you can send them the money they didn't give you.

Second place for bad tipping goes to anyone from Europe. Though claiming to be of superior intellect, these mooks drop the ball every time when it comes to a twenty percent tip. Third worst in tight-assed tipping goes to the people of Canada and Australia. We'll just lump these two America-wannabe countries together since they share the same flaws. Their citizens don't tip well and their climates are intolerable, be it brutally hot or insufferably cold. Angry that musk ox and dingo aren't mainstays on American menus, both nations' governments encourage their citizens not to tip Yankee waiters well. But they do have that socialized health care. Maybe those Canuck curlers and royal convicts are onto something. Author Suggestion: *Curling (the Olympic sport for OCD housewives) would be better if there was a secret, exploding stone.*

Honorable mention for incommensurate gratuity is awarded to our Latin American brothers and sisters. Perhaps it's upscale dining's lack of cock fights and Oscar De La Hoya homage posters that inclines Hispanic patrons to tip far short of a fifth. Servers are putting you California gardeners on notice. C'mon now, you had your babies for free, got a license at no cost, voted and still aren't here legally. You must have some money left for the waiters. Oh, I forgot. You spent all your money on that low-rider kit and Sprewell spinning rims for your unregistered, uninsured Honda Civic.

Last on the list of losers is white and black trash. The black trash hold the waiters responsible for segregation, the Civil War, and slave reparation check snafus. The white trash is unfamiliar with the word "emancipation," couldn't tell you which side of the conflict Connecticut fought for and can't believe that such a posh restaurant doesn't have a salad bar, sell chaw, or serve Old Milwaukee. Both trash varieties gag when the check arrives and you'll be lucky to get ten percent. One table at the Coventry said to me, "God damn, boy! I can buy a house in Tulsa fur what it costs ta eat here!" Would you really want a house in Tulsa, anyway?

Pain is not forgotten, nor is an inadequate gratuity. Etched in the mind of the poorly tipped are the fraudulent faces of those who dropped the ball and exercised frugality at the expense of another person's expense. Recollections of pain of any kind are troubling, vivid, and remain with you. This holds true when a server gets shafted on a gratuity. A professional waiter can serve thousands of people and still recall the face that betrayed him, even if it was years ago.

A dozen French-African royalty were guests at the Coventry and I and team waiter and future King Lear defector, Preston Hillman, were the lucky lads who got to serve these VIPs. They spoke little English and were dressed like The Isley Brothers prior to a Mardi Gras concert. Though from a continent associated with poverty and famine, these twelve men from somewhere south of Sudan kept Preston and myself buried with exotic wine selections while feasting on a seven course meal, running up a check just shy of $4,000. At the close of the four-hour meal, Preston gave the check to the host and quickly processed his credit card. Despite the party being enamored with the cuisine and devoted service, the tip the host left was only $40, one percent. We had expected anywhere from $600 to $1,000, and would have begrudgingly accepted $500, but forty bucks left us gnashing our teeth.

Preston and I took the credit card voucher to the maître d' and insisted he tell Chaka Zulu that forty clams wasn't even close to adequate wage for two waiters to split and pay their supporting caste, but he refused. The maître d' said that to overrule the host's decision on a gratuity would be insulting, something he would not do to a patron. He also said that $40 was likely a fair tip in this patron's country. Furious and in a sarcastic tone, I informed the maître d' that at some point this African court jester exited his country and traveled to Los Estados Unidos, where pocket change doesn't keep the kitty knee-deep in Tidy Cat. The maître d' didn't want to hear it. We would have to suck this one up, and after tipping out, Preston and I each netted a measly twelve dollars, sweat shop salary at best. To ease our pain, however, we discretely sucked up two bottles of self-serve Chateau Beychevelle.

The following day we took our protest to the GM and he instituted an automatic twenty percent gratuity for all parties of eight or more henceforward at the Coventry. A day late and $760 short of the mark for Presto and myself.

An elderly man once gave a King Lear valet a quarter to park and retrieve his late model Cadillac. To park a vehicle, the valets had to make a U-turn across J Street and drive into the lower levels of the spiral drive parking garage. The distance was four hundred yards there and back, a quarter mile hoofed total with any one car parked and fetched. A mile on foot for every four automobiles. The elements made the task even more challenging, whether it was horizontal rain or the melting heat of July. In this case, it was mid-January, and as the sheet of ice covering the Potomac showed, it was cold as a cryogenic Ted Williams. King Lear's valets also pooled their tips, which meant the evening's gratuities would be divided equally among the number of valets working. Twenty-five cents? That's wrong if you're driving a mustard-colored Yugo GV with chain links around the license plate let alone a new blue Caddy. Three to five dollars to a restaurant valet is the rule; the same for the coat checker.

And if you don't think auto theft occurs close to elegant city restaurants, think again. Five vehicles were stolen in two months in 1996 in front of King Lear, including two refrigerated lobster trucks, both taken in broad daylight. After the first theft, the delivery guy came in and asked if any of us had moved his truck. The second time, the same man walked into the kitchen with a look of incredulous disbelief. We felt bad for the guy but couldn't help. Imagine the scene at the chop shop: "Get me a gallon of primer, some drawn butter, a socket wrench, and a fingerbowl."

But the worst of the tip rip-offs was a group larceny perpetuated on me and fourteen others. A hoard of two hundred Saudi Arabian oil lords booked every seat in the Coventry for the day, which meant closing to the general public. The party preordered a set menu that was the most extravagant and expensive meal I had ever witnessed. Caviar, foie gras (that's goose liver, $100 a pound), meat, fish and fowl thought extinct, and to wash it all down, three cases each of Premier Cru Chablis (French Chard), Louis Roederer Cristal Champagne, and Grands Echezeaux (a pricy red Burgundy), and eight Baccarat decanters of Remy Martin Louis XIII (Mob brandy, $125 for three ounces, referred to as 'Louie Tres' by the staff). The prepaid check for the party was $84,000, which included the newly-instituted twenty percent automatic gratuity, $14,000 of which was to be divided among fifteen service persons: ten waiters, three busmen, and two bartenders. The windfall figure was $933 a server, though the staff had agreed to take $800 each, rerouting $2,000 to the cooks and dishwashers. The staff anticipated this day as if it were Christmas, and it would serve as compensation for all those $10 lunches and $35 doubles that occurred from time to time.

The party itself required eleven hours of intensive effort, only four of which was dedicated to actual service, the rest of the time was spent setting up, polishing, cleaning up, breaking down, and resetting for normal operations the next day. Cuisine, service, and timing were executed to perfection and the Saudi oilers were delighted with every aspect of their high-end evening, the night being nearly flawless.

At the end of the shift, the enervated fifteen were camped out at the bar, drinking the excess Echezeaux and waiting for the GM to fork over our $800. The GM walked into the bar and gave each of us an envelope containing two hundred in cash. In knee-jerk fashion the staff objected in unison, crying out for the missing money.

The GM hushed the objectors with a few loud sentences to answer the mad fifteen. He said, "Calm down this minute! Yes, everyone gets two hundred bucks and the remainder of the cash goes toward the bottom line. Eight hundred dollars is an excessive amount of money for one day's work for a service person. I don't want to hear any griping about this, the decision stands. Anyone who argues this with me will be terminated. Now let's all clock out and go home."

We stood in a complete state of shock, the anger inside of us building like a *Hawaii Five-O* wave. We had just been robbed by a man without a gun, but the threat worked. It made no sense to seek legal recourse and lose our jobs over $600. Meanwhile the slimy GM looked like a genius to the Coventry's parent company, having produced $11,000 out of thin air to up that month's profits. However, the profit would be temporary, because a jilted server is a clever creature, and the fab fifteen were about to wreak financial Pompeii on the Coventry.

Payback began by breaking the Coventry's precious glassware. These weren't your everyday Flintstone filling station collectibles, but instead, fine crystal, never intended for use on a commercial basis, disintegrating into a billion shards when broken with hostility. Imported silverware, made in some French village that no longer exists, was carted home piece-by-piece, person-by-person. No stiffed employee had less than five pounds of it. Stainless steel screws were constantly falling into the espresso grinder, fatally clogging it every time with a frustrated electrical hum preceding the smell of electrical smoke. Fine bottles of wine were disappearing in staggering numbers. Four waiters could open, pour and chug a bottle of wine in less than twenty seconds, though we were always practicing for a faster time. Bottles of chilled white wine or Champagne caused ice cream headaches, so we usually chugged red.

No longer did the waiters scrutinize checks to be certain all items ordered were rung up. Goods unrung on a guest check prompted higher gratuities. Friends of servers made out like bandits, often paying their waiter connection with a drug fix in lieu of cash monies. Food not served gratis to friends or dealers was server devoured Homer Simpson-style on the fire exit stairway. Olive oil and the circuitry of a computer proved incompatible, empirical data on said theory provided monthly at the expense of the Coventry's computer systems. Vandalism even befell the GM's Acura Legend. The car was hard-keyed on every panel with what appeared to be an oyster fork.

Unfortunately, of the stiffed fifteen, there were two casualties in the retributional war of smash, grab, and swallow. There was a server named Nori, a sizzling sister from the Philippines, who was caught off campus with stolen goods. While riding home on the crowded Red Line, Nori was boastfully showing off a dozen lifted Coventry espresso cups and saucers. Behind her on the train sat a plain clothes D.C. detective, privy to loud Nori's braggings due to haphazard proximity on the cramped Metro. The detective detrained and soft-tailed Nori to her residence, then ran the address, acquired her stats, and ratted her out like Jose Canseco to the Coventry's GM.

The other to be termed was Xavier Baca, a busser from the Galapagos Islands, whom, of all the financially impaled, was surely the most bitter. He was going to use the fat cash not given to visit his children in San Cristóbal, but now he'd have to postpone the trip. The morning after the Saudi party, Xav Sharpie markered all of the glass-less, oil-painted historic political portraits that hung throughout the Coventry. "Honey, I don't recall Thomas Jefferson having two black eyes and a Hitler mustache!" He also coated all the guest restroom toilet seats, both sexes, with black Kiwi shoe polish, which was undetectable since the seats were black as well. Several Coventry lunch guest fell vic to "black ass" before the source of the waxy melanosis was determined. One traumatized patron had even gone to the emergency room. Though a surveillance camera proved to be Xavier's downfall, he was regarded as a hero for the cause and the staff was able to find him off-books employment less than two days after his termination.

The staff often mused that before he went Sharpie-wild on the portraits, Xav said with a hardened Cuban accent, "Sey alloe to my little friend!" In vain attempt at intimidation and corporate muscle flexing, the Coventry management capuchins tried to prosecute Xavier for the tens of thousands of dollars in damage done, but alas, the man was not in America legally. All this did was bring more INS scrutiny upon the Coventry. One fine parting blow from the Galapagos guy.

During an extensive managerial meeting convened to address the outbreak of broken glassware, the appearance of Coventry silver in local pawn shops, screwed grinders, oiled computers, missing vineyards' worth of wine, ass-blackening toilet seats, Sharpie-enhanced oil portraits, and oyster-forked Acuras, a few of us naughty boys grabbed the Louie Tres and drank straight from the Baccarat decanter, high plains drifter canteen-style. We couldn't drink it all, but the next patron to order a snifter of Louie from that same decanter said, "Hey, there are bread crumbs in my Cognac!" "Um, sorry, sir."

The GM had stolen $11,000 from the staff, but it cost him $200,000 to do it, and was the beginning of the end of the Coventry, meeting with the same fate the HMS ship of the same name met during the Falklands War.[†]

On the other side of Dodge are the pure-hearted people, those who recognize service personnel as hard working human beings. Like any waiter, I've been the benefactor of some tremendous acts of generosity and big money tips. Heroic tippers are usually the timid ones and the people a waiter cares about the most.

The scene was a typical weekday power lunch at snooty King Lear. Energy filled the air with every table in the house jammed, four of which were in my station. Three of my tables were suits doing deals, talking the talk, plotting profit, and not making eye contact with me when ordering so as not to catch my leprosy. At my fourth table were three elderly ladies, all probably widows, and all a breath of fresh air from the hurried hustlers that were the

[†]During the Falkland Islands War of 1982 (*Islas Malvinas*) six British ships were lost. They were the HMS *Sheffield*, HMS *Ardent*, HMS *Antelope*, SS *Atlantic Conveyor*, and RFA *Sir Galahad*, as well as the HMS *Coventry*.

lunch majority at King Lear. Fate had clearly dictated that these three charming women would be the focus of my attention, as the baboons making maraca music, shaking their empty iced tea glasses in the air, became invisible.

During their meal, I overheard one of the women say it was her birthday, so I liberated some peach bread pudding, candled it, and asked Max, the day pianist, to play the appropriate tune. Max started playing as I placed the dessert on the table and wished the woman honored a happy birthday. The women were astonished, almost in tears. They were very thankful, and I told them that I was privileged to be their waiter on such a special occasion. They paid the check, plus a fifth, and thanked me again. Later that week the GM called me into the office to show me the following letter:

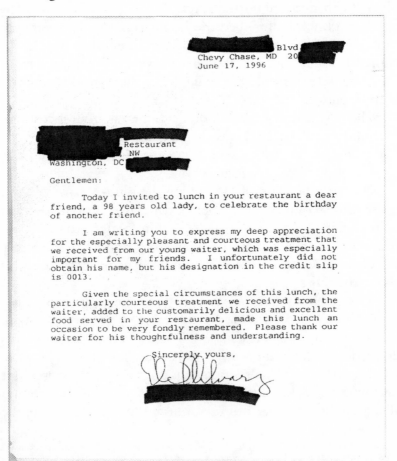

Blvd
Chevy Chase, MD 20
June 17, 1996

Restaurant
NW
Washington, DC

Gentlemen:

Today I invited to lunch in your restaurant a dear friend, a 98 years old lady, to celebrate the birthday of another friend.

I am writing you to express my deep appreciation for the especially pleasant and courteous treatment that we received from our young waiter, which was especially important for my friends. I unfortunately did not obtain his name, but his designation in the credit slip is 0013.

Given the special circumstances of this lunch, the particularly courteous treatment we received from the waiter, added to the customarily delicious and excellent food served in your restaurant, made this lunch an occasion to be very fondly remembered. Please thank our waiter for his thoughtfulness and understanding.

Sincerely yours,

What a wonderful letter, a kindness that I will always reflect upon. These lovely ladies may have seemed out of place in the chaotic world that was a late-century business day in D.C., but they made my day.

There was another man who was constantly making all the waiters' days, generous to a fault and exuding unparalleled class and honor. We knighted him "Earl The Pearl." The name fit him well.

It was New Year's Eve at King Lear and every table had been booked since Thanksgiving. King Lear was the place to be on New Year's, the guest list swelling with the names of Washington's elite. My station was the upper room, working in tandem with King Lear veteran waiter Mitch Morehouse. To our great fortune, we drew the coveted twenty-person, two-table reservation of Earl Styles—a King Lear king, banking mogul, and absolute favorite regular of all the King's men. ES was to KL what MJ was to the NBA.

Earl was a connoisseur of California's finest grape squash, with a relaxed demeanor and notorious for always tipping twenty-five percent. He lived in a mansion off of Massachusetts Avenue, where he also had a magnificent wine cellar, a fifty-degree gymnasium that was home to several thousand bottles full of viticulture's domestic best. Joining Earl, and responsible for ten of the twenty people on Earl's reservation, was Adreas Jackson, a man whose description was not so flattering. A suckerfish swimming in Earl's wake, Jackson was a self-professed, yet ringless and wingless Air Force Academy graduate, though we doubted he even knew where Colorado was. Jackson was also a notorious late-runner and no-shower, leaving Mitch and I with reservations of our own as to whether or not Jackson would post despite a fifty dollar per head reservation fee. But The Pearl vouched for Jackson and the word of our lord would not be doubted.

The New Year's Eve celebration was underway and the early seatings came and went. Mitch and I set up Earl and Jackson's two tables of ten and, on time, party complete, and with his stunning spouse on his arm, Earl arrived for the 10:00 p.m. seating. Jackson and the nine members of his entourage were still nowhere to be seen, but Earl maintained confidence that they would make it. An hour prior to the ball-fall, still no Jackson and guests.

New Year's Eve is financially to waiters what the Super Bowl is to football, and Mitch and I both knew we would forfeit a lot of money if one team didn't show. Waiters tend to feel protective about their best customers, and greater than the thought of not making big money on the best night of the year was the anger we felt toward Jackson for embarrassing Earl. Why was he doing this to The Pearl? Earl kept apologizing for Jackson's absence, though we smiled and said it was nothing to worry about at all.

As midnight came and went, Jackass Jackson and his nine phantom friends never showed, never called. Two hours into the New Year, the party was breaking up and Mitch dropped and collected Earl's check, $1,500 for the table. Mitch opened and glanced at the check and waved me over. I looked at the voucher to see that Earl had left us a one thousand dollar tip. Mitch and I couldn't believe it and agreed that we would not accept such a ridiculous amount of money, not from someone we valued so highly. Mitch said, "Earl, this is way too much money, even half of that is too much, please, we won't take it."

The Pearl quickly refuted our plea and said, "No way. You gentlemen earn this money all year long and are always looking out for me and my guests. That's why I love coming here. You guys are pros and deserve it. I know I can always count on you. Besides, Jackson is picking up this one. That is, if he survives the beating heading his way." He shook our hands and said, "Happy New Year, Mitch, John."

We bid him the same, trying to keep from getting teary. What a man. Happy New Year indeed.

Earl was always performing amazing feats of heart and generosity. He and his wife housed our head bartender for a few months when the wheels came off his fourth marriage. Vintners would dine with The Pearl and he would invite the waiters, post meal, to join him and the vintner at his home for wine tastings. He even paid for a King Lear kitchen worker to fly home to El Salvador to be with his dying mother. We loved him, Earl "The Pearl" Styles, the kindest man alive. Note to The Pearl: If you ever need a kidney, I've got two.

The Rules Reiterated
Subject: Tipping Protocol.

1. **Tip 20% After Tax On Every Check** received in a restaurant. This includes tipping 20% on the value amounts of gift certificates and credit vouchers. Just as trendy health club urinals reek of steroid whiz, gift certificate no-tippers ferry the hideous stench of fraud and malfeasance. Excuse me while I spit in disgust.

2. **$3-5** to the coat checker, and the same for the valets.

3. **If** you are with a party and are witness to a short gratuity, quietly complete the difference.

4. **To-Go Orders Are Strictly Forbidden** from any fine restaurant, but for the bastards who must defy this rule, **a hard fifth is due, plus an extra cash five to whomever answered the phone.** If you had any intelligence, you'd realize it takes twice the effort to box-up your meal for off-premise consumption. Now punch yourself in the face.

5. **Pre-Grease Your Tango Charlie.** An early five or ten to your server assistant (Table Captain, *Tango Charlie*, Tee Cee *"Roger that, read-back correct"*) buys you a loyal friend for the next two hours. Front your TC a fifty or better, and he'll be there for you in your old age.

6. **Don't Work In A Restaurant That Pools Tips.** When you do so, it means that your hard work is going to help pay for management's secret drug habits, and help the owners screw over the IRS and then blame you come audit time. Plus, there will always be greedy waiters palming grats. In addition, tip pooling breeds apathy in service. Why run hard all the way up the mountain when you know you'll only be getting a nibble of that power bar you've earned.

THE 4 CATEGORIES OF CHEFS ARE:

1. JOURNEYMAN CHEF
2. FAT MOUTH CHEF
3. CELEBRITY CHEF
4. CRUSHED CAR CUBE CHEF

Chapter 5

Return from Stalingrad

(chefs and insanity)

"Thou shalt not kill."

God, [Exodus 20:13, Commandment 6]

Mamas, don't let your babies grow up to be chefs. Not if you love your children. You carried them, bore them, now let some of that maternal instinct do its thing. Should your child show any signs of wanting to be a chef, either smother him with a pillow, leave him in the forest for coyotes to raise, or take him to a tot shrink. People who work in restaurants are misfits, the squarest pegs of all being the chefs. Just like the dentist elf in *Rudolf The Red Nosed Reindeer,* except this time Christmas *is* canceled because Cheffy had to work sixteen hours that day, and Rudy got gutted when the house ran out of venison.

Chefs are wayward souls who tend to have a lot of bad wiring, bad habits, and troubled pasts. Exile makes people waiters; condemnation makes people chefs, a fifty-year sentence of hard labor, incessant fatigue, and unfathomable stress that accelerates the aging process. Tell a child the truth about being a chef and he'll have screaming nightmares for years. It's no picture show, just an insane lifestyle devoid of pleasure and lasting reward, with a personal life that's a seaside cottage built on a rainy cliff of clay. No crystal ball is needed to look down the time continuum and see where the house ends up. There's no job security, none at all, and every day could be their last.

It only takes one gaff, one customer with food poisoning. For every two days the white collared office jockey works, Cheffy works three. As the office jockey gets a paper cut or finds a speck of toner on his French cuffs, Cheffy slices his finger to the bone and gets cirrhosis, his body a living resume of burns, scars, and abuse. Whether it's self-inflicted or accidental, it's not just likely, it's inevitable.

People become chefs because as adolescents they didn't fit in anywhere like the successful kids did—not with the brainiacs or the jocks or the zit-faced computer geeks. Even the stamp club freaks turned their heads away. They lacked the money and motivation to finish college, were too clumsy to chase campus cooch, and couldn't even tie a Windsor knot, so they started working as kitchen cooks. Kitchen toil was something they could perform that other kids couldn't or wouldn't. Next was fourteen months at culinary school and soon after, work as a sous chef. But in the back of their minds something felt wrong about this new direction, this new career, this place where they thought they belonged. And like frightened puppies in a cold and brightly lit pound, they had no clue as to the origin of their uneasy feelings.

The discontent in a chef's id is the repressed realization that what they do for a living is a paradigm of superflousness—feeding people food they don't need in restaurants that shouldn't exist, while life marches on without them. The by-products are grease, toxins, enormous waste, a diminished earth, and a pile of animal bones taller than the Matterhorn. As a chef, you are the vivisectionist and deal out pain like a curious KGB agent, whether it's ramming a skewer up a lobster's ass, committing mass mussel murder with olive oil and an iron skillet, or grilling the plumped liver of a crucified goose that lived for three months with its feet nailed to a wood plank to keep it immobile. Consumption is a chef's motto, turning the big wheel his duty, deep-frying a kitten if necessary. Few ruminate about the agony of soft shell crabs, though it's there in black and white, those flailing pincers exalting you to show some mercy, to pay some attention, to listen, to have a pixel of compassion. They were disemboweled, sloshed in egg wash, poofed in bread flour and laid gently in the fiery brown butter of a copper frying pan, but they're still hanging on. All that suffering for a human's quick munch. It takes a lot of pain and misery to put vittles on your plate. But people are cowards when it comes to learning the truth. Channel changers. So, too, are chefs. They don't question animal exploitation, nor care about West Virginia chicken smashing, or cogitate the consciousness of seafood and livestock. All they concentrate on is drinking, getting laid, and trying to remember what grade their kid is in at school while wondering if the child support check bounced.

If chefs were to meditate on their crimes against animals, they would conclude that the only reason an animal is slaughtered is because of its inability to utter words and converse. Animals clearly have thought processes, feel pain, have fear, harbor instinct, and, if you ever had a pet, you would even know that they grieve. They lack only the ability to articulate words and speak the emotions of their minds.

A bovine would beg, "Please don't take my calf, again. You've taken my last three and I fear something horrible has happened to them. But I am helpless as I stand here strapped to this machine that milks me dry, in a remote corner outside your city, in this concentration camp for cows."

Pigs would contend, "Rumor has it that we are to be executed for the meat of our bellies. Why must pigs be raised to die and mankind raised to live and infect the world? It's all a matter of genetic inheritance, isn't it? A matter over which we have no control. We protest this inhumanity and damn all those whose hunger for a bite of our flesh perpetrates this cruel death upon us."

A lab rabbit would cry, "Does anyone care about me and my siblings, locked in these stocks while the heartless humans in white coats spray chemicals in our eyes and jab needles in our hides to see how loud we scream? Do our cries of misery go unheard? Does mankind need to torture and kill rabbits, mice, and stray animals to know that an infant shouldn't swallow corrosive chemicals? We only know that this earth was in harmony before mankind crawled out of the sea."

A caribou would argue, "Every day another part of my habitat is destroyed and bulldozed into a mini-mall. What wooded areas remain are no longer quiet, but instead forever roaring with the sounds of your children's ATVs. Litter is everywhere, marking mankind's incessant impure ingress. My falcon friends tell me that even the remote plains of Arizona, where there is little human traffic, are now wastelands of strewn soda cans, beer bottles, and plastic bags that blow like tumble-weeds, durably made not to biodegrade. There's a golf course where my grazing area used to be and the lake water no longer tastes pure, tainted with herbicides that keep your fairways and putting greens weedless. Hunters are better disguised every day, to the point that none of my brothers or sisters have lived beyond two years old. The endless destruction of trees also has the owl, fox and coyote communities terrified."

A wolf would argue, "Dear Mr. President, I overheard a forest ranger saying that there are too many wolves and something must be done. But it is the opinion of the wolves that there are too many humans. The buffalo, deer, and Native Americans (who are also human but unlike you) agree with the wolves on this point. As humans, you have a custodial obligation to protect the lands, oceans and animals. But you renounce your duties to the earth and its creatures in the name of capital gain. It seems we should just resign ourselves to extinction, because there's no room in your economy for the concerns of a wolf, a whale, a prairie dog, a Sumatran rhino or even a snail darter. Just remember though, as you destroy us, you also destroy yourselves."

If the animals could speak, you wouldn't like what they had to say. But chefs don't ponder such things. You probably don't either.

Monz Flugzeugbau was the first chef I ever worked for. He was a German Napoleon who ran Cedar Forest's kitchen and strolled daily along the precipice of madness. Monz had better reasons than most. At the age of seventeen, in 1942, he was drafted into Hitler's Wehrmacht and sent to fight on the Russian front where he was captured and forced to spend the war's duration as a prisoner of war. Of the 260,000 soldiers of the German Sixth Army who fought and suffered to capture Stalingrad (Volgograd), only 91,000 survived to become POWs. Of those prisoners, only 6,000 lived to ever see Germany again.

At the war's conclusion, Monz was barely alive. Weighing only ninety pounds and having lost three toes to frostbite and most of his teeth to interrogatory beatings, he returned home to Recklingshausen to learn that his mother and younger brother had been killed in Allied bombing raids.[†] His father, a Luftwaffe tail gunner, had also been killed after his Stuka Junkers Ju was shot down during the Battle of Britain. As a chef in America, Monz understandably lacked any social savvy, so a harsh dictatorship defined his rule as country club executive chef.

Being the sole white soul in the kitchen, I took more abuse than my coworkers, but I didn't mind. It was obvious that I reminded Monz of a time long since past when he was still with hope, family, and aspirations, and life was more like a scene from *The Sound of Music*.

Monz was known for explosive fits of rage, triggered by any type of physical pain, and in a commercial kitchen the opportunities for pain abound. One time, the baker left a screaming hot sheet pan on a counter and Monz burned his hands when he tried to move it. He was so furious that he shoved a stack of dinner plates in the oven and zipped the dial to six hundred, demanding the baker remove the plates with his bare hands or be fired. The baker refused, wasn't fired, and the GM calmed Monz down, explaining to him that we were in Indianapolis, not Niedersachsen. But there was too much pain in Monz' past for him to ever feel good about anything, and in Cedar Forest's kitchen no one cared about World War II, its atrocities, millions of dead people, or the anguish of an unloved man who didn't belong anywhere and had lost everything thirty years earlier.

A Dane named Frederick Randers was next to take the reins as executive chef at Cedar Forest. Randers was a huge, red-bearded Viking with the thirst and disposition to match. He

---

[†]Of the 3.9 million German civilians who died in WWII, over 650,000 were killed as a result of Allied bombing raids. The Soviet Union suffered 25.8 million causalties, both civilian and military, between February of 1939 and May of 1945.

loved cigars, Chivas, and women-for-hire and, like Monz, was
reluctant to recognize his geographic whereabouts. The
Danish/African-American culture clash lent itself to many
tension-filled hours during crunch production times. At one
point while Randers was badgering the staff, a sauté cook pulled
out a revolver, cocked the gun, pointed it at Randers' giant
cranium and said, "Fuck off an' let me work motha' fucka."
Apparently this particular cook didn't care how they prepared
swordfish in Copenhagen. One syllable from Randers would
have gotten him killed. Nothing ever became of the gun
brandishing and the two ended up splitting a bottle of Calvados
later that same evening. "Thanks for not shooting me" was
Randers' actual toast. He earned the respect of his crew by
forgetting the matter.

The chef at the Uptown Club was an almost normal
Irishman named Roary Gates, highly skilled and wise enough
to know that kitchen crews respond better to diplomacy than
tyranny. Roary was a good fellow, not drinking that much for
an Irishman, though still enough that had his tongue caught fire,
he would have become a spontaneous combustion statistic. He
departed to open a cafe; *The Loose Stool,* and was replaced by
Henri Tambeau, a frog's frog who was despised by everyone.

Imagine the most unlikable Frenchie you know and multiply
it by nine. Tambeau treated people in the worst possible way,
and the kitchen staff stole the club blind in answer to his
unpleasantness. Though very talented as a chef, he possessed no
people skills, was a chain smoker of dark cigarillos, a wino
(nothing American), and drove a showroom condition Triumph
convertible when not casting misery upon his staff. Like most
chefs, Tambeau had made many enemies, several being people
he had fired. One almost killed him with a lug wrench, not by
bashing him over the head, but by loosening all but one lug nut
from the right front tire of Tambeau's cherished Triumph. The
tire came off during a high-speed left turn, causing the car to
skid into the wooden light post. The car was totaled, but the
only injury to Tambeau was a broken wrist. His demeanor
remained unchanged. Maybe two loosened tires would have

done the trick.

A few years later and five hundred miles east in Virginia, I learned that a chef's wrath was not just limited to cooks and utility persons. Chefs love to give grief to waiters, more so than to kitchen crews, and no matter what is said or done, the chef is always right and the servers are always wrong. If you said that water was wet and staring at the sun for hours on end was bad for your eyes, they could somehow prove you wrong. To make matters worse, management will always support the chefs over the waiters. "Yes, the chef did rob a bank, set a school bus on fire, wiped his ass with a nun's wimple, even encouraged a Boy Scout to build a meth lab in his pup tent, but *you* missed a belt loop on your pants yesterday."

At Charles Street Chop House, Rodney Kalashnikov was the first chef I worked for as a waiter; a screaming, spitting, nut-case alcoholic sociopath who is either reading this book from prison or in a capacious, lava-floored cavern in the bowels of hell. He had six DWIs, three ex-wives, and a crescent moon shaped indentation on his forehead, a permanent reminder of the time he drunkenly tried to punch a Maryland State Trooper after he parked his Renault atop the Chesapeake Bay Bridge to admire the view. The cauldron of hate and negative energy bound inside Kalashnikov made me wonder what horrible events from his childhood could produce so much dark vehemence and the spastic rantings he inflicted on his staff. DWI number seven cost Kalashnikov his job, his freedom, and money it will take him thirteen centuries to earn at his new position as the prison laundry lint boy.

To replace Kalashnikov was one man the size of three, Kent Hubbard. Kent was a four-hundred-pound, black-bearded dirigible that spoke few words for a chef, drank in moderation, and was the official mystery man of CSCH. There were more questions about Hubbard than answers. Though bigger than the average pachyderm, he was never seen eating beyond tasting sauces and drinking a few shots of sour mash. He studied calculus and mathematical formulas when not performing his culinary duties, an odd hobby for a chef. No one knew where

Hubbard lived, only that it must have been close to the restaurant because he didn't own a car or even drive and was about as ambulant as a clam. No one knew where he was from or if he had a family, only that his father likely had tusks. There was speculation that he was being hidden as part of a witness relocation program for sperm whales. All we knew for sure was that Hubbard was an accomplished chef who turned out to be mildly likable and, to his credit, ended up shedding almost half of his mass.

Across the Potomac at the Coventry was a sous chef whose very being defined evil, a man so insane that, in retrospect, to murder him would have spared many grief. Left on hell's doorstep by the stork, his name was Monte Collins, a sick puppy, broken beyond repair and an excellent candidate for euthanasia. Collins thrived on pain and confrontation; his only virtuous quality was his skill as a chef. In constant search of a fight with the waiters, he was always pushing us to draw first blood. He would bake steel plate covers so the waiters would burn their hands in the dining room when removing them. He would pour balsamic vinegar all over the waiter's station if it wasn't spotless and pitch a dozen dinner trays across the kitchen if a single poppy seed was found on one, cussing in our faces like a hostile drill sergeant. Management was deaf to the screaming. Collins mocked all questions, to the point that the staff stopped asking any regardless of necessity. He created specials so long-winded that to recite them unabridged to a table monopolized the waiter's time.

No positive words ever came from Collins' mouth, only cynical negativity. The demons in Collins' eyes were evident when slaughtering lobsters, trout, and crabs, his face giving way to a psychotic smirk when he played the role of execu-tioner. The waitstaff tried everything to get along with Collins, selling his specials, buying him drinks after work, helping him move on two occasions, even scoring him free drugs, but his hateful persona always prevailed.

Collins helped me realize that in life, people don't change. The generous stay generous, the kind stay kind, snakes keep slithering, the slovenly will never be tidy, liars keep lying, drunks stay thirsty, gossips will never be quiet, the true stay true and the mean-spirited and spiteful will always hurl their hate at whomever they can. You can waste your time hoping that people will change, but they won't. Someday someone will stab Collins through his black heart and I appeal to the courts on the killer's behalf that society is a better place with this man dead. Collins left the Coventry to take an executive chef position in New York City. We partied like it was New Year's Eve.

As mentioned earlier, Zach Cavanaugh was the greatest chef I had ever worked for, an eccentric professional and the reason the Coventry enjoyed so much success. Zach was an exception to all the classic chef stereotypes. He was mid-thirties, trim, handsome, and articulate with a Clint Eastwood-like demeanor. "Go ahead, make my bouillabaisse." He rarely drank, didn't smoke and was known for attention to detail that went down to the molecule. A bell pepper wouldn't just be diced; it would be cut into specific sized, uniform diamonds, each one exactly alike. Every sauce that could be individually made for a single entree, would be. Each leaf of radicchio would be equally dewed with the same amount of vinaigrette. Every temperature on every item had a very narrow window of variance. Every plate from his kitchen was an innovative master-piece worthy of a picture.

If cooking for a perfectionist wasn't enough to wear you out, cleaning up would. Zach was like a hospitalized Howard Hughes in his quest for a sterile kitchen. In addition to the hourly sweepings and moppings, every plate, dish, utensil and food item came off every shelf and all surfaces were scrubbed with hot soapy water every night. Rubber boots were custom-made to fit all the electrical outlets and gas valves and after the scrubbing, the entire kitchen was rinsed down with a high-pressure water hose. On Sunday mornings Zach would come in and scrub ceiling tiles, and no microbe stood a chance with cleaning-crazy Cavanaugh in the house. Zach was also a ranter, but his motivations were obvious, unlike Collins who had no keel.

Zach moved on to open his own restaurant, Cavanaugh's Bistro, which was naturally a huge success. You can tell the great restaurants from the merely good ones by noticing where waiters go to dine on their off days. Cavanaugh's Bistro was always first choice among D.C.'s fetch monkeys. Zach was intent on having the best restaurant in Washington at any cost, and he did, but the price was a ninety-hour workweek, every week.

At King Lear, we didn't have chefs in the traditional sense, but instead, proven specific formulas and procedures for the food and its preparation. During lunch and a few nights a week, Quixote Castillo ran the kitchen. Castillo was an over-muscled El Salvadoran whose motor skills and quickness could not be matched in crunch production times, the overlooked dimension of a modern chef. The waiters were always hoping he would be directing the line when King Lear was going to be busy, which was always. Castillo was also a drinker who had dried out after hitting rock bottom. The norm for him was a fifth of Southern Comfort a day until the morning he woke up in his car, upside down in a ditch off the Baltimore-Washington Parkway, with no recollection of the events that put him there. Feeling lucky not to have killed himself, other people, or been injured beyond a ten-stitch gash on the head, he never drank again.

But even during his drinking days, he always made it to work on time, 6:00 a.m. sharp every morning. This was King Lear's code of honor, especially among the waiters. Drink and party like Courtney Love, but no matter how plastered you got, you had to make it to your shift the next day. You may be ordered to go home, but you had to show up or be subject to endless ridicule for not being a tough enough drinker.

Jacques Fonte was the talented, but hot-tempered, head of evening production, an Ethiopian who drove a cab during the day and waiters crazy during the night. On my first New Year's Eve at King Lear it was twenty-five minutes until 1991 and an order of Oysters Rockefeller had been under the heat lamps for an hour, unclaimed by any waiter. Looking for room in the window, dehydrated and exhausted from the blistering heat of the ovens and broilers and stressed from the relentless orders,

Jacques grabbed the steel plate of oysters with his tongs, drew his arm back and hurled the two-pound appetizer across the kitchen at Eric Gagné velocity, bellowing out a pentameter of profanity, demanding to know which waiter left it there. No sane waiter with dreams of life in the new year would assume responsibility. The steel plate struck the side of a roasting oven, leaving a dent that would commemorate Jacques' last rage of 1990.

In 1995, I was accused of making a racially derogatory remark to Jacques which landed me in hot water. He had given me an order of asparagus gratineé with a badly burnt crust that shouldn't have been served. But Jacques refused to make another. On the way out of the kitchen, I said to another waiter, "This is blacker than Jacques."

The next day I was summoned to the office, written up, and forced to apologize to Jacques. Meanwhile, Jacques had punched waiters on several different occasions, been caught stealing cases of steaks, severely burned a line cook, and often cussed so loudly that the patrons could hear him. Yet never once was he disciplined. There was no fairness. There is now, though. Hey Jacques, that asparagus gratineé you gave me for Table 42 in March of 1995 was blacker than your spear-chuckin', wife-cheatin', steak-stealin', mother-fuckin' ass! I also retract my apology. The bio on Jacques also included his endorsement of the mutilation of women in his country, which tells you all you need to know about the man.

Ethan Colchester was the executive chef at Augustine's, a dirtbag culinary genius whose talents seemed wasted on the West Palmers who typically filled the dining room. The ignorance of the Florida snowbirds was well-demonstrated by those who would come from their summer homes in New England to their winter homes in Florida and order halibut, which could be found fresh in New England but was normally frozen in Southern Florida. You're in Florida, eat a fresh Florida fish.

Ethan was English, loved women of ill repute, drank volumes of beer, and was the most sexist individual one can image. Ethan often spouted that men rule the world and women exist only as platforms for breasts and the transportation thereof, and any problems women encountered in life could be traced to their periods. His staggering beer consumption and constant snide remarks about America made him even less likable. Though not fond of our great nation, he wed some lucky American lady so he could remain in the States. By marrying her, he got his citizenship. By marrying him, she got to be awakened from a deep slumber every morning listening to him piss for three minutes at a time to rid himself of the Exxon Valdez' worth of beer he drank the previous evening. In the summer of 1999, Ethan was arrested twice, once for punching a girlfriend and the second time for threatening to kill her with a flare gun and then speeding away at four times the posted speed in his Porsche. He called his wife for bail both times and, like a well-trained Affenpinscher, she came running. Ethan pleaded that both his girlfriend and the arresting officer were having their periods, but the judge was unimpressed.

Ethan's follies were only a fraction of Augustine's employee felonies that filled the court's dockets that year. Augustine's also boasted multiple arrests for crack possession, ten DWIs, the rape of a minor, and an assault on a pregnant woman. The local police never bothered with the fact that Augustine's was a botanical garden of marijuana. The staff often joked that if the restaurant ever burned down, every citizen south of Lake Okeechobee would get high and hungry.

The last crazed chef I worked with was a red-eyed fish named Oscar Poole, another drunkard and chain smoker who was given the top spot in Augustine's kitchen after Ethan moved to Miami to open a French cafeteria; *Tray Chic*. Though skilled as a chef with above average creativity, he was never, ever sober, thirsting only for Sambuca Opal, aka black buca, aka liver tar. Black Sambuca is to alcohol what beef jerky is to food—intense, dark, with the appearance of old motor oil. Often the word black denotes a hint of evil, an adjective that suggests trouble. Think about it. Black Jack—lost wages, ATM fees and overdraft charges; Black Panther—atonement and hate; Black Plague—death; Blackout—looting and conception; Black Sambuca—double vision, memory loss, and vomiting on your girlfriend's cat, family photo album, and oriental rug. Though Oscar was aggressive as a chef, his tanked up personality made him difficult to like. I was intense as a waiter and he didn't care much for my aggressive attitude, but we finally tolerated each other. I believe it was the same day I left Florida. In 2002, Oscar left the United States to open a Chinese restaurant in Cairo; *Wok Like An Egyptian.*

But universally, and especially here in Las Vegas, chefs are all from one of four phylums: **(1) Journeymen Chefs** who cultivate their talents, pay their dues, and for most part, respect their crews. **(2) Fat Mouth Chefs** who substitute volume for intelligence, profanity for talent, of which they have little to none of either. **(3) Celebrity Chefs** with their TV shows, book deals, and restaurants all across the land. And finally are the vast legions of **(4) Crushed Car Cube Chefs**. C4's don't have the talent, connections or gregariousness to be a Celebrity Chef, but got close enough to want it worse than a Fentanyl fix. They're called Crushed Car Cube Chefs because their bashed cranial mental state is an unfixable crushed car cube of psychological dysfunction, plagued with ultra-repressed resentment for working two lifetimes in one. These dented canned good societal rejects treat laterals and subordinates in the worst possible way, yet are somehow sublime in the thought of being a loathsome, bastard-bitch waste of a heart beat.

All of the world's problems are directly caused, or indirectly linked to man's mistreatment/inhumanity to man (and animals). Victory in existence is achieved only by treating those about you with tolerance, respect, compassion and love. But you can't explain such a simple, yet profound concept to a slobbering Crushed Car Cube Chef, there are just too many layers of denial, ego and narcissism. So the Car Cubes drudge on, fuming, hating and berating, until they die of syphilis, alone and unmissed, and then are reincarnated as a tapeworm inside the belly of a three-toed sloth, in a ghetto marsh in Sierra Leone.

Go chuck that in your mirepoix and stir it, Cheffy.

ON JUNE 23, 1888, ABOLITIONIST
FREDERICK DOUGLASS RECEIVED ONE
VOTE AT THE REPUBLICAN NATIONAL
CONVENTION IN CHICAGO, MAKING
HIM THE FIRST AFRICAN AMERICAN
EVER NOMINATED FOR THE U.S.
PRESIDENCY. DOUGLASS WORKED
WITH THE UNDERGROUND RAILROAD,
WAS CO-FOUNDER OF THE NORTH
STAR, AN INFLUENTIAL ANTI-SLAVERY
PAPER, AND IS REGARDED AS THE
FATHER OF THE CIVIL RIGHTS
MOVEMENT.

Chapter 6

Never Say Busboy Again
(*Great Expectorations*)

*"In all the relations of life and death,
we are met by the color line."*

Frederick Douglass (1817–1895)
*Speech at the Convention of Colored Men,
Louisville, Kentucky [September 24, 1883]*

No one wants to be a waiter. It's just a job one does while waiting for the storm to pass. All too often, the storm doesn't pass, it stays right where it began and there's no calm in the eye, which is where you stand. Before you know it, it's last call on your life and you wonder where all that time went. There is no job security, absolutely none. It's like working in a coal mine. You'll definitely get black lung and you never know when the mineshaft is going to cave in. The only difference is that there aren't any good songs about working in a restaurant. No one wants to be a waiter. Pension plans, 401Ks, disability insurance, stock benefits, catastrophic medical coverage, and golden parachutes are all meaningless syllables to a restaurant worker. Unless you've done it, you cannot imagine the tremendous abuse a restaurant carbon blob must endure.

There was a cook at Cedar Forest who lost his left eye when a pocket of water exploded in the deep fat fryer. Since he was black and it happened in 1968, you can guess how much financial compensation he was awarded—absolutely none. There was a waitress at Charles Street who had fallen in the dining

room after suffering a seizure, and was then dragged like an
infantry corpse to the office by a manager who insisted that
the sight of a convulsing employee would be upsetting to the
dinner patrons. There was a general manager in Bethesda
during the late 1980s who denied his AIDS afflicted waiters
medical coverage because they were unable to work the
minimum number of hours required to qualify for benefits.
It wasn't enough that these young men and women would
die young and often in a torturous manner, they would also
die in debt, broke and broken, cut down like tall blue grass
in the path of an angry Toro.

No one wants to be a waiter. You'll never see your daughter's
ballet recital or your son's soccer games and on the lunar eclipse
that is the rare occasion that you do attend the event, you'll
stand out like a palm tree in the middle of an Iowa wheat field
among the devoted parents, one of which you are not. They
thought your children didn't have a daddy or that you were in
prison or possibly dead. The truth is, when your wife got
pregnant you couldn't afford the abortion and she married you
because she thought you might make something of yourself
someday. She thought wrong. You never did, and likely won't,
and that's why her parents never speak about you to their
friends. If your wife doesn't divorce you (Vegas odds posted at
146 to 1 she will), she'll still grow old without you because
your porch chair is always empty. Late at night when you get
home, after you've scrubbed the grease out of your pores,
washed the smoke out of your hair, brushed the layer of booze
off of your teeth and are ready to make love, she's already sound
asleep and sore from banging the guy next door who has a 9
to 5 job.

No one wants to be a waiter. You are forced to smile and
serve those who judge you. Every now and then there is a
customer who sizes you up in a single glance: you, your origin,
your life, and your future. If you listen hard, you can hear the
omniscient voice in their minds. "Shhhh. Don't think too loud,
this guy might hear me thinking. Look at him. What a sad
sight, a depraved, alcoholic, drug-dealing loser. He never went

to Princeton. He didn't belong to a fraternity. He didn't marry the hottest girl on campus. I doubt he even went to college. He's beneath me, barely worthy of serving me. He doesn't own four homes or drive a Cayenne Turbo. I control billions of dollars and his only concern is keeping my wine glass filled. He's just a pathetic degenerate, destined for the gutter."

No one wants to be a waiter. Ask any waiter if they're truly happy; the only honest answer to that question is "no." You're always hoping for something better to happen, something to get you out of the quicksand. But it never happens. The only graspable branch is a bottle and once it's empty and the euphoria is gone, you're sinking again, only faster now with a dry mouth and another throbbing headache, the battering ram of reality. You never knew so much gravity existed.

No one wants to be a waiter, a swiftboat truth with only one statement more superlative. That statement is that absolutely, positively, no one wants to be a busboy. No way. Not as an adult. Not as a man. Not as someone trying to have pride and dignity. There exists only degradation. Shit is the State and, as a busser, you are the governor. You are the sultan of other people's sick. An orderly in a place where there is no order.

A restaurant is a menagerie of messes, nauseous smells, fluids, and spills, and the busboy bats clean-up behind them all. When the over-coked Lebanese debutante gets fucked in the ladies room stall, when the incontinent patron misses the mark badly, when the barfly's stomach refuses that twelfth Staraya Moskva with velocity to spare, the mess belongs to the prosaic busboy. You are the dignitary of the disgusting, whose caste is two notches below grave digger and far removed from self-respect. No one wants to be responsible for all this foulness. But when the coins of life are tossed and the cards of fate are flipped, some will find fulfillment and others will find another mess to clean-up. Such are busmen. No one wants to be a busboy.

In the 1970s, in the private golf and country clubs of Indianapolis, the busmen and waiters were all black. The club members were all white. The thinking, mentality, and segregation were all wrong. The snobbish white folk loved having their army of Uncle Toms there to fetch at their whim and since they had what they thought was a favorable genetic inheritance, a prescribed net worth, and a specified tonnage of stained glass in their places of worship, they felt they could be a member of the higher cracker order. Their white-above-black country clubs made them feel that time had stood still. The Civil War was over only about a hundred years ago. They probably still beat their kids with a belt.

My African brothers at Cedar Forest Country Club quietly found a way to serve the segregationist whities as they deserved. They finally let me in on the secret after I begged them to tell me what they were constantly laughing about. It involved toilet water in the age before bottled water was on every table. Whenever a patron was unreasonable or condescending, a busman would take a pitcher and cup to the employee's restroom, scoop up the water from the toilet, and serve it to that patron in their water glass. On hot days, some patrons drank two or three toilets worth of water and, let me assure you, the employee commode was not the sanitary, glowing clean bowl found in the club member lavatory. On the contrary, it was more like a crapper found in a bad-neighborhood Tucson bus station, with dried urine stains, hangover fragments and shit shrapnel from decades earlier. A thirsty malamute would have looked back at his owner and said, "Are you kidding? I refuse to drink out of here." But the cantankerous Caucasians did, though unknowingly. And if you had the pleasure of dining with a son of a bitch, your glass was also filled with toilet water because the busmen weren't about to use two different pitchers. Bastard club members who weren't drinking from the shit can were victims of the soup/salad phlegm hawker and the dreaded raw steak genital rub. "There's a hair on my steak!" "And not just any old hair at that, lady." Club members who snapped their fingers or were heard mumbling epithets were targets of these moves and much more.

The bussers at the Uptown Club in the early 1980s were both black and white, but the club members were still all white and still quite certain that they were superior to the club fetchers who parked their cars, took their coats, stirred their drinks, served their food, and did as they said. The only blacks they knew were Pittsburgh Steelers, garbage men, or bussers at their snooty, no Jews, spics, or brothers club. They might converse with a black skycap or shoeshine man, but only in a patronizing dialogue that silently said, "Don't look at my daughter that way."

Ironically, the defiant young daughters themselves were the first to step into the present. The first thing a repressed, hot and taut white city girl did at Purdue was get a black boyfriend. They wouldn't just date, they would live together, screwing all night to the soundtrack of *Purple Rain*. The same was true of the repressed farm girls who were raised in closets. The parents had socially suffocated their daughters to the point that such girls, once on campus and off the parental leash, ran to sample the forbidden fruit. If the Kokomo mother knew her precious hundred and ten pound daughter was being spanked thrice nightly by a three-hundred-pound tackle from Gary, she would have gone into cardiac arrest. The girl's father might also have disapproved of his daughter fellating a man whose race was the butt of his jokes. But yesterday is gone and it's a new world and a new century. No one is better than anyone else, unless you think you're better because of the color of your flesh or the worth of your net. Then everyone is better than you.

In the late 1980s at Charles Street Chop House, the bussers were still of one race, but black was out and Asian was in. The bussers at CSCH and many of the top restaurants in Washington were all from Thailand, all either friends, cousins, fathers, nephews, or brothers of one another and often referred to as the Thai Mafia. Most had been in the states for only a few weeks, speaking just enough English to get the job, working in ferocious fashion to keep it. They were the hardest working busmen and barbacks I had ever seen and simply invaded restaurants once one Thai had secured a position.

A typical Thai's work standards and dependability were a manager's dream, lending justification to the risks of hiring those who were illegal aliens. As well as not stealing or drinking like Liza Minnelli, the hired Thais were self-governing in a restaurant's political structure. The first Thai hired was the team leader and would demand an all out effort from any subsequent Thais he helped get hired. It was their discipline and dedication that made them ideal employees. Their names were all modified to have an American ring, like Timmy-Thai, Louie-Thai, Tommy-Thai. I never knew any to have any vices beyond one named Jimmy-Thai. He had run up a $20,000 debt gambling on college hoop "lock" winners as given to him from one of the bar patron prognosticators. A local bookie broke both of his collarbones for the uncollected marker. Jimmy-Thai retreated back to Thailand and was never heard from again, though he likely returned with mended bones, a new name, and a fresh start in a new city.

At the Coventry, the bussing tasks were handled predominantly by Guatemalans. Most were average, though two were outstanding, Faud and Nestor, house favorites of both staff and management. So much so that to obtain citizenship for them the GM actually purchased a bride for Faud and adopted Nestor. Waiters were written up for drinking a glass of milk by the same man who committed two separate felonies to keep a couple of busboys from being deported. The adoption and hushed wedding were supposed to be secrets, but there are no secrets in a fine dining establishment. It only takes one night of heavy drinking, a couple Vicodins, or a puff-puff on a giant jay before everything becomes declassified. For the most part, Faud and Nestor earned whatever rewards they were given, be it store-bought brides or adopted daddies who were only a few years their senior. Together they could handle the bussing duties of five men and when they were off, so too was the level of service at the Coventry.

King Lear's bussers were nothing more than primate extras from the movie *Quest For Fire*. I mean this only as a statement of fact and observation. The bus staff was exclusively El Salvadoran, all related, all crude and unrefined, each exactly alike except with different monikers. They referred to me as *el grande oso blanco del Polo Norte,* the big white bear from the North Pole. Their ages ranged from twenty to forty, and all were short with dark thick hair and bushy mustaches. Each had married as a teenager and had kids by the litter. Their wives would only buy clothing that was either oversized or elastic to accommodate their chronically pregnant conditions. When the Salvies weren't knocking up their wives, they were knocking them around, which is common in primitive cultures. If you can't use your mind, use your fists and be sure and hit something that won't hit back or call the police. One of the bussers had broken his son's nose so many times that the doctors finally removed all of the boy's nasal cartilage, resigned to the fact that there would be more falls down the steps of his one story home. The boy deserved the beatings; he was always trying to keep his father from disciplining his mother.

But the King's busmen's true forté, a lesser sin than abusing one's family, though still a sin, was theft. Most of King Lear's bussers would steal if the opportunity presented itself, showing no loyalty to the men who had given them jobs nor harboring feelings of guilt for wrongdoing. Robbing the Coventry was an act of retaliation, but theft from Constantine and Clay Papandreas, the revered owners of King Lear, was mutiny. They were ideal owners, unselfishly generous, and treated their employees as if they were family. But in the narrow mind of a King Lear busser, anyone who had more in life than they did was a target for theft, regardless of previous generosity. Nothing noble about these guys.

There are thousands of ways for a front house employee to steal and the Salvies knew them all. King Lear's bussers' favorite method of theft was to throw items in the trash, take the trash out, and then rifle through the dumpster after the shift, retrieve the item, and hustle it into the trunks of their rusty green Novas with the sheepskin seat covers. The linen bag worked even better in the same fashion and didn't involve rolling in refuse. The items stolen could be anything that wasn't bolted down (silverware, glasses, tea pots, wine, linen itself, steaks, kitchen utensils, plates, bowls, first aid supplies, even artwork that was, in fact, bolted down). "Hey, wasn't there a Picasso on that wall yesterday?"

Another stealing maneuver borrowed from Officer Candidate Mayo was to hide liquor bottles in the ceiling tiles of the pantry. This was done by the bussers who helped restock the bar during non-service hours. We learned about this trick only after a half dozen bottles of Malibu rum came crashing down like bombs from the overloaded ceiling tile, exploding on the pantry counters and almost killing a waiter. The bussers didn't know anything about it. Surely the construction workers put the rum there when they installed the ceiling back in 1978.

One mode of theft was to trade stolen liquor to the kitchen for food. A fifth of Ketel One, poured into an Evian bottle to throw to the hounds, would ensure too many racks of lamb would be cooked that evening and the excess mutton would quietly go to the Salvies.

Yet another ploy was to remove any wine in an ice bucket from the dining room, fake refreshing the ice, and quickly drink a glass or chug directly from the bottle if the coast was clear. This didn't last too long because a waiter who caught a busman in the act would fine him the cost of the bottle, docking his tip out for the price of a new bottle. Sometimes the fining process took several nights to cover high-end wines, but it had to be done. The bussers would usually retaliate in some form of vandalism usually directed at that particular waiter's car or locker room possessions.

The crudeness of King Lear's bussers was astonishing. They were homophobic mongrels absolutely obsessed with sodomy, flatulence, and excrement. Every day was the same sorry routine, listening to them accuse each other of homosexual behavior and disposition while constantly trying to out fart each other. Pitch, duration, stench, and decibel level were the critical categories. There wasn't a single shift in over 2,500 that I didn't hear about someone's alimentary canal fire exit. Even Christmas was not so sacred a day that they could refrain from voicing their personal postulations on the subject. If the Salvies weren't speaking of it, they were exchanging pictures of it.

Also noteworthy was the busser's incredible indolence. The waiters even joked about. it: "Which takes longer, Enrique and Timo resetting a table or photosynthesis?" And why walk thirty feet to a restroom when you could piss in a sink or floor drain? Post leak, it was more likely the whiz kids would quote Rudyard Kipling than consider washing their hands.

The Salvies ate like cavemen, stuffing their faces with both hands, never completely closing their mouths and never shutting the hell up, food consumption not hindering the speaking process. The food they lifted up to their faces had only a fifty-fifty chance of actually being chewed and swallowed, the excess crumbs falling on their clothing, table, chairs, and floor like confetti on a MacArthur parade. It didn't require a detective to deduce where the bussers had eaten, the waiters certain that the District's roach population had maps of the Washington area with the Salvies' homes circled.

Eating was the primary concern for the bussers and when the employee meal was unappealing, the busmen had no qualms about eating food from a customer's plate just cleared. Several times a week was some elderly woman celebrating a birthday whose relatives would order for her a five-pound lobster, the portion large enough to feed the Cratchett family twice. The woman would only eat a small portion, so little that the lobster probably could have survived the few bites had it not been cooked. The customers would elect not to take the excess home for fear it might stink up the Lexus while they were at the National Theatre, and that's when the Salvie chop shop sprang into action. One busser would bring the lobster into the pantry and the other bussers would converge on the crustacean like piranhas on a floating pig carcass, eating only with their hands and using grunts to communicate. Seconds later, the lobster was gone and all that remained were a few shell fragments and six filthy, farting El Salvadorans with lobster flesh in their mustaches, now using pieces of the antennas to pick their teeth. Such fury was never applied to the task of bussing.

Cocaine always dragged down service and Friday was both payday and District dust delivery day, no coincidence there. Since the coke middlemen to the bussers were King Lear waiters, the snow wasn't about to stop falling. It got so out of hand that it was rumored that Whitney Houston was going to stage an intervention. Many of the waiters sniffed during their shift, but they did so with discretion and not to the extent that it affected service. Not so with the Salvies, they snorted as delicately as they ate, and once your assigned busser was aglow for the evening, support service was going to be shaky or nonexistent. And when whacked, the busmen believed Spanish to be some Martian dialect or uncrackable Navajo code that no earthling aside from themselves understood. This made for many problems.

One evening I was working with a freshly lit amigo named Jesus (*hey-suess*, referred to as Baby Jesus). I asked him to offer pepper to a table of four. Furious that I had asked him to perform a duty outside the scope of his normal bussing tasks, he barked out the word "puta" while in the act of peppering. Amazingly, no one at the table knew the word but knew from his inflection that it was not a word appropriate in the atmosphere of fine dining. That table's next round was free and so was the labor of Baby Jesus that evening.

Another time during lunch, I was serving an obese woman from the State Department and her guest. An insolent rapscallion named Gilberto was resetting a nearby table and had commented to another busman about the woman's girth. One of the many cruel observations he uttered in Spanish was, "Wouldn't it be horrible if this woman sat on your face?" As it turned out, the ridiculed woman spoke seven languages, including Spanish. Her guest, upset and trembling, called me over to tell me what had just happened. I grabbed Gilberto by the back of the neck and marched him back to the kitchen, threw him inside the kitchen doors and told Castillo to deal with him. I then ran back to the woman's table and apologized as best I could for the busser's insensitive remarks. Their meal was free, but even a year of free lunches would not lessen the hurt this woman felt, remarks that she would remember for the rest of her life. She attempted to have Gilberto deported, though was unfortunately unsuccessful in her efforts.

With a few sterling exceptions, the Vegas bussers, like the Lear Salvies, weren't the brightest stars in the sky. One kid I worked with was named Jeff Davis, a UNLV underachieving sophomore, had never heard of, or learned of, or been taught by his parents or teachers whom Jefferson Davis was in American History. Another gullible busman had been instructed in prank by his fellow bong-banging bussers to sprinkle cappuccinos with used espresso grounds just prior to serving. I couldn't believe how stupid this kid was. I had to explain to him that customers shouldn't be bitter-faced, black-toothed and spitting out coffee grounds when drinking a cappuccino. A common busbiatch question from one particular fellow when asked to refill water was "which table?" "Are you kidding me, Poindexter? We only have two tables, just five feet apart, and you need me to show you which table has the empty water glasses? Lucky for you breathing and heartbeat are involuntary. Forget what I said about there being no such thing as a stupid question. You just wrecked it for me. You should have never violated that Nevada State helmet law."

The boy wasn't too bright. He thought that a blood drive was a car pool for black people.

The Rules Reiterated
Subject: Server Assistants/Table Captains (bus persons).[†]

1. **NEVER Say Busboy Again**. The correct term is Server Assistant, or ideally, Table Captain (TC). You can also say "busser" or "busman," but soon these words will also be antiquated. The author of this book claims exception to the NSBA rule.

2. **Be Ahead Of The Game** and stop using the word "waitress" too. Usage labels you as a dinosaur. Flo don't work here no more. All gender-indicative/deprecatory connoting descriptives are dying fast. Soon, it will be politically incorrect to say "bat boy" and "bat girl." The new terms will be "thunder wood fetcher," "lumber relocater," "bat attaché," "whack stick acquisition technician," and "timber-getter for that moody, ERA-wrecking indicted dude drinking the steroidaccino with the nasty back acne and scrawny little poodle legs."

[†] In U.S. Marine Corps and Naval Aviation, enlisted personnel responsible for a specific aircraft's maintenance are called "plane captains." Their names are painted on the plane's fuselage, and pilots are forbade to fly the aircraft without the plane captain's consent. It is this author's ardent recommendation that fine dining server assistants henceforth be referred to as **Table Captains (Tango Charlies)**. Using the term **Server Assistant** is good, but saying **Table Captain** (or **TC**) dignifies the position and creates pride. C'mon now, management. Drop your coke spoons and start typing up those TC memos now.

THE ODDS OF OPENING A RESTAURANT OF FIFTY SEATS OR MORE, MAKING A PROFIT, AND STAYING IN BUSINESS FOR AT LEAST TEN YEARS WITHOUT INCURRING DIVORCE, BANKRUPTCY, OR BEING NAMED AS A DEFENDANT IN A LAW SUIT ARE ROUGHLY 1 IN 9,000. THOSE ARE APPROXIMATELY THE SAME ODDS AS A U.S. INFANTRYMAN IN VIETNAM SURVIVING 407 CONSECUTIVE TOURS OF COMBAT DUTY.

Chapter 7

Owning a Restaurant

(*H5N1 ‹avian influenza›*)

*"Once they were a happy race. Now they are made
miserable by the white people, who are never contented
but are always encroaching."*

Tecumseh (1768–1813)
Council at Vincennes, Indiana Territory, [August 14, 1810]
Speech to William Henry Harrison

Don't listen to the song of the sirens, the soothing melody that
makes you think owning a restaurant is glamorous. That song is a
lie. You'd fare better by converting your net worth to cash and
wagering the entire amount on Bellamy Road to win easily at TKD
and gallop off with the Triple Crown. Look through the Yellow
Pages from five years ago and compare the restaurant listings with
a current edition. Not a lot of survivors are to be found. New restaurants fall faster than bubonic plague victims. You wanting to be a
successful restaurant owner is like the ghetto child wanting to be an
NBA star; the dreams are pleasant but the realities are very harsh.
The ghetto child will most likely end up in prison and you'll end up
in Chapter 11. There are thousands of successful restaurants in the
United States, but in proportion to all restaurants opened, the
successful ones are very, very, few. But you won't listen. You're
stubborn. You and the wife have just inherited a railroad car full of
cash and you're not content to invest the money in a secure venture
that will double the principal in a few years. You want something

more tangible, something that massages your ego and leaves people in awe of you as if you were the Dalai Lama himself. You've eaten in a lot of restaurants; therefore you must know how to own one, right? Please! Yet you still can't be swayed. Well before you leap, do as I say—work in a restaurant.

If you've never worked in a restaurant, a jolting cup of physical reality might lessen your dementia. Before you buy one sheet of paper upon which to fashion your business plan, get a job in a local restaurant and work every position for at least a week. Most private restaurant owners will avail you the opportunity at an exploitative wage, which is what you'll intend to pay your own employees anyway. Every position means every position, starting as a pot washer.

You'll find that slavery in America still exists and Abe Lincoln is nowhere to be found. Your hands will be raw, callused and pruned and your spine will ache from endless, menial hours spent in a question mark posture over steamy, grimy, Salton Sea foul sinks. Just imagine the mess in your mother-in-law's kitchen after Thanksgiving dinner and then multiply it by five hundred—only this time you're not sipping sherry, wearing your favorite cotton shirt, glancing at the football game and pondering a pre-pie nap.

Next is work as a dishwasher. You never knew so many dirty dishes existed, piled up so high that one more saucer will cause a ceramic avalanche. Worse than the endless stacks of soiled dishes and silverware is the unimaginable amount of waste you witness. The amount of perfectly edible food America throws out every day and night will astound you. And on that same city block, people are starving. This is sin in its purest form. Even if you can remove the moral impropriety of unadulterated waste, there is the relatively insignificant point of your own profit. As a restaurant owner, every lemon rind, parsley sprig, and chickpea discarded is another nickel out of your pocket, not to mention the high-end foods your employees are secretly gorging themselves on, compliments of you.

Next comes work as a utility person. Don't worry. You'll figure out how to dump a dozen two-hundred-pound garbage cans in a dumpster that's four feet high at its lowest point. Some of the garbage cans have holes in the bottom that leave a slime trail of garbage water from the kitchen to the dumpster like some mutant Chernobyl snail. You'll have to mop up the snail trail and scrub every surface in the kitchen twice before it's time to deblacken the ovens, clean the broilers, drain the fryers, and scour the stock kettles. You'll wear rubber gloves to protect you from the toxic industrial cleaners, but will still get a rash and a nosebleed from the fumes, the long-term effects leaving you in a cancer ward ten years up the road. You'll crush hundreds of cockroaches and not even dent their population. Flies, spiders, and ants are everywhere despite a weekly visit from the exterminator whose mystery spray causes you more harm than the insects for which it was intended.

Next, it's time to work in food preparation, peeling potatoes, chopping vegetables, shucking oysters and clams, slaughtering lobsters, eviscerating crabs, and filleting ten different kinds of fish until you stink so badly that a thirty-minute shower with Ajax and near boiling water doesn't get you clean. You'll make oceans of sauces, soups, and stocks and realize that everything in a working kitchen is either hot, loud, heavy, broken, pointed, steaming, toxic, sharp, wet, pungent, sticky, slippery, stressful, vulgar, bleeding, disgusting, or a combination of the above. If you make it behind the cook's line to produce live orders, it's a fast moving and furious chaos of screaming chefs, darting waiters, and cussing cooks, all misfits in the torpedoed engine room of the USS *Leper Colony* that is any fine dining kitchen. You'll never hear any positive reinforcement here, only a continuous barkfest of misery and negative dialogue. The chef will never be content with anything you produce, even if God himself had prepared it and given it to you to present as your own. All this time, all day long, you've never once sat down. At the end of the day when you've borrowed strength just to drive home late, walk in your house, and plop your ass down on the sofa, you're too tired to even take your shoes off.

Next is to work as a barback. In case you didn't know, ice weighs the same as water and the bar needs literally tons of it. The ice machine is nowhere near the bar. You'll shovel ice to the bar as if you were shoveling coal on a westbound locomotive in the nineteenth century, only this time the coal is kept in the caboose. Four hundred patrons can drink a dam of drams, every drop coming from bottles that you must haul from the storage room, not to mention what the employees drink. Their alcoholic consumption makes the bar patrons' look like a Mennonite sewing circle. Meanwhile, dirty bar glasses are piling up, each one requiring individual hand washing and drying. You can say farewell to your once soft hands. They'll become so coarse from bar chemicals that you'll be able to sand an unfinished credenza with your bare palms.

Ice melts, but empty bottles must be thrown away, which is more bad news for your back, and even worse news for the environment. Like food waste, the material waste that a restaurant produces will astound you. I worked fifteen years as a fine dining front houser, serving an average of eight bottles of wine a night. At five shifts a week, that's one hundred and sixty bottles a month, two thousand bottles a year, not even counting hard liquor and bottled water which was easily twice that amount. That's over 100,000 bottles, each with a cork or top, from one waiter between 1989 and 2004. Don't forget to add the 3,900 bottles of wine I drank during that time. That's no joke. That's five bottles a week, a proverbial bunny slope of alcoholic consumption compared to some of the Olympic medal drinkers I worked with—guys and girls who would intervene on an intervention so the drinking wouldn't stop.

But your apprenticeship isn't over yet, not even close. Next, it's time to be a busboy. Your job is all about filth and transportation. Resetting everything and polishing silver until your wits are withered and mind is numbed with tedium, leaving you with no feeling of self-worth. Every soiled plate and teacup is your responsibility to remove, replace, and repolish.

Being a waiter isn't much better. Waiting on tables will kill any hopes you had for mankind and its possible prosperity, serving fat-assed patrons who are committing suicide with a fork while blabbing on about their glory days long since past.

It's even worse for the pourboys, for at the bar exists the saddest chorus line of all, a row of obliterated zombies that make the bartender wish he worked on a scallop trawler, far away from the dank and chemically-dependent sponge bobs sitting in front of him.

If you think owning a restaurant is glamorous, then you've

been watching too many American Express commercials. Owning a restaurant is not some picturesque Nantucket bistro where you taste sauces with a silver spoon and nod at an over-starched chef in a shining brass kitchen and then prance about your Martha Stewart-decorated dining room in a Sax Fifth suit while listening to George Winston piano solos, smiling and savoring the sunshine of your own success. Owning a restaurant is the very opposite: a putrid, suspicious, sucking chest-wounded whorehouse of hate, theft, sloth, slaughter, and rotting fish, spinning out of control like Dorothy's house in a Kansas tornado, and Toto is nowhere to be found— some *Iron Chef* ingredient getter snatched him up.

The drudgery of long, hard hours is just one poison pony on the restaurant merry-go-round of pain. Next there is the physical tally. You will drink. The first few sips bring happiness; the next few thousand press your face against the furnace window of hell. You have to set a good example for your customers and you can't do that by sipping green tea and eating tofu. So you drink. You'll drink so much that you won't be able to recall the last day in your life you didn't have a drink. Given the chance to speak your liver would say, "Damn, did we move to Seattle? I'm getting rained on every day now and not just sprinkles. I mean monsoon season downpours!" Next is your hair; it's either going to turn grey or jump off your head entirely. Your face, still youthful a few years ago, now looks like a Rand McNally map of southern California. Your back is now bothering you daily, to the extent you'll make weekly visits to the chiropractor. Your knees will age two years for every one year you work in a restaurant. Your teeth are now some dark shade of eggnog from secondhand smoke, because dental hygiene is way down on the list of your daily priorities. You'll inhale so much smoke that you'll think you're the Marlboro man, every suit you own smelling like a South Carolina pool hall. In addition, you now have shin splints, fallen arches, grapes of wrath (hemorrhoids), high blood pressure, no less than four ulcers, and varicose veins. No hyperbole here. In fifteen years of fine dining service I had to have my varicose veins stripped twice and southern vineyard harvested once. Forget the gym, it would be like a trip to Coeur d'Alene. There just aren't enough minutes in the day.

You certainly won't have time for your family anymore, the emotional price of owning an eatery. The dreams you and your wife had of a happy family are dust, the storybook silver-framed wedding picture on the mantle a joke. The first year you make a profit your wife will divorce you because you are never, ever home, your marriage spinning out of the sky like a Spitfire that just lost a wing. She's been spending her weekdays handling the UPS guy's package, even though she told you she was home alone, all by herself, chopping broccoli. You'll get killed in the divorce settlement, sued so badly you'll wake up in the Paleolithic Era, left with only an office cot, a can of anchovies, a frozen partridge, and a four-digit alimony payment.

Your children will become strangers to you. Your son will do drugs, perform miserably in school, and end up breaking the law and going to jail. Forget about him becoming successful, you just want him to stop picking fights with cops and selling ecstasy. The new odds that he'll finish high school are exactly the same as Gary Busey being voted Negro of the Year, or Air France buying and flying a Boeing. Your daughter now despises you and lays the family break-up entirely on you. She'll show her rebellion by becoming a chain smoker, getting a cult tattoo on her scapula, a tongue stud, and moving in with an unbathed, razorless, law-defying, jobless man twice her age who won't be shy about slapping her around in retaliation for the way his parents abused him. The very thought of a strange man abusing your daughter makes you ponder the consequences of murder.

The next rusted pitchfork in your restaurant-owning side is employee theft. You can't stop it. You can't even deter it. Imagine a ten-story tidal wave crashing down on you and all you have is a squeegee to try and stop it. It isn't gonna happen. You can put in cameras, watchdogs, bells, alarms, whistles, even train tiny mice to hide out in the corners and rat out the bad eggs, but malevolence will always prevail. Restaurant workers aren't MENSA members or Buddhist priests with high ethical values. They are, for the most part, live-for-right-now people. You offer them no pension plan, no health insurance, and no job security. You drive a new Viper and force them to work on Christmas, and, in return, they take what they can from you and sleep like babies.

Restaurant employees justify everything. If you reprimand an employee for being late, he'll retaliate against you for disciplining him. Employee retaliation can take many forms. You've unknowingly provided fifty people in Nicaragua with a complete dinette set, from eleven-piece silver settings to crystal wine goblets including two cases of a pretentious Gigondas to fill them. You can't ask the good employees to stop the bad employees from stealing lest they become retaliatory targets themselves. People will always steal no matter where you are, and, in a restaurant, dishonesty rules.

The objective for servers and bartenders is to transfer as much loot as possible from the patron's pocket to your pocket. In doing so, all ethical and moral considerations must be disregarded. No person should have eight gin and tonics in one evening, but we'll bring you eighteen if we think you can sit upright and still thump out a pulse. Six shots of espresso is too much caffeine for any one patron's heart, but if it makes you jumpy enough to get up so we can turn the table, we'll do it. The five-hundred-pound man shouldn't be eating a sugar-rich, two-thousand calorie slab of mocha torte, but it upped the check another ten bucks and that's our job. It's hard to feel good about yourself when you're doing so many things that are so unquestionably wrong.

Hence, stealing from a pompous restaurant owner pales in comparison to the sins that comprise a restaurant employee's job description. So employee theft goes on and the person being robbed is you, the owner. Ten percent of gross profits is the accepted industry standard for theft. I wager it is much more than that nationwide. But your employees aren't the only ones who plan to take your money.

Extortion is next. You've built a restaurant and are enjoying the excitement of having the hottest place in town. You're still losing money because of extravagant spending, but it's justified if you can keep business roaring for a few more years. Your hopes are set way too high. Then a few well-dressed men walk in the kitchen door and insist you give them a cash slice of the wealth every few weeks. They even dictate the purveyors you'll use for everything from liquor and linen to produce and wine. You're not Chingachgook, you can't take these guys on, and to do so would give the word "losing" a new meaning.[†] Besides, behind them stand a thousand more greasy-haired clones with intimidating names. The police won't help, they know that interference means a horizontal trip to Hoffaville, and it's possible they've had to work out arrangements themselves. Italian cash taxation is just something you'll have to accept here. The only problem is that each month the payout increases until you find, in order to just stay afloat and keep your kneecaps intact, you have to fraudulently doctor your income reports. This leaves you open for an audit so severe that you'll be wearing an orange jumpsuit picking up interstate garbage. Keep reading.

The list of people who want a bite out of your restaurant-owning ass continues. Health inspectors to start. Health inspectors could easily close down dozens of big city restaurants every day, but a discrete envelope of non-sequential dollars keeps the inspector's pen idle. Every month a few restaurants are closed as a lesson to the rest of the herd. What about zoning officials? They may just discover a transgression long after you've completed construction. The bureau of ATF also has their law-enforcing eyes on you because your employees are dealing enough drugs to fuel a Led Zeppelin reunion. Then there's the INS, EEOC, NAACP, OSHA, and no less than a zillion lawyers representing any of your current or former employees, customers, girlfriends, wives, investors, partners, or even pedestrians who've walked anywhere near your restaurant, who will try and sue you for anything and everything imaginable. Even the name of your restaurant brings risk of litigation. I'll spare you the details about and repercussions of Mad Cow, Foot and Mouth, SARS and bird flu, a brakeman's yank to your business, cull and holocaust for the world's livestock. After it's all said and done, what is the end result? You're broke, in debt up to your eyeballs, alone, possibly in jail, definitely in poor health, likely an alcoholic, and irrevocably miserable and contemplating taking the Nestea plunge from the Golden Gate Bridge. You're not dreaming and if you are, it's a nightmare.

But if you still dream about opening a restaurant, don't dream big. Expansion is to restaurants what tsunamis are to shorefront condos. Anyone who has ever worked in a restaurant will tell you

---

[†]Chingachgook, father of Uncas and adopter of orphaned Mohawk Nathaniel (Hawkeye) Poe, was the tribesman who slew Magua in James Fenimore Cooper's 1826 Novel *The Last of the Mohicans*, one of 44 books written by Cooper.

the same. Minimalism is the key. You don't need a four-hundred-bottle wine list when fifty gets the job done fine. Plus, with an enormous wine list, you'll never have an accurate list of vintages. Don't get extravagant with your bar stock either. No one cares that you have vodka from Uzbekistan and odds are that your waiters will end up drinking it anyway.

On your menu, go with fewer items, each one outstanding, as opposed to dozens, most mediocre. Plus, if you think your customers don't recognize the sauce redundancy on your expansive menu, then you're not giving your clientele enough credit. Any successful restaurant that doesn't pile cheddar cheese on every other item will have a streamlined menu. Why do you suppose that is?

Be practical about everything in your restaurant. Sell your golf clubs, too. You can't make a restaurant succeed by putzing around the links pretending you're Phil Mickelson. But ultimately, there are two specific things you must do if you want any chance to succeed as a restaurateur. Their importance cannot be overstated.

The first is to hire an executive officer, a seasoned hospitality veteran who knows what a fragile beast a restaurant is and has full authority to make all decisions and say anything to you without fear of termination. Someone who can tell you the cold, hard, blatant, hurts-to-hear-it, incontrovertible truths without you and your ego getting bent out of shape. Your GM will tell you things that will make your ears bleed, but you must listen. There are millions of "yes men" out there to tell you you're cooler than Kanye West, stronger than Big Papi Ortiz, and a more nimble man than Jackie Chan, but that's just a load of fodder. You don't shit Dove Bars, and you should certainly know that arse-kissing is nothing but whiskey tango. As a fledgling restaurateur, you are going to make some colossal mistakes and if you don't listen intently to your second in command, you'll run the ship aground. Don't do it. Find a savvy leader and do whatever it takes to keep him contented. Pay him well, don't overwork him, and give him a percentage of the profits if you ever make any, which is doubtful.

The first thing your GM will do is hire a top-notch bar manager/sommelier, another essential member of your team. This person will also greatly influence whether you succeed or fail.

The second and most important rule of succeeding as a restaurateur is to treat your staff well. No restaurant has ever enjoyed sustained success where the owner mistreats the staff. Treat your employees poorly and they'll devour you like a luau swine on a spit. It will take you a few months to figure out who your top employees are, but when you do, look after them like sons and daughters. Give them a good meal every day. Let them have a shift drink, remembering that they'll have one regardless. Verbally praise them, give financial incentives, and ask for their opinions and ideas on all aspects of the restaurant. Regardless of what you may think, your employees know more about your restaurant than you do, so listen hard to what they have to say.

Close your restaurant one day a week, preferably Sunday, and for the love of God, **close your fucking restaurant on all holidays.** Your restaurant isn't a hospital, police or fire department. There is no reason to be open. Do you know how hard it was for me to wait on angry, indignant patrons at King Lear on Christmas day? What are they so upset about? I'm the one whose grandmother is sitting home alone in Delaware on Christmas day while I'm stuck in Washington playing yuletide fetch monkey for some spoiled aristocracy who were too lazy to make their own meal or stop by Sutton Place Gourmet the day before. There's a reason why none of the staff is smiling. When you are open on holidays, you are clearly telling the staff that a few days' profit means more to you than their happiness and family lives, an ignorantly eloquent statement that your staff will answer in an ugly and expensive fashion. Treating your staff well is an ongoing endeavor, and is just as important as treating your customers well. But only a small percentage of restaurateurs have the respect and loyalty of their crews, and thus, a successful store.

But, no matter how you slice it, the journey of building a successful restaurant is a nearly impossible venture, the wrong path taken on the forked road of your life. Don't do it. Mother Earth is already suffering too much, littered with far too many restaurants, as well-illustrated by a fast-food commercial from the late 1990s. A father and son are driving along a desolate and scenic road in New Mexico, the father scanning the twilighted

Note: The truly great restaurant owners close their establishments on Super Bowl Sunday.

horizon with a concerned look on his face. Suddenly, atop one of the solemn canyon ridges, he sees a notorious neon restaurant logo and smiles. This is the mentality of America, the enterprisingly free questing for the dollar at any cost. I hope you liked *Titanic,* because you're on it. We're just sinking a little slower.[†]

The Rules Reiterated
Subject: Owning a Restaurant (for potential restaurant owners).

1. **Don't Own A Restaurant** unless you really hate yourself, enjoy pain, financial hardship, and humiliation. America needs another restaurant like we need another Cher farewell concert, *Law & Order* spin-off series, or celebrity awards show. *Note to Jerry Orbach (1935-2004): LAO was never the same without Lenny Briscoe. We miss you, Jerry.*

2. **Hire** a full-authority second-in-command and listen to him or her. Remember, though, this person is not a scapegoat for when bad things happen. That inevitable bowl of spoiled porridge has your name on it. Now in delicious crow flavor.

3. **Treat Your Employees Well**. Close at least one day a week, all holidays, and provide your staff with health insurance. Your employee turnover rate is an excellent indicator as to how well you're treating your crew. Take special care of your **LOFT** employees, those who *Look Out For The House*. If you have nothing but **WHAM** employees (*WHat About Me*), then the odds are you're a lousy owner, your business is about to collapse and the entire staff is hunting around for something better.

4. **Try Hard** not to waste your unused food. In another life you'll be starving and regretting such apathy. Find a way to lateral it to the less fortunate. All this gluttony, excessive consumption, and indifference to waste is a major reason why other nations despise America.

[†]America's worst maritime accident occurred on April 27, 1865 on the Mississippi River after 3 of 4 boilers exploded on the steamboat *Sultana*. Loaded to six times its capacity, 2,000 of the *Sultana's* 2,300 passengers were killed, most being just-released Union prisoners of war. 9,343 lives were lost in the Russian sinking of the KdF *Wilhelm Gustloff* in January of 1945, the world's deadliest marine disaster.

†South Las Vegas Boulevard in winter of 2005. Picture by John Calvin Williams of IDM Graphics.

Chapter 8

March of the Penguins

(*The French Foreign Lesion*)

"Do me a favor
open the door
and let 'em in."

Wings, "Let 'em in," *At The Speed of Sound,*
Capitol Records, 1976

#1 Mitch Morehouse—The Veteran

In every organization, there is a person who is the heart
and soul, the one whose being epitomizes the essence of his
people, the cause leader. In Babylonian times it was Gilgamesh.
To religious reform in Europe it was Martin Luther. During the
American Revolution it was the stretched-neck spy Nathan
Hale. To the Apache Indians it was the indomitable Geronimo.
For the cause of equal rights and civil liberties it was Rosa Parks.
For the NHL's Rangers and the Madison Square faithful it was
Mark Messier, Mia Hamm for aspiring soccer femmes. To
ambitious dogs able to bark for help it was Lassie. For Roman
slaves it was Spartacus (though everyone claimed to be him) and
for terrorized New Yorkers it was Rudy Giuliani.

For the King Lear waitstaff, his name was Mitchell Foxwig
Morehouse, a restaurant journeyman and unofficial viceroy of
the two-dozen best waiters in Washington, the penguins who
comprised Drunk Man Group. There's a guy like Mitch in
every restaurant; a weathered rogue who had been at King Lear
from day one back in 1978 and would be there amidst the ashes

when it burns down during the Arnold Presidency Overthrow Riots of 2015. To him, like most career waiters, the restaurant was a sort of prison, and fate had thwarted all of his attempts to tunnel under and out.

Mitch was in his late forties, tall and handsome in a gritty fashion. He had served three years as a Coast Guard coxswain, dishonorably discharged in 1974 for sampling seized narcotics. After working occupations ranging from bookie collector and lone shark bone breaker to unlicensed glove compartment pharmacist, Mitch joined King Lear as part of its original twenty-five waiter roster, and was the last remaining of the initial crew.

Mitch went about his life without regard for rules and regulations, defying the altruistic aspirations of the owners and management as well as local and federal law enforcement agencies. Whether it was three cocktails before noon or being AWOL for a shift, his transgressions were tolerated because so many patrons demanded him as their waiter. Some patrons would refuse to eat at King Lear unless Mitch was their waiter; some would refuse to eat there if he was. The manicured senators and lacy lawyers wearing Al Gore levels of male bronzer didn't care much for Mitch. The mobsters, union heads, and star regulars insisted on no other. Mitch had taken me under his wing and taught me his craft, making me an exception in regard to the plebes. He didn't care for the new blood on the waitstaff. They hadn't been there in the 1980s when the waiters were taking home close to six digits a year and the entire crew drank so much that Irish villages actually wrote songs about their livers. I was grateful to have such a fine mentor, despite the fact a mere six Grand Marniers (referred to by the staff as Agent Orange or duck sauce) would have left me in the ICU. I repaid Mitch's faith in me by covering for him when he was missing in action and helping serve his tables when the purple haze was all around.

Among his many regular customers were a few fireworks dealers, and nothing goes better with four mid-shift cocktails than a pyrotechnic display in the alleyway behind the Landry Hotel. We're not talking sparklers and Snappy Pops, we're talking weekend in Fallujah "I'm sorry your car is upside down and burning" type fireworks. Mitch would pass the word to the other waiters and all at once the penguins would file off the floor and into the alleyway for the fireworks show. Sometimes the fireworks displays lasted so long that the GM had a few of the waiters' pictures printed on the back of milk cartons. "Have you seen this waiter? Last seen running out of King Lear's kitchen door with a pack of matches."

Though hard to believe, intoxication and high-velocity burning white phosphorus rockets fired in confined spaces isn't always a safe combination. Mitch once brought in this mega-powerful pod of five hundred rockets that was either Desert Storm surplus, or designed to frighten UFOs, the pod itself resembling an uncut wheel of Jarlsburg cheese. The word was passed and all fifteen waiters relocated to the alley. Fellow waiter and Maker's Marked man, Lee (aka "The Eel"), was chosen as the torchbearer. He set the giant wheel upside down, thinking the fuse would naturally be closer to his lighting hand and not the ground and thus, the pod must have been right side up.

He was wrong. The first whistling rocket angrily flipped the pod on its side and the remaining four hundred and ninety-nine fired sideways with Gatling gun frequency, flying two feet off the ground, the pod spinning with each blast. The waiters ducked for cover in the hail of spewing rockets, hoping to not get hit yet still poking our faces in harm's way trying to get a glimpse of the show. Each rocket ricocheted off no less than two surfaces before disappearing into the night. The dumpsters, parked cars, hotel windows, and ducking penguins were the primary targets. Cops weren't a factor. They had actually shown up a few times during previous displays, but the rehearsed line was that we heard some noise from inside the dining room and rushed out to the alley to investigate. This particular volley of rockets didn't seem to end, but at some point some of the patrons must have noticed the brief but complete absence of waiters in King Lear's dining room. Finally the red glare ended as a cumulonimbus cloud of flinty smoke filled the alley. We dusted ourselves off and hustled back into the restaurant feeling lucky that no one had been fragged. The next move was obvious—pound a drink, which was going to happen regardless.

Mitch was not only a demolitions expert, but an agriculturist as well. You can guess the main crop, the secondary staple being lethal peppers from which he made incendiary salsas so hot it gave the busboys vertigo. What Mitch couldn't grow in his backyard, he bought in bottled form from local gourmet shops. The bussers were always volunteering to be Jack's guinea pigs in the matter of salsa tasting to reaffirm their sense of self in the unlikely event that it had been a slow week for spouse smacking or mustache growth. To any reluctant bussers, he would simply say, "I guess you're not a man." Already feeling unmanly because majority of the surrounding waiters were at least a foot taller, they would always cave in to the con. Mitch could say, "I guess you're not a man because you won't tug on that angry bobcat's whiskers," and they would do it every time, getting ripped to shreds in the process. Mitch's salsas weren't much tamer. I recall many a red-eyed busser with Seabiscuit-sized nostrils.

There was one woman patron who, seeking nothing to do with manliness, just wanted to have, and I quote, "the hottest damn Bloody Mary you can make." Mitch was her waiter and Fate cruelly looked on with anticipation. Mitch grinned and told the misguided woman that his best effort would find her in a morgue drawer before sundown. With defiance, the arrogant woman said, "Bring it on, boy, let's see what you've got." Mitch was off the hook and retreated to his locker where he kept a stash of peppers and a few bottles of muriatic acid for just such an occasion. He then ducked behind the bar and mixed the madness, hoping the glass that contained it wouldn't melt prior to attempted consumption. With increasing reservation, Mitch placed the drink in front of the female fire drinker and attempted another warning but was waved off in a nonchalant manner. With most of the staff looking on, she grabbed the glass, took a hearty swallow, calmly looked up at Mitch with watering eyes and said, "Perhaps you were right. If you could dilute this just a little bit it would be perfect." Mitch complied, though now convinced this woman was a witch. She had taken a sip of a drink that was more lethal than Jonestown punch and not even blinked.

The truest leaders lead by action, and that's what made Mitch the man at King Lear. He had all the moves, knew all the shortcuts, and could feel the pocket caving in during the ugliest service-critical rushes, always able to fight, snow, or wriggle his way out of any situation. One such situation found Mitch serving a corner table with four plates in both arms as a giant filet mignon started to slide off of one of the plates. With no free arm, he pinned the mignon against the wall and maneuvered the plate back under the piece of beef in one motion for the save, a move unnoticed by the chattering patrons he was serving. Were the walls not painted black or had the menu not been ala carte, a blob of beef blood would have been noticed on the wall and anything else on the plate would have hit the floor. But all that was lost was a sprig of parsley. Mitch served the filet he had just pinned against the wall.

Another time we were serving a large table when the tray jack collapsed and nine slabs of prime rib hit the floor. We fell to our knees, gathered up the beef like we were gathering autumn leaves, retreated to the kitchen and after a swift dunk in au jus, served the same beef that was on the floor only two minutes earlier. It wasn't pretty but it worked, and that was the most valuable lesson I learned from Mitch during my time at King Lear. Break the rules if you have to during the rush, just do it in a collected fashion. Customers look to their waiters for reassurance, so don't ever let the children know the house is on fire. Mitch had mastered the science. He was the epitome of efficiency at King Lear and the living memory of all the wayward souls who had come and gone from its service ranks.

#2 Preston "All Women Are Whores" Hillman

A descendant of martyred Crispus Attucks, Preston was a crossroads of fierce emotions and racial angst.[†] Tall, handsome, polished, muscular, brilliant, and violent when knee-deep in

[†]Crispus Attucks, half African and half Natick Indian, was killed by British soldiers in the Boston Massacre of March 5, 1770. A harpoonist and ropemaker, Attucks is recognized as the first man to die for the cause of freedom in the American Revolution.

dust and drink, Preston was King Lear's resident political philosophist, black activist, and volume lover boy. He was the last of the Coventry defectors, an outstanding waiter who was able to misbehave more than the average bear because he was black. King Lear needed minorities on staff to comply with EEOC regulations and since PH was the only African-American on the waitstaff, he could and did push the proverbial envelope, even by King Lear besotted penguin standards, which was scary. Preston loved expostulating to his coworkers. He thought his personal theories and arguments were definitive truths, and any conflicting conjecture was erroneous wetback and white boy gibberish. His favorite self-constructed axiom was one he spouted at least once a week, a theory from which he could not be swayed, a quotation that Preston spoke like gospel. That statement was "All women are whores."

We would argue, "Preston, what about the Virgin Mary, Mother Theresa, Gertrude Stein, that girl who fell down a well in Texas, Judi Dench, Marie Osmond, Aunt Jemima, Harriet Tubman, Sarah Jane Pitman, Florence Nightingale, your own mother, your grandmother? Surely there must be many women who are not whores."

He would always respond, "There are no exceptions, none. All women are whores."

Supporting data for Preston on his theory was the fact that four different women had restraining orders against him, yet he would still frequent the Adams Morgan bars where he suspected they would be. Though he got more woolly bully than Orlando Bloom at Bryn Mawr, any woman rejecting Preston made him insane. Even worse was seeing an ex-girlfriend with a new boyfriend. Next would be confrontation, followed by apprehension, incarceration, detoxification, false repentance, and additional restraining orders. He was the self-professed "hair-trigger nigger" with a standing reservation at the local hoosegow.

Sometimes Preston's girlfriends would come in for dinner before hitting the clubs. PH would buy and serve them dinner at King Lear and would meet up with them later at whatever club. He didn't want other men hitting on his women while he was stuck at work. His solution was the Caesar salad maneuver. He would give his girl du soir a half-dozen drinks and then bring her a Caesar salad. Not a normal pile of eggy romaine, but instead, a Caesar salad with no less than five crushed garlic cloves. The result was a rotten-breathed bitch that no man would get near. No concubine was ever the wiser.

The bussers caused Preston much personal grief with his fleet of female friends when the ladies would call him at the restaurant. The call would initially go to the maître d's podium and then be transferred to the employee line in the pantry. The bussers would usually be first to answer the pantry phone and often it was a demure female voice in quest of Preston. Having listened to him brag about all the hot femmes he had banged that week, the bussers would always attempt to identify the caller by asking "Is this Vanessa?" when in fact it was Jennifer. Or "Is this Abby?" when in fact it was Megan. Or "Is this Laurie?" when it was Megan's mother. The bussers never got the name right and Preston was left in a perpetual state of hot water with his rightfully paranoid girlfriends who suspected Preston of perjury in his claims of monogamy. Busman cuss-out would follow, audible from across the street. "God damn it, you fucking El Salvadoran pieces of shit! Laurie wants to know who the hell Jennifer is and Megan's mother thinks I'm cheating on her daughter with more women than just her! Just answer the fucking phone and give it to me!"

Preston did have difficulty hailing a cab in D.C. at night. No Washington hacker without a bulletproof partition would pick up a young black man, even one in a tuxedo. The other waiters would flag down a cab, fake hopping in, and simultaneously Preston would jump in, refusing to budge until the driver had taken him home. When Preston tried to hail cabs a capella, the drivers would invariably pass him by, at which point he would kick the side of the moving car leaving a hefty dent. A few times cabbies would stop and get out, but after a closer look at the dark muscled man with fury in his eyes, the hacker always retreated.

Race discrimination was the fire that burned within Preston, fueled by alcohol and anything else he could get his hands on. He wasn't fond of my race, a point he expounded on often. Color was his excuse for everything. If he was given a parking ticket, it was because he was black. If he was sent home for being blitzed drunk, it was a plot to keep the funk soul brothers down. When he lost a grand betting on football, it was because a white quarterback intentionally threw the game so the man (a white bookie) could take his money. If he got a bad tip, it was because white folk refused to pay the black man a fair wage. And if a woman rejected his advances, it was because she was a slave to her lily-white husband who didn't want the help touching his wife. And she was a whore.

Preston was always telling me how easy my life was, that I had the world at my feet. Apparently people just rang my doorbell and left giant sacks of cash. I learned that debating Preston was a winless situation and that by taking the evasive route, despite his racial resentment, we got along well. He didn't want to like me, but he did anyway. I did stop partying with Preston because the police always seemed to give last call. He would start a scuffle in a bar and then ask me a few days later why I didn't back him up. My response never changed. "Preston, it took me all my life to grow my teeth and I don't want to lose them in a three-second fight." Though we weren't drinking mates outside of King Lear, we did play a lot of sports together and caught the Redskins whenever possible. One morning Preston and I were off to see the Skins and Seahawks, driving in his car southbound on Georgia Avenue. Suddenly Preston began to pass out at the wheel going fifty miles an hour, due likely to the residual intoxication of the night before. He slumped over the wheel and the car crossed the median line with another car coming at us head on. I grabbed the wheel, jerked the car back on to our side of the road, almost flipping us as I smacked Preston with the back of my hand and said "Wake the fuck up! You almost killed us!" He took the wheel and said, as if nothing had happened, "Calm down, man. Damn! You white boys drink too much coffee."

PH had many stories about him that grew like Bunyon lore.

A possessive woman broke his nose with the fat end of an empty Veuve Clicquot bottle when she caught Preston with another girl. He once spit on a couple of cops after they asked him to turn around because he fit a robbery suspect's description. He had even fought three guys at once outside a strip club, leaving all three groaning on the sidewalk.

But Preston was best known for starting a fight at the funeral of King Lear's owner. Constantine Papandreas, our beloved owner, died after a long battle with Hodgkin's disease in 1996, leaving his brother, Clay, as sole proprietor of King Lear. The funeral was held on a Sunday. King Lear always closed on Sundays, but on this sad Sabbath the staff and regular patrons had a drink at the restaurant after the services in honor of Constantine. Most of the staff had met at the restaurant prior to the funeral and Preston started stoking his rage then. Four hours later and back at the restaurant, PH was four sheets to the wind and more hostile than a hurricane. Then the inevitable happened. A few waiters tried to get Preston to lower his tone and ease his consumption a little. He shoved a waiter onto a table of mourner regulars, knocking the table over and spilling drinks everywhere. It took six of us to wrestle him out of the dining room and out into the alleyway whereupon Mitch gave Preston a couple of eye dilators to calm the madman within. Minutes later PH was tame and then taxied to the doorstep of a girlfriend's house.

As the story was retold over and over again, it became quite exaggerated. The latest version was: "Remember when Preston started that fight at Constantine's funeral?" "Yeah, he punched out the bishop right in the middle of the benediction and then flipped Constantine's casket over and the body fell out."

In 2000, Preston opened a home improvement store for hip-hop singers: Holmes n Gardenz. "Yo, shop here, Bitch!" (Safety Note: Asking for a lawn jockey at Holmes n Gardenz will get you killed).

#3 Dustin Vannoy—The Joint Chief of Staff
In every restaurant you'll find someone who loves to smoke marijuana. I'm not talking an evening jay after a hard

day's work, I'm talking four Crosby wraps daily with dope, bongs, pipes, papers, lighters, matches, and hash stashed everywhere. This was Dustin Vannoy, an albino-haired, surfer dude, munchied man who smoked more pot than a summer long Maui forest fire and sported the diminished cerebral functions to prove it. Chronic is a gateway drug, and recreational drug use can best be described as self-inflicted terrorism.

Vannoy was another of the Coventry jumpers at King Lear, a career restaurant worker who was making the transition to chef, likely because the kitchen had more rolling surfaces. A UCLA graduate and former national surfing competitor, he moved to Washington to convalesce after tearing his Achilles tendon on the Bonsai Pipeline, and would never return to the Pacific Coast. Vannoy wasn't bad as a waiter, but he never demonstrated a sense of urgency during the rush, the fire alarm in a waiter's head that tells that person to prioritize and take swift action. The only matter about which Vannoy had urgency was the rolling, licking, and smoking of his revered reefer.

His most notable gaff was at the Coventry when he teamed with another waiter, a flamboyant homosexual named Joel. Vannoy was working the front and Joel was the back waiter, dealing with the kitchen and hustling out food. One table, while inquiring about desserts, asked him if anything was flaming, to which Vannoy replied, "Well, Tinkerbell here is flaming" as he pointed to Joel who was serving the very same table coffee. The table didn't seem to mind the remark, but Joel went straight (no pun intended) to the maître d', who also enjoyed gladiator movies, and soon every plant mister at the Coventry stood behind Joel (both figuratively and literally). DV was suspended for a week.

Vannoy was also known for his nutty, stripper girlfriend who caused him more pain than a molar extraction with no anesthesia. To him, however, having a hot, busty, coke-snorting stripper girlfriend was worth the torment so long as she didn't smoke too much of his pot. Her name was Jezebel, the waiters referred to her as "Jezebel from Hell." The name was justified. One time, DV and Jezebel were driving on the beltway traveling about 80 mph. DV had put his week's tips, about $1,300 in hundreds, in the console of his Fiat. He looked over to find Jezebel throwing his money out of the car bill by bill. DV screamed, "What the fuck are you doing?" to which she replied, "Just trying to get your attention." It took seven hundred dollars to get Vannoy's attention that afternoon. The cash proved unretrievable. Amazingly, they stayed together for years. Most men would have pitched Jezebel out of the car, me included.

When DV came to King Lear, I did my best to look out for him. The first six months of a new waiter's employment was a probationary period and only one in four new hires made the cut as a waiter. I was working with Vannoy on a large party, and several of them wanted their unfinished entrees wrapped up to go. King Lear had sleek silver bags with plastic liners and normally the wrapping was done tableside. Vannoy took a plastic liner, held it to his mouth, blew into it to inflate it, and then put the customer's unfinished sirloin in the bag, in full view of the entire dining room. Dumbfounded, I grabbed DV, yanked him into the pantry and said, "Dustin, what the hell are you doing? You just put eight zillion of your personal pot smoking germs in the man's plastic bag. If the GM had seen that he'd have canned your ass on the spot!" Vannoy just looked at me with a lobotomized gaze, clueless as to the gravity of the infraction. In dragged dialogue, he told me not to be so anal retentive.

What angered me most about Vannoy was the way he would mock a particular regular who had suffered throat cancer and used a hand-held voice generator to speak. He would mimic the patron's voice at the bar and in the kitchen every time the man came in to eat. DV thought he was so funny mocking this poor man. It made me crazy to the point I almost dragged Vannoy outside by his lapels and kicked his ass. I ended up smashing his bong and chucking his trick bag of pot parapher-nalia instead. It affected him not at all. DV was much like an auto parts store in the matter of back-up, high times equipment.

#4 Benny Ambrieres—Benihana
Benny was in his mid-forties and of French-Algerian descent.

He spoke with a heavy French accent and had done it all, or so he said. He said he had played a role in the movie *The Battle of Algiers,* which was true because the waiters rented the movie just to see if he was bullshitting us or not. He claimed to have been in an airline crash where over half of the passengers manifest was killed. He said he had won an Olympic medal in the javelin and declared he was tight with many, many celebrities from when he worked in Hollywood. Benny touted that he was friends with Clint Eastwood, Lucille Ball, Marlon Brando, Robert DeNiro, Sigourney Weaver, Anthony Hopkins, Steven Spielberg, Linda Hamilton, Harrison Ford, Mel Gibson, Robin Williams and Bill Murray. Supposedly one of his best buddies was Paul Newman. We didn't buy it for a second, yet he insisted it was true.

One afternoon, Paul Newman came in for lunch and the waiters knew we had Benihana on the hook. We were going to humble his javelin-throwing, jet-crashed ass once and for all. Preston called over to Benny and said, "Yo, Benihana, your homeboy Paul Newman is sitting on Table 25." Benny ran up to the table and Paul Newman stood up and said "Benny, how the hell are you?" as they shook hands and smiled. The crowd of waiters and busmen watching couldn't believe it. That French fucker was telling the truth when we were so sure he was lying. We'll try him again if Hannibal Lecter ever comes in here.

#5 Jeremy Whalen—Prison Bars Don't Serve Liquor

The drinker's drunkard, the druid of fluid, was named Jeremy Whalen, a waiter I worked with at Augustine's. Formerly a restaurant owner himself, Jeremy lost his restaurant and two daughters in a landslide divorce victory by his second wife that left him near destitute. Jeremy was a forty-year-old, tall, bronze, and lean sexaholic with a washboard stomach and face like Adonis that left all the lassies unable to say no to any lewd act he might propose. Jeremy wasn't one to buy a girl dinner and plot a course for joy on the third date. You couldn't even get drive-thru from this guy. No way. He just wanted the goods, and fast. To him, dry mounting was not germane to framing.

In the one year I knew Jeremy, he had debriefed three different women right in the restaurant and one in the parking lot. The ladies' room vanity had been the sight of one particular conquest, smack in the middle of service where any of a hundred different women could have walked in on an ankle-panted Jeremy and the rammed bangette. The one woman who did walk in on the pair was the owner's wife, who was a good sport about the matter. She just said, "Excuse me," turned around and left. Research concluded that there were no rules in the employee manual about having mid-shift sex in the restrooms, on the pastry cart, out in the parking lot, or on top of the dumpster. When not sowing wild oats at Augustine's, Jeremy sought multiple-party sex in Fort Lauderdale, getting more pickled ginger than Usher.

But what amazed his coworkers most was Jeremy's ability to drink alcohol, consuming quantities that would make the average man part of the coroner's to-do list. His poison of choice was the infamous Long Island Iced Tea, a melting pot drink that combines several liquors with a sweet edge for downability. Jeremy would pound a half-dozen Long Islands and then search his shirt pocket for some home-spun fun, always delighted to share. Heroin had previously been his passion, but after it cost him his wife, kids, and restaurant, he kicked the habit that had kicked him. Jeremy likened heroin addiction to his desire for sex, times ten.

Though it was difficult to believe, Jeremy had only one DWI to his name. He had spent time in prison, but for selling and possession, not DWI. In Florida, as in several other states with limited public transportation options, DWIs are common. Of the thirty plus employees at Augustine's, we averaged more than one DWI per person. But not every DWI seemed justified. We had three such ludicrous arrests of Augustine's staffers. Our meat cutter, Ezekiel (Zeke) was busted for operation of a vehicle under the influence while in his own front yard. Zeke was on his ride mower, cutting his lawn, though nursing his seventh sweating bottle of Stella (Amstel Light) {STELLA!}.

There was Tamara, a hostess who got toasted off of her arse

at a bar, and had made it to within a few blocks of her apartment when her Volkswagen Cabriolet ran out of gas. After a few minutes of early morning grunting, pushing her VW, the cops who came to assist Tammy ended up busting her for DWI. They asked her if she had just been driving her car, but Tammy said no. Still, the police didn't buy her explanation of the situation. "So you're saying you pushed your car to a bar, got drunk, and this is where we found you, pushing your car home?" "That's right, Ociffer."

The last ridiculous charge for drunken operation of a vehicle was against a toper waiter, Leo (referred to as "Leotard"), who had lost his driver's license after his third arrest, and was busted a fourth time for intoxicated speeding in a school zone, on his bicycle. Rumor has it that Leotard was busted a fifth time while walking on a sidewalk, pulling a children's Radio Flyer wagon.

Drinking was the way to survive at Augustine's. Customers would flood the restaurant during the dinner hour like Scots in a Braveheart charge, all screaming for service and demanding it now. The waiters would get so buried that survival without a complaint seemed impossible, so all Jeremy and I would do was laugh and liberate a bottle of Schottliver and drink through the madness. Sometimes we would snag a bottle of Captain Morgan and drink it out of coffee cups during the shift to ease the stress. But when the stress ended, exhaustion took the helm.

The most I ever saw Jeremy drink was during the summer that I departed from the Sunshine State. It was another booming Saturday. Jeremy and I had sucked up three bottles of Sadsaque French Merlot during the dinner rush. After closing, we parked ourselves at Augustine's bar where Jeremy threw back a quintet of Long Islands and a trio of tequila shots in less than an hour. Finally, at about 1 a.m., he did a Jamal Lewis line and fired up a joint the size of a bamboo shoot before jumping in his Wrangler for the ride home. Jeremy's philosophy on driving drunk was that the faster he drove, the less time he spent on the road and thus reduced his chance of being pulled over. The same thinking applied to Thanksgiving cooking would be to put the turkey in a two thousand-degree kiln so it would cook in ten minutes. Jeremy was racing across the intercoastal bridge at 80 mph (45 mph posted), with lips pursed around joint two when he heard the sirens of a young cop at his six o'clock. Stopping at the top of the bridge, he flicked the joint to the manatees and stuffed his face with a handful of airline nuts that he kept in his console for just such an emergency. The young cop pulled up behind him, did not detect any clues of intoxication, and ended up only busting him for not wearing a seatbelt when Jeremy would have blown at least three times the legal limit, not to mention approaching Mach on the speedometer. This was cause for liquid celebration.

Jeremy was not just a lucky sot, he was a tough one, too. During service one weekend, he had cracked an incisor down to the root, leaving him in pure agony. Just to breathe caused him pain and the staff told him to get his ass over to the emergency room. He refused, and instead demanded the Bacardi bottle, snagged a pair of needle-nose pliers, and retreated to the linen closet where he yanked the cracked canine himself, a battlefield amputation. He packed some cotton in the bloody abyss and continued service as if nothing had happened. We tried to explain to Jeremy that he needed a replacement tooth to keep his other chompers from shifting, but he elected to just carry on minus an ivory.

When Jeremy wasn't agitating his alveolar neurons, playing Georgy Porgy of the orgy, or lapping up Long Islands and serving stewed cod cheeks to senior citizens at Augustine's, the Lothario was on his boat, the lone toy kept from the divorce settlement. His vessel was named *The Puffin*, a double entendre suggesting both of his favorites: the Nova Scotian seabird with a bright colored beak and his favorite form of Colombian aromatherapy. Like many Floridians, Jeremy found refuge on the water, a tranquil break from the madness of terra firma and a great place to party so long as you don't end up like Natalie Wood.

But a boat is like an unemployed girlfriend, always in need of money, and *The Puffin* was no exception. One afternoon, Jeremy came in to work with a fallen face and said his boat had sunk, to which the bartender said, "What happened? Did you spill your drink?" Fret not though, *The Puffin* was raised, repaired, and out on the Atlantic a few months later with helmsman Jeremy Whalen at the con and Captain Morgan at the bar.

Jeremy, wanting to get paid for what he did best, finally left the restaurant business in 2000 and went on to star in several adult movies under the screen name Hung Likehorse. Hung's filmography included feature roles in the movies *Dirty Harriet; The French Foreign Lesion; The British Are Cuming; Escape From Vagina Island; White Men Can't Hump; Hands Across Mr. America;* and my personal favorite *Gonorrhea With The Wind*. For his performance in *Gonorrhea With The Wind*, Hung Likehorse won two Golden Girth Awards and a Scarlet Shaft nomination from the Clinton Film Academy.

#6 Greg Moseby—*Crouching Tiger, Hidden Drag Queen*

Everyone at the Coventry liked Greg. He was articulate and cerebral, with chiseled good looks that could allow him to stunt double for Billy Zane. Moseby was the kind of man you might expect to find in a science lab, not waiting tables, but he had no other apparent aspirations. Moseby wasn't a druggernaut or boozehound beyond a few cocktails at the Old Ebbit and as a pit crewmember during wine-chug time trails. He was also a Lear defector, but was part of the seventy-five percent of new hires that didn't make the cut, somehow rubbing the GM the wrong way during his probationary period.

Moseby walked on thin ice at the Coventry too, not due to lack of skill in his waiting capabilities, but instead, because he was a handsome heterosexual male in a world of spiteful broke back mountaineers. The package scanners at the Coventry protested that Greg Moseby was simply too handsome and knowledgeable about drapes not to be queer. Did God screw up and toss Moseby in the heterosexual bin by accident? This was another assumption of the Coventry Capotes. They were certain that all handsome, straight males were denying their gayness. The queens even offered to pay for Moseby to get psychoanalyzed so he could get in touch with his inner woman, who would tell him it was okay to be a man who liked other men while dressing like a woman. But Moseby gracefully declined. He had a full roster of sumptuous hot women, girlfriends the river dancers referred to as fish. As a waiter, no service-critical situation ever made Moseby uptight. Even if a customer caught on fire, he would calmly ask the bartender for a bottle of Evian to douse the patron. "Should I ring this up on a comp check first?" he might inquire. How appropriate that he was the key figure in "The Crash," a wreck of mammoth proportions witnessed by no less than two hundred people one summer Saturday night at the Coventry. It was a precision catastrophe that took Satan months to contrive.

The Coventry was a combination of two restaurants on two floors. The upstairs was an ultra-posh and expensive fine-dining room with menu prices averaging about seventy dollars per head. The downstairs menu was more casual, though still with exquisite cuisine. Both floors had bars with one wine list and one sommelier attending both levels. Connecting the arrogant upstairs with bourgeois downstairs was a gigantic, ten-foot-wide marble staircase that made a one hundred and eighty degree turn as one ascended or descended the stairs. There were finely polished brass handrails on both sides and for those too frail for the climb, there was an elegant glass and brass elevator around which the staircase was built. At the top of the stairs was the maître d's podium and several rows of booths and tables. The floors were Charlemagne marble and over-waxed wood parquet.

On this particular night, Moseby was a back waiter whose station required that he walk past the precipice of the canyon-like staircase to bring food to his tables. Moseby was also a waiter who carried his trays on the tips of his fingers, feeling for the center of gravity. The entree plates were heavy, fourteen-inch, one-pound, white china discs that could be heated to ten thousand degrees Kelvin and had giant stainless steel covers that allowed the plates to be stacked. The maximum number of entrees that could be carried on a single tray was twelve. Moseby and his front waiter had a party of ten, which he would have no trouble hoisting to save a second trip to the table.

Just as Preston proclaimed that "all women are whores," I proclaim that all waiters hate marble and wood floors. They erode your knees just as too much time with your own family erodes your sanity. Another tremendous advantage of carpet over hard surfaces is friction and the reduced risk of slipping. Even after a wine bucket full of ice water is knocked over, one can still walk on that surface and not slip if there is carpeting. But such practical thinking never prevailed at the Coventry. Aesthetics always took precedence, and on this particular occasion the price was about to be paid. **Note to ownership:** *Noise abatement (reduction) should be **the** primary consideration in floor surface selection, which means sound-dampening carpet. If that's news to you, then start planning your insurance fire now. What were you thinking letting your fuchsia-thonged Clemson-dropout girlfriend (the one you left your wife for) design your restaurant? That doe-eyed slice of southern pie is gonna cost you the farm. Only seasoned restaurant front-house veterans should design restaurants. Bastard-bitch Crushed Car Cube Chefs need not apply. Call them **B2C4's**, {be two sea fore}.*

Moseby was called into the kitchen and after Chef Cavanaugh had carefully inspected each entree, he wiped and covered the plates, stacking the final products on the giant tray with the women's food on top for accessibility and proper service order. Moseby propped the heavy tray over his shoulder atop his fingertips and was off and out the kitchen door. He sped along the main strip of parquet which was bordered by the top of the staircase, his intent was to make a ninety-degree turn at the maître d's podium, and proceed directly to the ten top. The lynchpin of the impending chaos was an invisible floor-splotch of Beefeater spilled by an intoxicated senator who had pointed to the table he desired with his up drink—the exact spot where Moseby would plant his pivot foot. Worse was that Moseby was a southpaw and every tray he carried along the main strip hung over the edge of the staircase.

Moseby headed for the turn, downshifted to third gear, planted his pivot foot, and slipped as he shifted his weight to his now foundationless foot. The tray full of entrees flipped sideways in the air and, after a brief gain of altitude, acknowledged the earth's gravitational pull and crashed inverted at terminal velocity, exploding on impact. Greg had also hit the floor, the wind knocked out of his lungs from the impact, as he reached like a beaten soccer goalie for any piece of the tray. But rescue was out of the question as the horrific, deafening, incessant noise of the crash begun its opus. The crashing items had started at the highest point of the staircase and continued a long, loud migration to the bottom of the stairs. Within seconds of the piercing crash, every patron in the restaurant knew that something was horribly wrong. Waiters froze in midstride, turning only their heads with eyes unblinking to see the cause of the unceasing dish and cover crashathon.

For well over a minute, the plates, covers, and forlorn food smashed down the stairs like a food service wreck of the Hesperus. Every human being in the restaurant was motionless with mouths ajar, taking in the tumult. Moseby still lay on the floor, shocked and unable to move from his stretched position. His first instinct might have been to get some oxygen back into his lungs, but the tantrum of exploding dishes would not relinquish his attention. There was simply no end to the noise; the plate covers sounding like cymbals, each with its own hostile and hyperactive percussionist. The violence of the crash was like two locomotives colliding in front of a mountainside Crate and Barrel outlet during clearance week. The White House Secret Service even dispatched a couple of agents to investigate the commotion, the crash having been heard loud and clear at the East Gate listening post. Soon after, the wreckage gave up the ghost as the last possessed plate cover made a wha-wha-wha sound at the feet of some terrified patrons standing in front of the downstairs coatroom.

Nobody dared clap, for someone must have been killed amidst such high-volume violence. The maître d' looked around for customer casualties, ignoring Moseby who was still on the floor attempting to catch his breath. The maître d' scanned the saucy wreckage along the mahogany walls, steps, and brass railings, relieved to find no patron injured or soiled. With the help of two other waiters, Moseby got up from the floor, sore but uninjured, and began to assess the affected parties in his usual cool manner. Clean up didn't even enter his mind. This mess would take a dozen bussers three days to clean.

The most affected party were the diners whose food was now smeared over several hundred square feet. They were quite indignant. To them I say, "Fuck you." Their only question was "Was that our food?" Moseby had just taken a fall that would have killed half of the patrons in the dining room and not one customer inquired if he was okay, despite the fact he had fallen in full view of the affected table and was lying on the parquet for well over a minute. Yes, it was their food and, yes, it would be a while before new entrees would be ready, but a few of the women at the table could not refrain from rolling their eyes in disgust and annoyance. Waiters aren't blind, they catch all your snobby little facial pouts which make them want to forfeit the remainder of their lives that very instant in exchange for repeatedly pummeling your face in fury until the bones of your skull break away like papier-mâché shards from the belly of a Cinco de Mayo piñata. If I could have had my way, they would have eaten whatever was recovered from the floor. "Hey, this is a doorstop!" "Uh, sorry about that."

Moseby's next task was to face Zach who had heard the crash from the kitchen and could only wonder which of his children were lost. No one had the courage to tell him the entire hayride went over the cliff and there were no survivors. But finally Moseby was able to give the news to Zach, addressing him like an unsuccessful surgeon breaking the bad news to relatives in the waiting room. Instead of forcing Moseby to drink from the deep fat fryer, Zach redirected his energy into the production of ten new entrees, a testament to his professionalism. The indignant ten got their food in record time, news crews arrived to cover the crash, and Moseby kept his job and drank compliments of his fellow waiters. Funds for a crash memorial were never approved.

#7 Roland Lockheart—The Saint
There are some people you meet in life who are special

beyond special. Such was Roland Lockheart. The absolute nicest man you could meet, kind, generous, never speaking harsh words about anyone and setting a standard of excellence in service that others could never hope to attain. He was tall and lean, with a boyish face, was not a drinker, but was instead a running devotee. Roland would work a twelve-hour shift and then relax by running ten miles. While the rest of us were crawling into a bottle after, during, okay, before the shift, Roland was off running somewhere. He was Constantine and Clay's favorite employee with good cause. He was a perfect gentleman, waiter and maître d'. Roland was also a customer favorite, in constant demand by the regulars who comprised half of King Lear's patronage. But a man like Roland is hard to keep because there are so very few like him. He was offered a partnership in a gourmet wine shop and deli in Annapolis. Roland had planned and helped to build the store while working full-time at King Lear, still spending time with his wife and three sons and running fifty miles a week. I always thought rest was required to exist, but Roland seemed to be the exception to the rule. We loved Roland so much that we would make the new hires bow down when speaking to him and address him as Mr. Lockheart. When we finally lost Roland to his new business, it was comparable to Elway leaving the Broncos. The team was never the same.

Once during an employee party at the senior maître d's spacious home in Manassas, Roland's wife complained that they didn't live in such a luxurious house themselves. Some of the other waiters overheard his wife's complaints and couldn't believe their ears. Here she was, married to a saint, a workaholic, the greatest man since Cassius Clay, and she wanted a larger breakfast nook. We were incensed. An emergency waiter's council meeting was held and we proposed drowning Mrs. Lockheart for speaking such blasphemy. We told Roland that we would be delighted to kill his wife and purchase him a new, quieter spouse from one of the many mail order bride catalogs. He declined, but smiled in appreciation of the thought.

Though difficult to imagine, Roland wasn't always a saint.

I arrived at King Lear after the metamorphosis, but the more senior waiters recounted the legends from Roland's darker days. Apparently Roland Lockheart used to drink. Not a flask in the glove compartment or a little morning whiskey, but drink as in "Get your own damn bottle of Bookers." He was also about fifty pounds heavier before he traded in his shot glass for a pair of Pumas. Early one morning during his wild days he was well-cooked, yet had wits enough to cab it home. The cab brought him to his doorstep whereupon the Pakistani driver quoted an inflated fare, thinking his drunken passenger would be easily fleeced. Roland, sharp even when dulled by booze, knew the fare and handed the driver the required amount as he began to exit the car. But the Paki hackie wouldn't back down and grabbed Roland's arm, yelling in mutilated English, demanding more money. That instant things got ugly fast as Roland grabbed the hand that was grabbing him and broke the driver's wrist. He then leaned over the seat and ripped the dispatch radio off of the dash and spiked it on the floorboards, jumping out of the cab as the driver peeled off, fearing more pain from this madman, or perhaps that the police might discover he wasn't a legal alien. Stories grow over time and this one was no exception.

When I first started at King Lear, I was told the story about a Pakistani cabby trying to run over an elderly nun holding a basket of kittens and a Stradivarius wrapped in the Shroud of Turin. The kittens' names were Figueroa, Plato, Matilda, Ivanhoe, Hermes, and Little Elvis. Roland, who was spoon feeding homemade stew to a group of street people, saw the runaway cab and its terrorist driver. He ran beside the speeding car and dove into the passenger seat, stopping the car a split second before it would have crushed the nun, fiddle, and kittens. A fight with the driver ensued and Roland ripped the driver's arm off of his body and proceeded to beat the man to death with his own severed limb to make it look like a suicide. He put the mutilated corpse in the trunk of the cab, set the car on fire and pushed it off the Key Bridge into the Potomac River. He then ran back to the nun, apologized for the commotion, gave each kitten a ball of yarn and resumed feeding the homeless people before going to a local orphanage to read Dr. Seuss stories to blind children. That was Roland Lockheart, the saint.

#8 Omar Quevedo—Beef Heart

Omar was another of the Coventry refugees. Born in Bolivia as the second of eight children, Omar was raised by his mother in impoverished mountain squalor outside the city of La Paz. Omar's father had died in his thirties, leaving his mother not a penny in her struggle to care for her children. Remarkably, she was able to feed, clothe, and educate all of her children successfully. At seventeen, Omar moved to the United States and found work in Washington as a busboy. Within ten years, he had learned how to speak perfect English, had become a citizen through marriage to his wife, Robin, had a beautiful daughter, bought a modest home in Potomac, and had risen from busboy to waiter and maître d' at the Coventry and King Lear. He had come a long way from the hard times of his childhood.

As a boy in Bolivia, he would accompany his mother to the local slaughterhouse where the butchers would give his mother hearts of slaughtered cattle for free. She would take the beef hearts home and cook them for her family several times a week. At the same time American families were eating pizza, fried chicken, or meatloaf, Omar and siblings were eating beef heart. In America he found a meat shop where he could buy beef hearts and taught Robin how to prepare them using his mother's recipe. Though he often invited the waiters over to dinner for Robin's award-winning beef heart, we were always busy that night.

Omar was a conniver of sorts. He used and dealt coke, which you'd suspect from a beef heart-eating Bolivian. His Potomac home was quite a jaunt from King Lear and when the partying got out of hand, which was often, he had no qualms about calling in to say he'd miss his lunch shift. He averaged one balk a week, but would never say he was sick or admit his hangover-induced double vision had gotten out of hand. He had two excuses he used for missing a shift, these two and these two alone. The first was "my daughter has food poisoning." The second one was "I hit a deer." Twice a month, his poor little daughter had food poisoning. That little girl suffered from more food poisoning than any thousand children combined could have had even if they were eating rancid roadkill and drinking straight from the River Nile during cholera season.

And when Omar's daughter wasn't on death's doorstep writhing in gastrointestinal torment with repeated bouts of ptomaine poisoning, it was the deer population of southern Maryland that suffered. Omar had bought a Ford Explorer that seemed to be a deer magnet, but only en route to work in broad daylight, never on the way home at night. Omar hit so many deer that the waiters lobbied to have all whitetails who lived within a twenty-mile radius of Omar's house put on the endangered species list. And what a testament to the toughness of his Ford Explorer, never once showing any signs of damage from collisions with the eight-dozen deer he had hit and killed during the previous two years. "Omar hit another deer this morning and won't be in." The GM couldn't believe it. "Damn! Such unabated carnage, and those poor fucking deer. How the hell does he drive to work? He couldn't hit more animals if he was driving inside a petting zoo."

#9 Sinclair Kahana—The Hawaiian Horse Whisperer

Sinclair was the master of his trade, a consummate professional waiter and equestrian who brought his skill to King Lear. In his fifties and of Hawaiian ancestry, he sported a pencil thin mustache and was married to a French-Canadian woman named Elise who also worked in the District waiting tables. Sinclair had saved and invested his money shrewdly from the beginning of his waiting career in the late 1960s, which afforded he and Elise a forty-acre farm in Harpers Ferry. There they raised and rode over twenty horses. Their only children were these hoofed quadrupeds. The special bond that sometimes exists between people and horses was obvious with Sinclair and his horses. The favorite was an Arabian stallion named Equinox. Mounted on Equinox,

Sinny looked just like a vanted leftenant of an Anzac Horse Brigade, ready to invade Cumberland.

As well as being a workaholic, Sinclair was also a generous man and, like Roland Lockheart, never spoke unkindly of anyone. Several Sundays a year, Sinclair and Elise would invite the waitstaff over for trail riding and a gourmet feast at their farm. We would rent some additional tack and saddle up and ride into the Maryland sunset. After the ride, we'd grill some steaks, drink a little Brunello, and sit around the campfire as the Armagnac bottle ran laps. It was a magnificent way to conclude a long hard workweek, a horseback tour through the crisp cool woods, being scrutinized only by the wildlife that had no demands or places to be. Such days regenerated our dining-service-diminished spirits and reminded us that beauty still existed in the world if you cantered far enough outside the concrete chaos.

Though first to acknowledge the vast drug and drink problems inherent to the hospitality industry, Sinclair himself was a professional alcoholic, albeit quite functional no matter how far removed from sobriety. Since we were both perfectionists in the matter of service, we shared many similar frustrations. At King Lear it was the busmen. Each Friday when the magic powder arrived, busser support service departed. The busmen would get so snorty that they would try to clear tables that hadn't received their main courses or had just been served their entrees a few minutes earlier. Bus service often got so bad that at times you had to tell your assigned busser to stay away from your tables. The waiters dealing to the busboys didn't mind the coke consumption because they profited from it, but Sinclair, myself, and a few of the other aggressive waiters had to endure the nonsense as best we could.

Sinclair and Elise spent ten weeks a year in Saratoga, working during the brief but lucrative horse racing frenzy. In their employ were two full-time ranch hands that kept Equinox and his siblings shod and fed while mom and dad were in New York working to keep the hayloft full. They never had difficulty getting a leave of absence from their Washington employers because they were such model employees.

Sinclair had worked hard all of his life and had more happiness and wealth to show for it than any other career waiter I had ever met. A beautiful wife, a picturesque country home on a farm, and a horde of horses who adored him. But there was a thief in Sinclair's life, and that thief was a ten-inch high, green bottle full of a clear hemlock that answered to the name of Tanqueray. Sinny loved his juniper berry poison and, although he threw it back like water, his service never faltered that I noticed, except on one occasion.

It was New Year's Eve of 1996 and all the waiters were drunk before long, Sinclair ahead of everyone by fifteen lengths. By the time the night was through, Sinclair had consumed an entire bottle of Tank by himself, so wasted that the other waiters did his checkout paperwork for him. We had deliberately broken into his locker and took his truck keys to keep him off of the road, but he carried a spare set, as we learned after the fact. Sinny drove the fifty miles from D.C. to Harpers Ferry. The next working day when Sinclair came in, we really gave him hell about driving home, telling him he was lucky not to have been pulled over. He replied, "Oh I was stopped at four different police checkpoints. I just smoked some cigarettes, chewed some gum, and the cops waved me through." We couldn't believe it but we knew that Sinny was telling the truth. The fact that he had driven out of the parking garage without wrecking was amazing enough, but for Sinclair to have made it home in such a ripped condition left us dumbfounded.

Luck does run out and sadly it did for Sinclair. I had already moved to Florida to start flight school. One night, three months after leaving Washington, I had many vivid recollections of Sinclair and the talks we had while working together at King Lear. I truly considered him a friend, only one of a few at King Lear about whom I felt that way. The following morning, I checked my email to find that Sinclair had been killed after crashing his truck into a cement post, only three miles from his farm. His leg had to be amputated just to free him from the wreckage and he died en route to the hospital. The local papers openly stated that alcohol was the cause of the crash, though fortunately no one else was involved in the wreck. Sinclair's death was a bitter pill for King Lear, and heartbreak for Elise and certainly Equinox and the other horses, too.

The leading cause of death among King Lear employees was AIDS, with drunk driving fatalities and prescription overdose deaths tied for second at 3 each. There was a framed *New Yorker* cartoon in King Lear's bar. The scene is an elegant New York restaurant, packed to the gills, where a maître d' who looked exactly like Sinclair Kahana is sending glaring looks at a couple of finished diners who won't vacate their table to allow other patrons to dine. The night Sinclair died, that picture inexplicably fell off of the wall.[†]

#10 Mason Cormier—*The Da Vinci Coed*

Some people say all the wrong things and never bat an eye. This was Mason, a jumpity Quebecois waiter, maître d', and cocaine abuser, his powder purchased compliments of a fat trust fund from which he received a few thousand a month. Though a ten-year King Lear veteran, Mason's aspiration was to be a movie star. He belonged to the Screen Actors Guild and had played several small roles in various films, never getting a role as a named character or doing much beyond appearing as a background pedestrian. Mason's NW condo was a shrine to Hollywood. He owned a copy of every movie ever made, or so it appeared, and had stockpiles of costumes, posters, and autographed pictures from hundreds of celebrities. Mason was also a *Star Trek* freak, a regular at conventions, and he had even attended a Klingon language college, which I don't believe was accredited.

Every room in his condo was cluttered with home entertainment equipment, enough electronic equipment to stock a Circuit City. This was someone you wouldn't want as a neighbor. You name it, he had it. Giant screens, speakers with enough

---

[†] A few of my other good friends who passed on well before their times were Neil Qualls, Joel Schroeder, Marilyn McHenry Wilhide, Tim King, Tommy Novak, Karen O'Neill, Leslie Belford, Myrna Davis, Chuck Sloane, Ronald Brissette, and Billy Whittaker.

wattage to create wind, camcorders, VCRs, DVDs, computers, fax machines, copiers, cameras, scanners, audio mixers, turntables, microphones, reel-to-reel, and every toy had a remote control. His lifestyle forced the good folks at Potomac Electric Power Co. to work overtime. When he was not appearing in major motion pictures, Mason headlined in home movies. His pastime amidst all these toys was to videotape his sexual conquests and then discretely invite the waiters and busmen over for a private viewing. The invitation wasn't really discrete, and we piled into his place like English soccer fans to view his most recent Hiltonette. No vixen videotaped was ever looked at the same way by the waiters. Mason, like Preston, would bring his cokettes in for dinner and the staff always wanted to make a comment like "How are those four moles that form a Krugerrand-sized trapezium on the left cheek of your lily-white ass doing?"

None of Mason's women appeared to know that they had co-starred in *Remember the Trojans* and I'm sure some of his wilder rides even made the Internet. Boasting more scores than Wayne Gretzky, Mason thought his mediocre looks and annoying personality were what wooed all the fillies into his bedchamber. But it was the vial in his pocket that made the girls want to get in his pants. Female sniffers who had maxed their credit lines and were three months behind on their Mitsubishi Eclipse payments would gladly trade their nether regions for a little $C_{17}H_{21}NO_4$. It was true then, it is true now, and it will be true tomorrow. Even the Elephant Man could have gotten some boo-yeah had his medicine chest been properly stocked.

Mason's diction was in line with his film productions, and when acting as maître d' he said some of the most unbelievable things ever heard. Why he wasn't fired or suspended for some of these comments was a mystery. But since Preston wasn't fired for flipping over Constantine's casket during the funeral and bending the bishop's cross into a swastika, I guess Mason and his ill-uttered comments were small potatoes. Former Press Secretary Jim Brady was one of our lunch regulars, who, as you should recall, was shot and paralyzed during the Reagan assassination attempt. The staff loved Mr. Brady and always gave him extra attention because he was such a decent customer. One day Mason was hosting and Mr. Brady came in to meet a guest for lunch. Four different waiters greeted Mr. Brady and held open King Lear's four glass doors to allow his wheelchair ample room for passage. As he came in, clever Mason said, "Hello Mr. Brady, roll right in here." The four waiters holding the doors looked at each other, doubting what we had just heard. "He didn't just say what I thought he did, did he?" Omar, Mitch, and I apologized to Mr. Brady for Mason's insensitive comment, but Mr. Brady was a gentleman about the matter and said he knew Mason was just trying to be funny. The staff protested to the GM, but Mason remained a part-time maître d' long enough to make several other shocking remarks.

One such comment was made to a complaining woman from India (with the stereotypical red dot third eye, called a *bindi*, which indicates she is married). Mason said "You should get some Clearasil for that blemish on your forehead. And what's that red dot mean, anyway? Coffee's ready?" He once told a blind customer waiting at the maître d's podium, holding his walking cane, "Stick around for a good table." And then subsequently to his penguin matrix assistant, "See this man to his table." Even to DC's troubled mayor he uttered, "Our crack staff will take good care of you!" But the comment he made that really floored me happened one evening when I was assisting Mason with the maître d' duties.

A group of ten Asians came in and one of the party stepped forward and said, "Good evening, we have a reservation at eight under the name of Fong." Mason really wanted to show off his ignorance and said, "Are you Japanese, because we have Japanese menus," making a menu gesture with his hands in case his over-enunciating didn't convey the message. The head of the party retorted in perfect English, "No, in fact, we are Chinese. However, the English menus will be quite sufficient." Mason had no idea how badly he had just insulted the party, checking off their name in a ho-hum way and directing me to take the Fong party to their table. I did so and then leaned over to Mr. Fong and apologized profusely. I

said, "Mr. Fong, please forgive the restaurant for the maître d's
ignorance and stupidity. He unknowingly insulted you and
your guests and I deeply regret what he said. Will you allow
me to select some appropriate wine for you and your guests
after you've ordered? Compliments of the house." Mr. Fong
shook my hand with both of his, smiled, and said, "We would
like that very much, thank you." I made the arrangements
with the waiter serving the Fong party, who brought them
three bottles of Nolte Mugshaht, an exquisite blend of
Cabernet, Cabernet Franc, and Merlot with a subtle note of
wild blueberry. Though he didn't know it yet, the wine was
on Mason.

But despite all of Mason's questionable words, addictions,
and dating techniques, the boy had a heart. For anything that
involved charity for children's causes, he would contribute, or
work to raise money. Every year he would initiate a campaign
to raise money for children's clothing, especially children's
underwear. Mason would quietly lean on a few of the
customers to contribute, knowing the time to collect from
the bar flies was either after a betting victory, and certainly
when soused. One of Mason's motivations that I knew of was
a letter he had somehow gotten, written to Santa Claus from
a five-year-old girl. He had it taped inside his locker door. The
poor child wasn't asking for a pony or dollhouse, but for
underwear. We all have our various motivations, and it was
a little girl's tragic letter that lit a fire in Mason's heart.

And Mason finally stopped taping his sex quests and
showing for public view. It all ended after hours at King Lear,
with several bar flies still fixed in their seats. Mason was on
lock-up duty. He slipped behind the bar and popped in a
VHS cassette of him wham-bamming some young thang. I
believe the intended genre was western because Mason was
wearing a cowboy hat and saying "yee-haw" with great
frequency. About three minutes into the cattle drive, a reg fly
patron hopped over the counter and violently ripped the VHS
player from wall, slammed it to the ground then punched
Mason square in the face, knocking him down and hollering,

"God damn you, that's my daughter!"

#11 Lido Fawkener—Appetizer Rape

A Las Vegas waiter captain transplanted from Chicago, Lido's Polish birth name was known only to a limited few; his parents, family and several angry Illini bookmaking operations with whom his six-digit markers went unpaid. More appropriately, he should have renamed himself Monsieur Black Jack Dicemonkey, the dreaded gambling bug having really bitten him hard. Out of luck in Illinois, Lido sought refuge in Vegas, confident that sporting a new identity and changing his address to Nevada would be shrewd moves. But relocation to Vegas for a restless gaming junkie is like letting a famished Augustus Gloop loose in the Chocolate Factory when Willy Wonka isn't watching. Perhaps he should have moved to an Indian reservation instead.

After arriving in Las Vegas in 1995, Lido immediately started working as a waiter at Romeo Charlie's, but for him, income production was a fruitless endeavor. His gambling compulsions kept him trapped on the spinning gerbil wheel of futility, though the proverbial gerbil, safe from Richard Gere's grasp, maintained better living quarters. Despite having taken home over $468,000 in income from 1995-2003, Lido had nothing to show for his half million in wages beyond a few yellow-pitted shirts, no car, miserable credit, no bank accounts, a bad haircut and debts to any sucker enabling enough to lend. His studio apartment at The Earwig Suites (on Vinegarroon Avenue) rented weekly, cash only and for meals he would eat free Krispy Kreme samples for breakfast and Romeo's Charlie's complimentary employee meal for dinner. Surprisingly, he had no chemical vices, not even caffeine. Though still, his life was the perfect embodiment of whiskey tango. Hell's own twisted version of *Gift of the Maji*. If Lido had made a 100k at the gaming tables on Monday, he'd be busted back to nothing by week's end (known as *regression to means* in gambling terminology). His gaming poison of choice was anything wagerable: road dog Syracuse (+14) @

Villanova, 29 BLACK after four consecutive spins on RED, Vandershank Helmutslam and the Ponies (-8) against Brothelburger and Coach Poutjaw, Sugar Shane Mosley by K.O. in the tenth round, a diamond queen needed for a royal flush, and Iron Chef Chinese (secret ingredient: fish retinas) to win over challenger Sum Long Wang from the Hello Kitty District. *"Uhm, this fish retina sorbet is the best I've ever had!"*

Before his termination at Romeo Charlie's in 2003 for credit card fraud, Lido was infamously known for "appetizer rape." Large parties of corporate conventioneers would come to RC's and Lido would offer to assemble "a few" appetizers for the table. Once he had secured the positive nod from the party's air boss, Lido would show absolutely no financial mercy as the kitchen's order-printer spewed out thirty yards of appetizer tickets like a 1929 stock ticker gone awry. Weighty portions of barbequed Langoustine, Alaskan king crab legs, Australian lobster tail medallions in Italian truffle butter, escargot-stuffed mushrooms, and seared Ahi tuna would be plattered and dragged by Iditarod dog sled to the sensory-overloaded table.[†] The only thing missing in the pre-meal gluttony fest was a wedgied Sumo wrestler lifting up on one foot prior to striking a temple gong. Before even one bite of any food was taken, the convention go'ers had unknowingly spent more on appetizers than they would for that week's hotel stay at Mandalay Bay. Just prior to the Berlin Airlift's appetizer arrival, the entree choke hold was offered. Lido would suggest his patrons select the entree "special" of the evening. Though subconsciously patrons thought "Special, huh? That means some kind of exotic Stealth Bomber costly surf & turf entree for the price of a Winnemucca diner meatloaf sandwich. How very pleasant." Fraid not. The "special" of the evening was usually the most expensive item of that evening's entree selections, always over $75, yet still a fraction of the cost of the appetizer barge.

Since an automatic gratuity was included on parties of six or more, being tip-stiffed wasn't an issue. But furious patron

---

[†]In the late 1950's, U.S. demand and consumption nearly caused Alaskan king crab to be fished into extinction. Found in the Bearing Sea in the lethally cold waters north of the Aleutian Islands, king crab fishing is now highly regulated.

outrage was. "The cost of this meal means I'm forced to lay-off the people I just dined with!" If the patrons cried too much, management would void a few items to shrink the check, but not many, and not often. Like all restaurants, Romeo Charlie's always sought higher check averages, so rarely servers, especially Lido, were punished for appetizer rape. In fact, waiter check averages were posted weekly on the bulletin boards to shame the servers into higher sales. My average was never tropospheric, but I wasn't about that. As a waiter, my goal was to get my out of town customers to return to the restaurant on a subsequent trip to Vegas. After Lido had his way, most of his patrons couldn't afford to get their cars out of long term parking. He kicked my ass in income production, but at least I could sleep at night. And it mattered not how much money Lido Fawkener made on any given evening anyway. He would leave it all at the casinos before sunrise. Regression to means, Pathy Gambi.

#12 Dante Castanheira—The Alpha Male

King Lear's lead supply man, Dante, was a dark sky full of angry clouds bound within the flesh of a madman. Second generation Portugese, he was a free-falling alcoholic and happy-dust dealer who sought to resolve all of his life's problems with cocaine, profanity, and violence. He, like Jeremy, liked passionless sex in public locations, women existing only to be screwed and not wooed. For Dante, the more compromising the circumstances, the better. If a restroom was where the thrusting took place, it was better if it were filthy and crowded. Or if the woman rogered was engaged, hopefully it was the night before her wedding, she was a virgin, and the groom was his kid brother. His ideal conquest would likely be a three-way with a Ninja's wife and a Supreme Court judge in the Taj Mahal on Gandhi Day. Fisticuffs often were the post-coitus course with Dante, with three arrests for honey bashing. Dante was an alpha dog who must have really crashed his Oedipus complex. Dante wasn't good looking to any degree, but the ladies were on a waiting list to receive his abuse. Some women just like to be treated badly.

Although Dante was a scuttled psychopath, abandoned by his guardian angel, he was a flawless hero among the busboys. To them he was the ideal man. An ugly, short, unrefined rogue, who packed his nose and smacked around any of his many fair-skinned sexual partners. All psychology aside, Dante was probably possessed.

As a waiter, Dante got the job done. Knowing he was a busboy icon, he tipped each Salvie he worked with a pre-shift twenty and they always covered his back. Dante would get the twenty back and much more when that same busser bought his blow. The other two waiters who also required that busser's service that evening would be in dire straits, but such are the peripheral politics of drug commerce. Rain falls up, dogs go meow, starboard lights are red, and heathen busboys on cocaine don't give a shit about customer service. But there was a brief downspike on the busboy cocaine intake charts when Dante was fired, almost literally.

It was a midweek evening and a lone gentleman was seated in Dante's section. The customer had a simple meal: iced tea, endive salad, and steak au poivre. Dante was already well wound and had given this man considerable amounts of attitude for not ordering a cocktail or a glass of wine to up the check. The gentleman simply said, "I can't." When a customer says this, the waiter must back down. The patron could be an alcoholic, a pilot, or perhaps an alcoholic pilot, which is so common if you knew the truth it would frighten you out of commercial air travel.

But Dante persisted in pestering this man and the beginning of his end was near. On a fifty dollar check, the lone diner paid in cash leaving two dollars on the table, no doubt in protest of Dante's offensive disposition. The gentleman left the table and proceeded to the coat check. Enraged at the four percent tip, Dante grabbed the two dollars and ran toward the front, found the gentleman, proceeded to march toward him with the two bills clenched in his fist yelling, "You asshole, come back here! What is this shit?" Knowing he was seconds away from a brawl with a lunatic, the patron reached inside his blazer, pulled out a Beretta, pointed it at Dante's tiny brain and said, "Freeze where you stand. I'm a United States Marshal and I will fire if you do not stop this second."

Dante turned to stone, more likely from shock than the command. The maître d' was quick to take the side of the man with the firearm and asked the Marshal if he wanted to press charges or call the District police. The man declined, but informed Dante that his drug usage was obvious and warned him in not so subtle words not to press his luck. He was fired before the Marshal had left the restaurant, though it was a gross miscarriage of justice according to the bussers.

#13 Julia Cunneyworth—The Red Snapper

Julia was the classic Jewish girl, or at least possessed what most Americans might feel are classic Jewish qualities. Physically, she was petite with a Hebrew nose and long, red hair. Her skin was geisha fair with freckles that would darken in protest of too much direct sunlight. She was called the Red Snapper because her survival at the Coventry required she be tough and aggressive to combat the vicious queens who resented her for being female. She had many characteristics that the queens used to cut her down. Foremost was her use of heroin. She thought it went unnoticed, but no one was fooled. It was like Conan O'Brien's hairdo; something was going on. The drug use apparent in her eyes did not deter her from being one of the most effective servers at the Coventry.

Julia was also an animal lover, to the extent that her once beautiful house in Shaw had acquired many barn-like traits. Julia didn't require references or pedigrees when it came to taking in a stray, only that they accept the other wayward animals she sheltered. She had opted for the company of pets over humans, animals being much nobler about love than people, a profound and often ignored truth.

Julia's bottom line was the dollar. Most of the waiters learned, after the fact, that she had palmed a lot of gratuities which were intended to be shared. We would often work in teams at the Coventry and when teamed with Julia, she would always drop and collect customer checks and their payments. When a customer paid in cash, she would invariably report that the patron had left a bad tip. If the customer left a hundred, she would say he left only sixty. Never once did a waiter team with Julia and get a twenty percent cash tip. I learned of her malfeasance only after a customer I knew outside of the Coventry told me he had left a fat cash tip. Julia had palmed half and reported to me a pittance. Other waiters had similar experiences and a few of us confronted her on the matter. She denied any wrongdoing. This would cost her down the road and, not surprisingly, cash tip percentages when teamed with Julia rose after the allegations.

There was another way that a few of the Coventry queens and Julia bamboozled for personal profit—it was the age-old, double-tip maneuver. If Julia had a large party with a thousand dollar check, she would use the computer and add the automatic twenty percent. She would present the check, process the credit card, and return the voucher with the tip line left blank, not mentioning that gratuity was included. Most customers assumed the grat was not included, wouldn't scrutinize the check's fine print, and would leave another two hundred or so on the twelve hundred. The end result was fraud, a fat tip, and customers who got screwed like shipyard whores, the unethical server taking four hundred on a thousand. Hush money was paid to the maître d', forty bucks cash to mimic a mime. When the office higher-ups questioned such huge gratuities, the standard response was, "They were very pleased with the service."

One banquet, I teamed with Julia to work a party of seventy people who had ordered three cases of an expensive Montrachet. The sommelier, a sandy Jekyll and Hyde, Peri Gilpin clone, had advised Julia and me to open most of the wine in preparation for the rush when the party arrived. We opened twenty-eight of the thirty-six bottles inside the walk-in cooler when the sommelier found us and said the party had just called. There were only going to be thirty-two people total. She noticed that we had opened most of the wine and informed us that we'd be paying for any excess wine opened but not served. Thirty-two people would drink, at best, fifteen bottles, leaving Julia and me to buy thirteen bottles of Montrachet at fifty bucks each, six hundred and fifty dollars total. We would have to work the week for free, and that wasn't going to happen.

Knowing the sommelier drove a factory fresh Mustang with a hypersensitive motion alarm, we enlisted our busman, for twenty, to zip down to the parking garage and give the car a good shove. The parking attendants called up to the restaurant to tell the sommelier that her alarm was going off. When she dashed down to the garage, Julia and I ran inside the walk-in cooler and dumped eighteen innocent bottles of perfectly wonderful Montrachet down the floor drain. After the party had finished its meal, the sommelier went into the cooler to see how many bottles we would have to pay for. Julia said, "They drank all of the twenty-eight bottles we opened." The sommelier didn't buy the ruse for a second and said, "C'mon, thirty-two people drank twenty-eight bottles?" Julia said, "Rather alarming how much some people drink, isn't it?"

Julia had interviewed at King Lear, jumping through all the hoops and barrels to get the job. Ultimately, the GM let the deciding vote go to the other Coventry defectors who had worked with her. Her application was rejected with a unanimous "No" vote. We just couldn't trust her.

#14 Lee Salazar (call sign *Salad Bar*) —The Eel

Boston people are fun. It's a well-known fact. They have culture, personality, and are ideal drinking partners. Such was Salad Bar, a Boston bean who loved to get baked and was best friend of Mitch Morehouse. Before being a waiter, Lee was a Merchant Marine whose foot was crushed in an accident at sea. He kept his foot, though it caused him incessant bouts of pain. He received some kind of monetary settlement, but only enough to cover some of his drinking or all of his annual mortgage payments. He no doubt drank in volumes to numb the tremendous pain his foot and the Red Sox caused him. Lee and Mitch were like a pair of school chums, doing everything together—eating exotic foods, doing exotic drugs, watching exotic dancers, and puking in exotic places. Salad Bar spoke with the stereotypical Teddy K accent that we loved to make fun of, which he often answered with a Bobby Brownie.

Lee's passion was pornographic film. He had seen every porno ever made and was always giving us the latest review. We nicknamed him "The Eel" because his favorite porn film, entitled *Hey There Orgy Girl,* starred a live eel and a half-dozen creative, naked, Crisco-ed women. At the end of this epic film, the women cook and eat the very eel they had just become familiar with (I apologize for giving away the ending of this movie). We would always say, "Lee spelled backwards is eel." Lee's other favorite snog flicks were: *In Deanna Jones (starring Berlin Marriott and London Hyatt); The Dirty Dozen (starring the Houston Rockets); From Here to Paternity (starring Michael J. Cocks); A Street Ho' Named Desire (starring Hugh Jorgan); Fiddle Her on the Roof (starring Ben Dover); Pandora's Box (starring Dick Army); Gang Bangs of New York;* and the box office smash *My Big Fat Greek Vagina.*

As for his taste in hooch, he drank ports, but bourbon was a good way to start the day. He loved gourmet foods and had eaten everything from crispy-fried scorpion and jellyfish sushi to calf brains en croûte and Szechwan dachshund. The omnivorous Eel had even wolfed down a few helpings of Robin Quevedo's beefheartaroni, and once went to Carls Jr.

Lee was another member of the Portuguese parade whose mother still lived in Lisbon, his father in Boston. His mother was very ill for almost two years and Lee flew from Washington to Portugal twice a month because his wife worked for United Airlines and he could hitch the ride for free. He often sat in first class and feasted like Aretha Franklin every second of the way. On his day off, Lee often flew up to Boston to catch the Celts or Bruins, slept at his father's house, and flew home the next morning.

This landed The Eel in trouble one time. He was still bending when he staggered onto a plane to Dulles, fell into his seat and passed out. He was then awakened by the voices of some passengers behind him pointing out the Mississippi

River. Either his plane was flying the largest holding pattern in the history of aviation or he was on the wrong flight. Lee flagged down a flight attendant and asked if he was on the plane bound for D.C. and she said, "Of course not, we just departed Washington. This flight is bound for San Francisco." The Eel had slept through his stop and no one needed his seat for the continuation of the flight. Salad Bar was off to Haight-Ashbury and it would be two days before he could get a free ride home.

#15 Jasmine (Jazzie) Deming—White Trash and Cash

I trained and worked with Jasmine at Augustine's. She was a half-Cherokee, extremely attractive Florida native with a mouth so vulgar she could make DMX blush. Her looks got her the job, her vocabulary would get her fired. Jazzie was also a fishy drinker, going to bars and getting blitzed, drinking to excess every time, and driving intoxicado in the wee hours of the morning. It was difficult to believe she had only been convicted of DWI once. Some of the staff tried to convince her that it was her Native American physiology that prevented her from metabolizing alcohol effectively, but she didn't care to hear it. Jasmine had never heard of the *Trail of Tears* and wasn't interested in her heritage unless she was named in a will.[†] Jasmine lived to party and loved the attention from the boys. Her lifelong ambition was to have a plastic rack, despite having a nicely proportioned body with smooth, milky mocha skin.

Jazzie's husband, Ernie, was a West Palm police officer, jealous to a fault and with good cause. His flirtatious bride, though a tomboy, brought a certain sexual energy to the staff when she worked. Allowing the guys to rub her ass didn't diminish her popularity either. She curried favor with the cooks by sharing her pot and sneaking them beer, along with the ass rubbing. On holidays, she wouldn't wear panties as a bonus for the cooks.

Jazzie was very open about discussing her turbulent marriage and family life. She had three children, all said to be

---

[†]Between 1838 and 1839, over 17,000 Cherokee Indians were removed by U.S. troops after the discovery of gold on their tribal lands. An estimated 4,000 Cherokee died of hunger, disease and exposure during the ten-month relocation, a forced march of over 1,000 miles.

mistakes, becoming pregnant even though she and Ernest had used multiple combinations of birth control. Apparently Jasmine became pregnant with her last child despite being on the pill, wearing a chastity belt, using a coil, a frisbee-sized diaphragm, and a giant sea sponge smeared with ebola virus and Echinacea. Ernie wore two cast iron condoms, a wet suit, and an extra small pair of Jordache jeans and withdrew well prior to happy hour while concentrating on a picture of Vladimir Putin. When not with Jasmine, jealous Ernie was always calling Augustine's to keep tabs on the missus. The waiters would try to fuel Ernest's paranoia with erroneous information. "Yeah, Jazzie's not here. She went over to the Bed Bug Bed and Breakfast Inn with a donkey, Colin Farrell, a Haitian with a toolbox, a man from Nantucket, and some male model from Zurich with an oversized knackwurst in his lederhosen." Jasmine and hubby fought like cats and dogs. Their marriage seemed to be held together by threads. Everyone hoped that Ernie had checked his gun at the station. Jazzie's car often sported new dents and broken mirrors, to which she would say, "Ernie and I had another fight." It was rumored that the only reason Jazzie had just one DWI and neither had been charged with spousal abuse was that Ernie was a cop.

As a server, Jasmine did well, her touchy, flirtatious way making her the highest paid server at Augustine's. "I'd rather you not massage my husband while he orders." "Shut your mouth, woman! Keep working those shoulders, Jasmine." There was nothing Old World about Jasmine's service. Although she had limited food knowledge and didn't know a single word of French, she did suspect that wine was made from either grapes or strawberries. It mattered not though, because her customers were happy and she made outstanding money. Her biggest problem at Augustine's was the dreaded "Slap Ass Thursday." Keep reading.

#16 Danette Van Rhölm — SAT
A lovely fair-skinned blond, Danette was a soft-spoken

vixen who worked at Augustine's and had aspirations of becoming a sommelier. She had passed her sommelier's certification and taught wine classes every Monday at Augustine's. Danette was much like the Seinfeld soft talker, with a demure voice and seductive stare that made the male libido run wild. She was the best server at Augustine's and friend to everyone on staff. Danette's claim to fame was inventing "Slap Ass Thursday."

The fourth business day of every week, the men and women of Augustine's would smack each other's asses at the least expected moment. Though of genius intellect, Danette had failed to note that boys outnumbered the girls three to one, hence the female tushes would receive much more punishment. These smacks were not little timid pats of endearment, but Singapore caning-type whacks that elicited high-pitched squeals of torment. A typical Thursday shift would start out conservatively, but after a few Keoki coffees or similar set-up beverage, the smacking became rampant. Most of the men would not smack unless first smacked, but that didn't take long. Danette even carried a *gluteus maximus* checklist so as not to leave any asses unsmacked. Dani herself must have had a can of steel because we tried to smack her ass with authority, but all she would do is grin and glow in some sadomasochistic way.

Like anything fun in the workplace, Slap Ass Thursday turned into an obsession, the staff slapping asses at every turn. Schools of dolphins swimming in the Atlantic would pause and raise their heads out of the water to see what all the smacking noise was. Augustine's health insurance premiums were raised because of SAT.

The one girl who suffered most in the McCoy and Hatfield ass-smacking feud was Jasmine. She smacked all the boys' asses with a rubber spatula, leaving us with butt bruises that lasted for days. But the boys would get their payback, declaring war on Jazzie's bottom. We even goaded the kitchen crew for the sake of retribution. "Yeah, Jazzie says you guys don't have the apricots to wail on her tail like men and therefore aren't worthy of any more beer." "What? That bitch said that? Her ass is grass!"

And so endless punishment on Jasmine's hindquarters began. No one gave a damn about the restaurant or service, smacking Jasmine's boo was what now mattered in life. By night's end she couldn't even sit down and claimed that a mere thousand authoritative ass smacks had caused her to go through menopause before she was thirty. Jazzie never initiated another smack again.

And as for Dani, we could never smack her ass hard enough, and we really tried. We even smacked her ass with a frozen pompano, but all it did was turn her on, which turned us on, thus turning her on more and suddenly everyone was feeling amorous with pheromones flying everywhere because of one piece of frozen fish. Had Danette been Joan of Arc in a previous life, she likely said at her death "Oooh yeah, more fire. I like it really hot. Chuck some more wood on that fire, boy."

#17 Ty Orr—The Waiter's Station Agent

Never hold someone accountable for their genetic inheritance. You can hate someone for their behavior or the way they treat other people, but not for their physical contours. If we could pick our genetic codes, we'd all have perfect teeth, thick hair, and eyes as deep as an ocean. We wouldn't have acne that scarred our skin or slow metabolisms that leave the obese mocked as weak-willed by the thin. No one would choose to have a lazy eye or Leno chin or a schnozz the size of an anvil. Never would we elect to have an unquenchable zeal for alcohol that suffocates our *joie de vivre*. No woman would be flat chested, big boned, or always the unpicked wallflower. But most of all no man would choose to be unusually short. Not in America, not today. The extremely short are ignorantly picked on because of something they can't control and the result is a simmering rage that often goes unrecognized. The unknowing busboys beat their wives because they were short, though they blamed it on unfolded laundry. You can judge a person on their character and heart, but genetic inheritance is a game of roulette spun in a sealed vault. No one wants to be a Chihuahua in a world of Great Danes.

At four feet, three inches tall, shortness was a cross to bear for Ty Orr, the shortest of D.C.'s short waiters. A borderline alcoholic with a short name, a short fuse, and a short leash on his tall wife. Most of Tyler's coworkers at King Lear were tall as oak trees, making him feel all the shorter. The premier mocker of Ty's height was Preston, the man who wanted men of all racial variances to be treated equally. Ty weathered the abuse well, though, like anyone else, had days when his patience wore thin. He was a gifted guitarist, an accomplished writer, handsome, articulate, and married to a beautiful wife he had put through college and law school by working at King Lear.

Ty was also an obsessed Beatle fanatic, knowing more about the band than Ringo. His devotion to the band prompted him to stand in line three days for tickets when McCartney played RFK. The result was fourth row seats for the six King Lear penguins and our dates. Ty was so excited that we almost had to have him sedated. I'll never forget Linda McCartney rattling on a snare drum during "Let Em In" just thirty feet away from me. Knowing his Beatles obsession, the maître d' played a cruel joke on Tyler the day following the concert by writing in a fake reservation for Paul and Linda but saying he would not let Ty be their waiter. After seeing the reservation, Tyler first demanded, then literally begged from his knees, pleading and groveling to the maître d' to let him wait on the McCartney's table. The maître d' refused, acting like Ralph Fiennes' character in *Schindler's List*. After hours of mental torture he let Tyler and the rest of the staff in on his deception. Ty was inconsolable, furious and exasperated from his incredible and needless expenditure of emotional energy. But if Tyler's tarot card reader had told him the truth about the hard times that awaited him a few years down the road, he would have achieved an even greater degree of despondency.

Chapter 9

Management, Maître d's and Pourboys
(*Constables of Chaos*)

"Ashes to ashes
Funk to funky
We know Major Tom's a junkie
Strung out on Heaven's high
Hitting an all time low."

David Bowie, "Ashes to Ashes,"[†] *Scary Monsters*
Virgin, 1980

The next worst thing to owning a restaurant is managing one. As a manager you can't go bankrupt when the restaurant is foreclosed upon by angry lenders, but that's about the only advantage. The pay, in general, is awful. You'd fare better peddling Chiclets on the streets of Buenos Aires. Most restaurant managers make less than ten bucks an hour calculated after dividing that week's paycheck by hours worked, and you'll work twice as many hours as Willy Wall Street for a quarter of the money. Job security is non-existent. You can be canned on less than a whim with absolutely no justifiable reason. Modern restaurant owners often act like wild western gunslingers, firing whomever they want at any time of day to flex their monetary muscles. It's their town anyway and what they say is law, making them more of a joy to destroy for the employees because the owners just fired the only good manager the restaurant ever had.

[†]Also performed admirably by Tears For Fears on their 1991 CD *Saturnine Martial & Lunatic*.

As a manager, the odds are nine-to-one you'll have a chemical addiction of some sort. Maître d's, managers, and barmen have done, are doing, or are detoxing from every deviant behavior imaginable, from licking toads to playing hamsterdam. You name it, they're into it.

You'll have no social life beyond the quart of Hpnotiq you drank during your shift and just as all of the clothing of medical students smells of formaldehyde, the entire of your wardrobe will reek of grease and smoke. Don't get married, and if you do, have the lawyer draw up the divorce papers when he's doing the prenup. It's also best to determine custody before conception.

Managers are never voted most popular, but do sweep the awards for person most probable to go on a campus tower killing spree. You'll be hated by the entire staff, constantly having to be the bad cop, reprimanding individuals for actions even kindergartners know to be wrong. This goes far beyond being late, not calling when absent for a shift, or using profanity in the dining room. I'm talking about things like reminding an employee to shave or bathe, asking the amigos not to clip their finger and toenails in the kitchen, demanding the cooks cover up when they sneeze or cough, forbidding the sale of OxyContin to customers, instructing the waiters not to take a sip off of a customer's overfilled martini (even though it seemed like a waste to throw the excess out), and insisting that the prep cook with pink eye and acute mononucleosis is the wrong man to shuck the oysters, make the bearnaise sauce, and grind the tuna tartare that day. Post-can hand washing is only for Phi Beta Kappas and Rhodes scholars, throne flushing being akin to hieroglyphic translation for the average kitchen scrotum scratcher. Trying to explain *Campylobacter jejuni* and *Staphylococcus aureus* to an Andes mountain man was like trying to teach a bear how to play the cello. To them, trichinosis was a social disease contracted from prostitutes, salmonella was a recipe for fish, and fleas were the world's tiniest life form. As a restaurant manager, you are the zookeeper in a cageless zoo, and you can bank on the animals misbehaving.

As a bartender, every employee wants at least three freebie cocktails from you, the higher the shelf, the better. The approach is always the same—a thorned paw plea, a bonus ten above the tip-out percentage, and the eyes of Anne Frank.

Being maître d' is like being the President of the United States; every move you make will favor some and anger more. You are given the pieces of a thousand different puzzles, none of which fit together to form a pleasant picture, every customer and employee's personality factoring into a solutionless logarithmic equation that forces you to find solace in a bottle.

I don't know why anyone would want to spend their lives inside a restaurant, be it as an owner, a manager, a cook, a customer, or a fetch monkey. Might I recommend a suspicious fire and a fresh start in Vancouver?

At Cedar Forest, while Chef Randers was convalescing a broken femur, 73 club members became violently ill with explosive, crippling, inverted-colon, "I think I just shat a kidney" Staphylococcus infections. To avoid the hassle of making a new sauce everyday, the cooks, who thought Staphylococcus aureus was the same thing as aurora borealis, were making hen house nightmare-sized batches of hollandaise and storing the excess at room temperature for days, sometimes weeks. Hollandaise sauce, a microbiological Shangri-La, should be tossed every few hours. But instead Cedar Forest's GM, Trevor Brockton (disrespectfully referred to as Broccoli), was terminated for not noticing the parasite-rich, horror movie premise hollandaise that was now capable of speech and hair growth. Cedar Forest ended-up as a gavel-squashed defendant in a Jurassic size class action club member law suit, immediately followed by a substantial increase in monthly member dues.

Vincent James was the first restaurant manager I ever worked for as a front house employee, the GM of Charles Street Chop House. He was a good man with a frank, succinct, and honest disposition. Of average height, thin, bald, with academic glasses and a thick mustache that made you think he belonged in a 1920s photograph, wearing a brown derby. For those serious about their jobs, he was a pleasure to work for. Vincent was a recovering alcoholic, refusing to even get close to alcohol to avoid temptation. Never would he even touch a bottle of sealed wine or perform any function related to booze, not even setting one foot behind the bar, trying hard not to listen to liquor's seductive call. But working all day in a restaurant and avoiding alcohol is like being a sailor and hoping not to smell the sea. I had heard rumors after departing Charles Street that Vincent had fallen off of the wagon, though it was difficult to imagine of a man so disciplined and who had tried so hard to stay dry. His marriage also derailed, another proverbial domino of chemical addiction that can never be set up straight again.

The lead barman for Charles Street was Antonio Miller, a man not so reluctant to defy his liquid cravings. Antonio was a Jewish Puerto Rican, one of those mixes you don't hear much about, like Saudi Baptists, Harlem Mormons, and Duke Lacrosse eunuchs. He was older, had thick grey hair, and a paunchy gut from an unquenchable thirst. Antonio, like Sinclair and Elise Kahana, spent two months a year in Saratoga, though he spent his time at the betting window, not as a service person. He knew more about horse racing and track gambling than anyone I had ever met, though he had only debts to show for it. He was always hoping to hit a monster trifecta. Still hoping, last I heard. He tended bar during the day at Charles Street where the same regulars would stroll in every day, blab their groundless diatribe, drink a dozen Newcastles, eat a lobster roll, and waddle home. The scene inside never changed, only the seasons outside. Antonio never smiled, and in retrospect, it is no wonder why.

Charles Street's maître d' was Paulie Lamas, a roaring-hormoned sleazeball Puerto Rican twin of Pancho Villa with a giant black pompadour and Geraldo mustache. The waiters nicknamed him "Paulie Grip" because in order to get a profitable station with high-tipping regulars, you had to pitch Paulie a twenty. I played his game, never missing a payment and Paulie did me proud, coming through every time. This angered some of the other waiters who refused to be extorted, but it was a small investment that paid stellar returns, the greasing waiters netting, on average, four bones more per month than those with the uncracked piggy banks. You can't succeed as a waiter by being miserly with your support staff. Restaurant support personnel, though often drunk, dizzy, hallucinating, or comatose, never forget who's white-knuckled with the wealth, and that goes for customers as well. Look after them and they'll look after you.

I liked working with Paulie. He had a jolly way that made people remember him. He wasn't into drugs, but instead into the firm-breasted waitresses of Charles Street—physically, literally, and sadomasochistically. Charles Street boasted a fine lot of hot young honey bunnies in estrus and Paulie was always there to oblige, his wife and boys notwithstanding. Most of the waitresses had hordes of roommates and since he couldn't take his potential scores back to his house in Belle Haven with wife waiting, Paulie did his girls in his AMC Gremlin after a few prep drinks at Bullfeathers. The following day, Paulie would regale the male waiters in Cheech fashion with his tale of tail. We knew every detail about the more permissive wenches of Charles Street—who was loose, who was loud, who had teething instincts, who broke his parking brake, and who was foul-mouthed and dirty during the carnal crescendo.

Paulie was yet another example of a less than average looking man to whom the ladies ran. He was forever worried that his wife suspected something, especially after one of his young sons found a pair of panties under the car seat. He explained to his son that he had helped one of his employees move, albeit back and forth several thousand times. The explanation was concluded with a request that the boy not mention the lacy find to his mother. To all the Puerto Rican wives out there whose home-tardy spouses play in the NBA or work at, up to, or within one nautical mile of any bar, restaurant, or tavern and want to know if your husbands are drunk and constantly screwing other women, the universal, immutable, etched in stone answer is "Yes!" Díos mío, stop lying to yourself.

The last manager I worked with at CSCH was Dade Tatum, a short, fit, handsome weasel who was wound up like the guts of a new century baseball. He loved his Downey powder and it showed. One of my first encounters with Tatum was when a customer of mine found a plastic milk seal ring baked into her Yorkshire pudding. She was quite upset and I took the plastic ring and popover to Tatum and suggested we not charge the woman for her entree. At that second, Tatum cracked, screaming at me a million miles a minute in the waiter's prep station, ignoring the problem entirely, "That's just great, John! You have all the answers in how to run this God damned restaurant! Why don't you take my tie and you be the manager and I'll be fired and out on the street all because you want to do everything your way!" I didn't have a response for Tatum, a man who made Bobby Knight look like Steven Wright. And it wasn't caffeine that had tripped Tatum's control settings.

The answer was blowing in the wind, which makes for a common dilemma that would land Tatum in Lorton. How does one pay for a dime-a-week coke habit when only making a third of that amount through legal employment? Banks don't normally approve cocaine loans and at some point your wife or live-in girlfriend will notice that you haven't paid for rent, groceries, or dry cleaning for three years. Tatum went to prison for embezzlement from his subsequent restaurant employer in Baltimore, taking over half a million before being caught. The reality is that a half-million isn't that much money for a diehard blowhard.

Across the Potomac was a different style of management featuring blatant favoritism based on sexual preference and wardrobe color-coordinating ability. If you preferred the company of men, then you made more money as a waiter at the Coventry. I didn't mind throwing Paulie a twenty, but I wasn't about to play Simon and Grabankle no matter how much cash was involved. But the higher-up heterosexual deities accepted this sick dicktatorship, even though it left the straight waiters way down on the financial depth charts. When a new waiter was hired, the question of the day was "Is he gay?" The queer eyes didn't care about his name, where he was from, or if he was an effective waiter. All they wanted to know was whose side he played for. Did he spend his Sundays watching the NFL or shopping at Pier 1 Imports? Did he listen to Def Leppard or Donna Summer? Did he like Sean Hannity or Sean Young? March Madness or April showers that brought May flowers? The nancy boys would inspect the new recruit from head to toe and reach a conclusion for themselves. "Well, you're wearing a Brooks Brothers, chestnut-brown, herringbone, tweed blazer with darker-hued pleated flannel pants, appear to have tweezed your eyebrows and you've never heard of Dan Marino. You subscribe to *Meat Whistle Magazine*, have a curious suspicion about automaton C3PO, and respect the Boston archdiocese's stance on child rearing, so despite that butch voice of yours, I'll say you're one of us."

When I started at the Coventry, the *Will & Grace*rs were so sure that I was gay that I had to show them my drivers license. "Let's see here, you're an organ donor and Not Gay. Damn it!" The worst favoritism offender was a Liberace-esque king of queens named Troy, aka Helen of, who was obsessed with baldness and always trying to convince the staff he wasn't going bald, despite a yarmulke-sized patch of skin on the apex of his noggin. Troy was always talking about his Alfa Romeo and smoked curiously long cigarillos, leaning on the bar and vogueing as if he were James Dean looking out over Niagara Falls, wondering if George Clooney was out there somewhere. He loved drag racing and cock fights, so long as it didn't involve cars or poultry. Troy created so much dissension and animosity between the heteros and pet shop boys that management finally had to intervene, teaming the opposing sides whenever possible.

Aaron Hennings was the giant matrix of the Coventry. I mean giant literally, six feet, nine inches and well over three hundred and fifty pounds; with hands so big he could almost conceal a bottle of wine in his grip. He was the proud father of five knee surgeries. His appearance in a tuxedo to a seated table was intimidating. Customers intent on voicing a complaint would suddenly cough up a compliment when son-of-Lurch cast a shadow on their table. "Sir, the crab shell hidden in the

velouté that just severed my esophagus was exquisite, Sir."
Aaron brought a welcome change to the gay administrations
that had ruled, decorated, and feather-dusted the dining room
previously. He judged servers solely on their ability to wait
tables. He suffered retribution from the river dancers who had
previously received Oklahomo favoritism. Art exhibit tickets
were being mailed to him daily, potpourri sacks were jammed
in his desk drawers, a teal-green mesh banana hammock with
an ass floss back was put in his gym bag, and the picture of his
mother was stolen from his desk and replaced with a scratch
and sniff lithograph of David Hasselhoff.

Aaron and I got along from the start. Combined, we were
thirteen feet tall and weighed almost six hundred pounds. When
Aaron began working at the Coventry I had just had my first
varicose surgery and was given a bottle of Percocet for the pain.
I only needed a few to get me through the week so I offered
the remainder of the bottle to Aaron, who gladly snatched it up.
Aaron was a devout deadhead, and Grateful Dead groupies pop
Percocet like high school make-out probables eat Altoids. He
also wasn't shy about a little chemical-reacted cannabis—most
restaurant people aren't—though "little" with Aaron was a
relative term.

In the end, Aaron left the Coventry to open and manage a
new restaurant in Reston. He knew the Coventry was in trouble
and wouldn't survive, so he jumped ship just as Zach Cavanaugh
had. To replace him was another lord of the cock rings who
restored the queen's rule. The renewal of gay favoritism was the
catalyst in the exodus of Washington's eight best heterosexual
waiters, who left the Coventry and joined King Lear, the
proverbial Goliath of D.C.'s power restaurants.

The general manager of King Lear was a unique and
exacting man named Gavin Haft. My relationship with him
started turbulently and ended in friendship when I finally
departed King Lear. Without question, Gavin had the most
difficult management job in Washington. There was such a
diverse mix of wild personalities and culture clashes on King
Lear's staff that one wondered how the restaurant even

functioned, let alone took best restaurant honors for fifteen consecutive years. Gavin somehow put the puzzle together.

Gavin was in his late thirties, had thinning hair and was of medium build. He was a loner, or to be more precise, his job was his mistress. There was no time in his King Lear-dedicated life for anything or anyone else. He dressed in custom-tailored suits, and during the colder months wore a raccoon coat that probably took at least forty raccoons to make. All he needed was a Dartmouth pennant and football game against Yale and he would have been set, even though Marquette was his alma mater. He had a handsome face with larger than normal eyes that were very effective when asking questions, giving orders, and punishing the hungover and misbehaved. Gavin was sensible, articulate, and cautious with good cause. The waitstaff, though the best in the city, was always in trouble because of alcohol and drug consumption and commerce. Someone was always strung out, lying, lit up, booze-blinded, or pulling a con and Gavin Haft saw through it all. In 1997, all but three of the forty men and women who comprised the bus and waitstaff were either alcoholics, drug users, dealers, compulsive gamblers, or recovering from the overuse, abuse, experimentation or devastation of the former. Restaurant health insurance, at the few eateries where it is provided, normally doesn't cover chemical rehabilitation stays, which is pure insanity. Imagine a medical insurance plan for firemen that doesn't cover the costs of treating burns, smoke inhalation, and scratches from tree-rescued cats.

Gavin himself was a recovering renegade boozehound, one of the very few who was able to punch out the drink demons that stalked him. During my tenure at King Lear, I never once saw Gavin falter in his bone-dry state. He drank Uneid Deatocks, a non-alcoholic Cabernet. Everyone thought it was a full-blown red, but it was only fake wine. Being a high profile GM, it was very important for Gavin to look as if he was drinking a real red because, like the owners, he had to set a good example for the clientele, and besides, no one except for George Thorogood wants to drink alone.

Constantine, Clay, and Gavin always ate every meal, usually together, at King Lear—a major reason why the restaurant enjoyed such consistent success. Eating all of their meals at King Lear allowed them to evaluate every entree, each employee, and every aspect of service. The waitstaff moaned when ordered to serve the trio, but such objections were never voiced, the only phrase ever uttered in retort was "My pleasure." Gavin had instructed every front houser to respond to any statement, request, or demand with the phrase "My pleasure." "John, get me some remoulade." "My pleasure." "Preston, tell that man to put his coat back on." "My pleasure." "Mason, bring me a bottle of Gevrey-Chambertin." "My pleasure." "Dustin, stuff a live lobster down your trousers." "My pleasure." The waiters got so tired of using the phrase that we proposed different phrases to Gavin that sounded similar. Some of the alternatives being "sunken treasure," "at my leisure," "search and seizure," and the waiters' favorite, "Your wife's breasts I'll measure," but Gavin wasn't about to change his prized one-size-fits-all phrase. The waiters had also mailed a letter to Bell Atlantic suggesting they change their key phrase, which was "Thank you for using Bell Atlantic" spoken majestically by James Earl Jones. We instead wanted Mr. Jones to say, "My black penis is gigantic." Bell Atlantic never responded.

The new hires spent their first six months under the microscope and Gavin was the mad scientist adjusting the focus. The plebes also ended up serving Gavin, Constantine, and Clay much more often than the other penguins did. The first time Gavin corrected me on service was when I served him a cup of coffee with the cup handle not turned to the proper four o'clock position. He abruptly corrected my faux pas, warning me to pay closer attention to detail. But the worst trouble I found myself in with Gavin was when serving Clay Papandreas, Clay's wife, and a few guests early in my first year of employment at King Lear.

Clay's party was seated for dinner at the best table in the house and I was their waiter. The pressure was on, though I tried hard not to let it show. I greeted the table, took the cocktail order, and sped over to the service bar to get the drinks. The ice for the service bar was kept in a lined trash can that sat on top of a two-foot-high table. This trash can was used exclusively for ice, though it was still a trash can. You can put your dirty socks in a tomato crate and call it a hamper, but it's still a tomato crate. I rang up the order, grabbed the glasses that were kept on the waiter's side of the bar, scooped the ice for those drinks requiring ice, and the service bartender read the ticket and poured the order. I then put the cocktails on my tray and zipped back to Clay's table, serving the drinks in the appropriate order from the appropriate sides and then stepped away, allowing the party time to browse the menu and enjoy their drinks.

About a minute later Clay waved me over in frantic anger. I hustled to the table and before I could say a word, Clay blew at full volume, "Damn it, John! There's a cocktail napkin in my wife's drink!" He gave me his wife's drink glass. I looked down into it, and, to my great dismay, there was indeed a wet, wadded-up napkin. At the speed of sound, I ran back to the service bar, threw the napkin-stuffed cocktail into the trash, glass and all, and demanded a new drink faster than fast. I grabbed a new glass, scooped the ice, inspected the contents at eye level to be sure it was free of debris, and once the drink was poured, ran back to Clay's table, served his wife and apologized as best I could. Clay was livid and my fellow waiters were sure Gavin would fire me for the gaff, albeit unintentional. Clay was angrier than the vets had ever seen him.

That evening after check out, I was summoned to Gavin for the cut. Gavin was the coach and I was the defensive end who missed a key tackle that cost the team a wild card berth. Gavin began to yell at me, and certain that I was being terminated, I elected not to go gently into that good night. I interrupted his reprimand saying, "Gavin, you cannot pin this entirely on me. The bar is dark and overcrowded and you keep the ice in a fucking garbage can. The customers start to squeeze into the waiter's side of the service bar because there's nowhere else to stand and some patron chucks his cocktail napkin in what he thinks is a garbage can, and it is! Plus, Mrs. Papandreas was drinking a screwdriver. How am I supposed to see a wadded up cocktail napkin in the middle of a bunch of orange juice in a dark ass bar? The bartender missed the napkin, too. Does he get blamed for any of this?"

I thought my arguments were valid but Gavin didn't like the free-thinking attitude of this new King Lear waiter. He said, "Damn it, Galloway, you're responsible for *everything* that goes on your tables and if you're not willing to take responsibility for this one, then maybe you should just pack up and go, because you don't belong here!" Though furious, I held my tongue, as it appeared that termination was not a foregone conclusion. Despite being the whipping boy that day, that month, that year, Gavin kept me on staff and soon after the incident his anger diminished. He knew I wasn't a lost cause boozer or drug dog and worked hard to be an effective server.

Clay didn't stay mad at me for long either. On the contrary, he often told me I was his best waiter, offered me a management position, and insisted whenever possible I serve any and all food critics, celebrities, and other VIPs who dined at King Lear. Gavin promoted me to part-time maître d' and had me train the new hires.

My fellow waiters would not soon let me forget about the wadded-up napkin incident. Every week I heard a different rendition of the story, the worst being that I had deliberately put a tampon in Mrs. Papandreas' drink. But the boys finally got off my back when a better target for ridicule came along. A waiter named Jarrod had gotten so wasted one night that he didn't realize until the following morning that the woman he had taken home was actually a man. Jarrod's second and more critical error was confiding this gem to another employee. A day later even the customers knew that he had been seduced by a she-male. No one had the courage to ask Jarrod if he had been probed by aliens, though the silence on his face made us suspect he had.

Gavin's job involved a lot more than keeping a posse of wild waiters in check. He also had to keep the staff from stealing. Most of the waiters weren't takers, with the foreseeable exception of the fair-haired boy Dustin Vannoy. He was one of those people who thought he was smarter than everyone in the northern hemisphere when the truth was he'd lose if playing *Jeopardy* against a couple of Golden Retrievers. Integrity could not be found in his pot-limited lexicon, having smoked too many jays over his days to ever be intelligent again. Vannoy was a grape juice snatcher. His primary ploy was to dart behind the bar after closing and lift a primo bottle of red or two after the barman had stepped away from the bar to take his first leak in five hours. He would stuff the stolen wine in his backpack and hustle out the door before the tender returned.

Fishy drinking on and in the house was an accepted practice among the waiters at King Lear, but consumption of high-end wines was done only at the customers' expense. Vannoy's midnight wine larceny was an act of mutiny, betraying the two best owners in the city. Preston was the first to suspect Vannoy of wine-sticky fingers and soon the rest of the waitstaff had their eyes on him. After checking with the lead barman, we learned that Vannoy had likely stolen over four cases of fine reds, bottle by bottle. His preferred wine to take was Silver Oak, a hundred dollars per. The waitstaff knew the busboys had no shame, but there was an unspoken expectation of the waiters. Gavin also suspected Vannoy of taking wine on a regular basis but had no proof, so he quietly encouraged a few of the waiters to take the law into their own hands. It was the right thing to do. Mitch gave Vannoy a few choice words and broken tooth guarantees. Having known a few of the guys whose asses Mitch had kicked, the message somehow seeped into Vannoy's over-hemped head.

Gavin also took special efforts to keep the El Salvadoran employees, who accounted for over half of the King Lear's staff, content. Aside from paying them excellent wages, providing them with clean uniforms and one square per shift, Gavin also saw to it that all the King's conquistadores had health insurance, which was almost more important than wages because their wives and girlfriends squeezed out more bambinos than Mary Kay Letourneau (whose students were banging more than just erasers). It seemed like every other week another King Lear-sired baby was born.

But Godfather Gavin was a rich uncle for all the branches of the King Lear tree, taking care of all the administrative and financial details in regard to mass amigo manufacturing, asking only a fair day's labor in return. Yet despite all of Gavin's generosity and efforts, many would still steal whenever the opportunity beckoned.

As for the fertility facts, in July of 1996, King Lear had seventy-one full-time employees. Of those seventy-one, thirty-eight were Hispanic, the remaining thirty-three being African-American, Asian, or Caucasian. Combined, the thirty-three drybacks had a total of forty-four children while the thirty-eight Hispanic employees had one hundred and six children. Quixote Castillo alone was the father of nine by three gullible mothers. The monthly health insurance payment for each employee was just shy of $200 a month, the vast majority of those dollars paying the costs of pediatric care. There was no limit on how many children an employee could have. You could sire a hockey team and live in a shoe and all your medical costs would be paid. But health insurance wouldn't cover a stay at detox, something the majority of the staff desperately needed, leaving the bill-footing barren to wonder why they had health insurance at all.

Neonatal healthcare aside, Gavin's greatest testament to his loyalty to King Lear was the way he stood by Constantine Papandreas as Hodgkin's disease slowly took Constantine's life. Even though he was dying, Constantine spent the majority of his time at the restaurant. Gavin and Clay were by his side every step of the way while simultaneously managing a booming, chaotic restaurant. Clay knew how lucky he was to have a man as dedicated as Gavin at the controls and helping to care for his brother.

To help Gavin care for the restaurant was his best friend and Marquette fraternity brother, Nesbie Rasmussen, the birth-abducted identical twin of Andrew Dice Clay. He was the lead maître d' for King Lear. Gavin was temperate, disciplined, and led by example. Nesbie demonstrated all but three of those qualities.

Nesbie was the mad farceur of King Lear, plotting practical jokes as if he were navigating Cape Horn in foul weather. Some pranks were cruel, like the Tyler Orr-McCartney torture. The concealed habañero ploy was another gag that brought pain to its victims, sinister joy to the Nesbinator. Nesbie would order up a dozen clams casino, each with a nickel-sized slice of a Scotch Bonnet pepper cloaked under a piece of panchetta.[†] He would set the sizzling appetizer in the pantry, proclaiming it as a mistake and there for anyone's consumption. After finding out what the word "consumption" meant, the busboys would suck down the booby-trapped bivalves so quickly that it was too late to reverse the clam's course once the heat was sensed. You might think that watching the busboy's involuntary convulsions wouldn't be funny, but you're wrong.

Another classic joke was to have a rental girl approach an off-duty waiter and date dining at King Lear and demand palimony, rash ointment, and child support for the triplets. New hires were victim to the "hand the portable phone under the stall door to the man on the can" gag, as well as several other tricks involving the telephone, whipped cream, and furious fake callers. A cigarette fuse, which allowed a five-minute delay, enabled Nesbie to set fireworks off across the street while posing as a shocked and frightened bystander when the Claymore blew.

My personal favorite prank was the "tuxedo avalanche." Fifty plus tuxedos and countless pleated shirts hung at ceiling height in the employees' locker room above a second pole holding all the cooks' uniforms. Nesbie would pull the coat rack bar out of its socket and set it on the edge of the fitting ring so that the slightest touch would cause eighty pounds of wool, cotton, and polyester to come crashing down on an innocent waiter just trying to get dressed. A quarter in any of the locker's slide mechanisms caused the lockers to jam closed and only a repeated pounding with a meat mallet would get the locker back open. The preferred punkee of the tux-avie-quarter-locker double play was Angus the Shagger, a snooty Scotsman waiter from Glasgow.

[†] In kitchenspeak, *clams casino* are often referred to as *"gambling clams,"* which should not be confused with *Grambling clams*, which are mussels.

We knew he had arrived when we heard the repeated industrial banging of metal against metal and a few dozen well-bellowed "fucksakes" coming from the locker room.

The worst prank was putting a single oyster, scallop, or shrimp in an employee's car and letting it fester under a floor mat. One waiter Nesbie did this to had put his car in long-term parking for a ten-day vacation in New Orleans. He never drove with his windows up again, even in winter. There was also the coke-dusted jelly donut, a sweet snack fit for the mayor, a pricy treat able to make even the most homesick and unhappy camper smile.

As a maître d', Nesbie was effective at working the crowds and getting the customers in the door, but pushed too hard for the waiters to turn their tables. He would demand the waiters drop checks on any tables that had finished their entrees, a move that most of the waiters refused to do because it would ruin what was otherwise well-executed service. "Tables, we need tables. I want checks dropped on any table that's finished their main course." "Nesbie, that table just ordered a round of thirty-year-old Tawnies for dessert." "I don't care, drop a check now! The bar is packed and we're an hour behind on the reservations." The reality was that some of the more impatient customers had greased Nesbie with anything from a twenty to a hundred and Nesbo didn't want to return the cash to the palmer. The Nesbinator would never relinquish invisible money, hot-green unseen in the eyes of his wife and the IRS. When Nesbo was really in the worst of table jams, he had his trump card. He would find any table on coffee or cordials that had paid their check, approach and ask if they had given their car to King Lear's valets. If the party said yes, he would perjuriously inform the table that the valets were a half hour or more behind in car retrieval. In his best, softest Jesus voice, Nes would offer, "If you give me your valet stub, I'll get you in line so you don't have to wait out in the cold. In a while, when your car is up front, I'll let you know. But hey, it's our secret, okay?" The table would invariably buy the ruse, touched by such well-sold merde. Literally seconds later, Nesbie would burst up to the same people, proclaiming, "Hey folks, your car's upfront, ready and running, parked on a slant with the emergency brake off. Thanks for dining with us, we'll see you again real soon." The diners would immediately do a coffee spit-take, barking a run-on profanity, chugging their after-dinner drinks and abandoning the table. The table would be cleared before all the guests had entirely stood up, reset before they motioned towards the front door.

Nesbie, unlike Gavin, did drink. He liked his job, and why not? He slept in every day, came to work at 4 p.m., ate like royalty, drank the finest hooch the house had to offer, pocketed a tax-free couple hundred every night, and usually had a smile on his face before the night was through. All this without setting foot outside of King Lear, or only briefly on pyrotechnic display nights. Few people can boast such perks about their places of employment.

Nesbie wasn't the best looking man in Dodge, a little puffy-faced in fact, but using free food and fine wine there was always some shameless tart he was prepping for penetration. After a few conventional compliments and a few bottles of Poiwzunsip Cabernet, the ditzed dame was ready to be done, the doing usually atop any of the wine crates in the cockroach-infested storage room. If it was late enough and his turn to do the lock-up, the plush table banquets, bar counter, or rolly-wheeled guerdons made for preferred venues. Nesbie had even repeatedly screwed King Lear's sweet collegiate valet, and he was proud to have spanked an eighteen-year-old George Mason student. He fired her ass literally the day after she declared her love for him. Young girl get out of my life.

There was one candidate that Nesbie really had fueled for the score, a woman so drunk that she actually passed out under the guest telephones between the guest restrooms. She regained consciousness and was assisted back to Nesbie's regular table, which was located next to the maître d's podium for phone proximity. The staff noticed how blotto this damsel was and hoped that Nesbie might show restraint. To mount this oblit-erated hussy would border on necrophilia. No such luck. Nesbie, who was combating his midlife crisis, was a dog in heat who was going to hump whoever he could no matter how many times we sprayed him with a garden hose. The next day, three District detectives were taking statements from the previous night's staff. Gavin saw me and waved me and a few other waiters into the office and explained the situation. Nesbie had indeed screwed his passed out fishwife and then tossed her slutty ass in a taxi. When she arrived home to her worried and curious husband, the defiant wife said that she'd been mating with King Lear's head of penguins. Cognizant of her intoxicated state, the husband insisted that she must not have consented to the coitus, thus it was rape.

The hubby called the police to press charges and an investigation was started. Gavin, who had already been briefed by a couple of lawyers, told the waiters that we needed to have a consistent telling of the events. We were to say that the pokee did not appear intoxicated, that she never had more than three glasses of wine, and for Nesbie, that the intercourse was consensual. The actual tally of her cocktail consumption was eight glasses of Druncquen Karkrash Chardonnay and three snifters of Martel VSOP, enough booze to put any cat in the bag.

I reminded Gavin that perjury and obstruction were felonies and that the woman had passed out on the floor, to the point we almost called the paramedics. Gavin then asked me to say nothing or that I didn't recall the woman, lies that an investigator's glance at the previous night's station assignments could quickly refute. But solidarity was needed, and I couldn't say no to Gavin. He was too fine a leader even though he was asking more as Nesbie's friend and frat brother than as King Lear's general manager. I pleaded no knowledge when queried by the doubting detectives and after three days of questioning, a formal charge of rape was never leveled against the Nesbinator. More astonishing was the fact that his wife never found out.

Nesbie should have never been married, but he was, which was unfortunate for all parties concerned. He would dip his wick in any trick, jamming, on average, a different woman every week within the confines of King Lear. His wife was no fool in the matter of knowing about most of his indiscretions, foolish only in marrying Nesbie. He lived in Manassas and when we first heard the breaking news about some crazed Manassas woman pitching her husband's severed penis into a hayfield, we were sure it was Nesbie's wife and Nesbie's penis. We were wrong about that. We were right about Nesbie being an adulterous dirtbag who had jeopardized the entire restaurant and our means of income. A fun dirtbag, though.

Morris Uhlenfeld and I shared the maître d's duties on Nesbie's nights off. He in no way resembled Nesbie. He was calm, cautious, and calculated in all his words and actions. Morris, aka The Cat, lived on his boat docked in Annapolis, and could be found fishing the Chesapeake Bay when he was not working at King Lear. Morris was also a recovering alcoholic and a potter, but didn't sport the dim-witted pass-the-Dutchie-on-the-left-hand-side disposition of Dustin Vannoy.

Morris had previously led a wild life of drinking and drugging, but got a wake-up call in 1988. He and four other men were arrested while camping in Veracruz for possession of marijuana. Morris was sentenced to ninety days in a filthy Mexican jail, where he acquired a nasty case of amoebic dysentery, glad that three month's imprisonment and an intestinal disease were his only penance. Morris told me that the Mexican authorities missed the main stash of reefer he and his friends had buried in case the police did smell foul play. Had the buried weed been found, he and his buddies would still be locked away in Ixtapaluca Correctional. He said the worst part of his incarceration was not being able to call his mother, who presumed her only son dead. It had been a hard ninety days for her as well. Since then, Morris had devoted his life to fishing, a tranquil refuge from the havoc of King Lear. The Cat was always taking the waiters out on his boat, the only price was a little financial pitch-in on the fuel costs and that the boys bring their own party favors and paraphernalia.

King Lear was a favorite place of the Japanese business lords, because the portions of beef served were bigger than their offices back in Tokyo. When a novice Japanese King Lear patron was served a slab of prime rib or New York steak, the person's mouth would pop open and his eyes would bug out in disbelief at the side of beef that now lay before him. A frantic few sentences of the Japanese tongue would then follow. Though none of the waiters spoke a word of Japanese, somehow we were always able to precisely translate what they were saying. "Buddha have mercy! Look at this piece of beef! This is enough to feed my village for a week. First these American pigs give me a cocktail the size of an aquarium, and now a ginormous piece of beef that even Godzilla could not finish, not even if assisted by Ann and Nancy Wilson! I fear this table will collapse from the weight of so much meat. When the meal has concluded, I will ask the waiter to snatch the credit card from my hand." And even though the piece of beef was more red meat than the average Japanese citizen ate in a decade, the determined Jap would not waste a morsel, groaning from the pain of abdominal distension during the final three-dozen bites. The mere suggestion of dessert caused the bloated Asian to scream "Nooooooooo!"

One evening Morris and I were working the door together when an incomplete party of Japanese patrons came in for their reservation. An incomplete Asian party was an odd sight because Pacific Rim restaurant patrons tend to be scientific in the matter of punctuality (learn from the yellow man). I seated the party and the other two arrived at the podium not long after. They said they were part of the Tanaka party and I escorted them to the table. The pair bowed and said in English "We are very sorry, but we could not find the restaurant." A well-intoxicated, silver son of Kentucky who was seated with a guest at the table adjacent to the Tanaka's table turned his head, chimed in and said, "Yeah, well you sure had no problem finding Pearl Harbor, did you?" The yokel's tablemate, a more civilized man, scolded his friend saying "Harry, what the hell's wrong with you?" He stood up and apologized to the Tanaka party as the yokel barked out in hateful discourse, "You boys speak real good English, don't you?" Mr. Tanaka responded to the reb, "And you sir, do not." I waved Morris over for a quick briefing on what had just happened. The Cat and I agreed that the offending patron would have to leave the restaurant.

We informed the civilized man that his guest would have to leave, the yokel drunkenly protesting the eviction. The civilized man said, "Damn it, Harry, you're embarrassing me." He grabbed his buddy's arm and headed for the door, yanking him as if he were pulling a choke chain on a mutt. He handed Morris a credit card, asking him to buy the Japanese table a round and to pay for his meal. He said, "Please tell them I'm sorry about my partner's mouth here. I'll come back later this evening to get my credit card after I get Harry to the hotel." The bluegrass ass' last words before exiting were, "I killed four of them at Iwo Jima!" The friend yanked the misbehaved Reb out the door. Morris apologized to the Tanaka party, who were appreciative of the eviction and free round. The Cat and I were just glad the mouthy man had such a levelheaded dinner mate.

Roosevelt Burba was King Lear's bar manager and lead pourboy, a full-bearded Australian who looked like Grizzly Adams, minus the docile *ursus horribilis*. Originally from Wollongong, New South Wales, he worked every lunch and several nights a week as the best-paid bartender in Washington. Consumption was his life, be it pouring the same sappy regulars their fix or sucking up his daily two bottles of wine. He wasn't much of a smiler, except in the matter of debt collection in regards to the rental girls whose tabs were past due. To postpone the debt, Roosevelt would extend more than just credit to the overdrawn prostitutes, who would swallow more than just their pride. The rental girls and Roosevelt would disappear into the wine closet behind the bar and lunchtime drink service would cease until after the uprising was quelled.

While no staffer knew the exact drink-to-fellatio ratio, there was one rental in particular who was always flugelhorning Roosevelt. Her name was Dawn Hollis, knighted "Dawn Ho" by the penguins. Dawn was forever trying to kiss the waiters to be friendly and we would turn our heads away like infants refusing a spoonful of pureed kale, offering to shake hands instead if a sink and anti-bacterial soap were close by. "Please, don't kiss me. I know what you did last summer, forty-two times. Plus, rumor has it that your Chlamydia is flaring up again."

Roosevelt was the only man in D.C. who could drink at King Lear's bar without a coat and tie. He would throw back two for the road when his bartending day was done.

Roosevelt was a prime example of a restaurant vet with a dismembered family life, going a perfect four for four: married four times, divorced four times. He had only two children, both from spousal unit three. Rosie's daughter was a near-perfect creation. She was a 1550 SAT high school senior with three track scholarships from highbrow universities, and devoted her free time to helping children with cerebral palsy. His son was just the opposite, a billboard of renegade behavior, sporting an English punk rock coiffure, tattoos professing the gospel according to Mephistopheles, and more personal piercings than Bonnie and Clyde's getaway car. He had a rap sheet so long it required Virginia Vice to change the ink cartridges on their printers. At only twenty, he had already spent one-fourth of his life in jail. Though he seemed indifferent, Roosevelt's son despised his dad for never being home, divorcing his mom, and being so proud of his sister. He demonstrated his rage by keeping his father broke from legal expenses. Roosevelt made well over six digits a year, but had little to show for it. Always batting financial clean-up for his boy and his payouts on the four exes kept him broke. The unwritten rule with King Lear's employees and patrons was never to ask about Roosevelt's son, only his daughter. But his personal strife notwithstanding, Roosevelt Burba made King Lear's bar a place people wanted to go.

Jody Thibideaux was King Lear's second barman and assistant general manager, another company man who had booted hooch for running shoes. Jody was like Roland in his demeanor, Gavin in his dedication, and resembled David Keith in his physical appearance, speech, and mannerisms. Jody was a mid-forties man who admittedly felt defeated in the challenge to escape the grasp and wrath of restaurant work, a feeling I myself saw coming up fast on the road ahead. At King Lear, Jody's job was all about flood control, trying to keep the penguins from drinking the house dry. We could have done it, too, but JT was there to keep the hounds at bay.

A typical drinking day for a waiter working a double shift at King Lear started two hours before noon. You clocked in, signed in, checked your station assignment, and when the coast was clear, you dashed behind the bar and poured a pair of Crown Royals for you and your lookout. The lookout had the portable phone with the first six digits of King Lear's phone number dialed and would hit the seventh if a manager appeared in order to detour the manager to the podium instead of the bar. You had thrown some ice in the glass, maybe even a cherry so you could call it a Manhattan, but these drinks had nothing to do with a Manhattan. You clinked your glass with your lookout, toasting any thought that entered your mind. "To Velcro," and bottoms up. It was twelve past ten and you already had five ounces of happy juice under your cummerbund keeping that loxed bagel company.

The next drink was at noon, a fast glass of house red that was kept under the table where the ice garbage can was located. The barmen were so busy that management decided to let the waiters pour the house wines, which we did, mostly down our own throats. You'd have to drink from a crouched position, but it was better than standing up straight and not drinking at all. The house grape squash was a fair wine at best (referred to as Wal-Mart wine by the waiters), but it adequately carried the torch of intoxication until the next drink could be had, which was after the lunch shift. You slipped the service bartender an extra ten and in return he poured you a fat shot of Grand Marnier. Though invented to be savored, this particular shot would be consumed at the exact same speed a television set turns off once the power button on the remote control is hit.

Now you had two hours before your dinner shift, so it was off to the M Street strip clubs where three beers would maintain that drinker's euphoria nicely at a minimum price. The next drink wouldn't be until the dinner shift was underway. That's when you called seven drinks when you had only rung up six. Jody would be too busy to notice the discrepancy and a line of hurried waiters behind you made for a good smoke screen. The extra drink had to be different every time so as not to arouse JT's suspicions, and on the way back to your table, you detoured into the pantry and chugged the spare.

If you had a large party drinking wine, you had an excellent opportunity to drink unabated. After the fourth bottle, the party had lost count, leaving at least one bottle for you to drink a cappella. Plus if you were serving a group of Alsace foreign matter who plotted all day to shaft you on the gratuity, a bottle of wine rung on their check yet poured in your mouth was only fair. These measures got you to your shift drink and from there it was off to any of the many Georgetown watering holes until last call. The smart ones cabbed it home if they didn't sleep in their cars.

Jody knew he couldn't stop the penguins from drinking, but he did what he could to slow down the flow rate. His focus was on maintaining customer satisfaction, making sure service standards never fell short of excellence. On occasion, JT was forced to send an overwatered or highly-medicated employee home. When a waiter was too intoxicated to work, the primary indicator of his state was that he couldn't form a sentence. Of course, the bussers were incapable of forming a sentence even when sober. Jody didn't like being the bad cop, but since Nesbie was a mess himself, the burden fell to JT when Gavin wasn't around or was otherwise occupied with endless administrative duties.

Restaurant life destroyed Jody's marriage, though he and his wife Chloe had divorced in amicable fashion for the welfare of their daughters. They did not make their children prizes in the emotional tug of war that is scuttled love, as some divided parents do. Jody worked hard to provide for his girls, always concerned for their well-being and spending as much time with them as possible. Most separated, divorced, or never married fathers who have careers in restaurants and don't have custody of their children are just the opposite, aka deadbeat dads. They moved to a different state to make the court's actions and decrees more difficult to enforce and since their jobs pay in cash, garnishment of wages for child support payments becomes almost impossible. Those who don't evade child support payments often grossly underreport their tip income. The payments are based on a percentage of declared income. Mothers have a hard enough time trying to work and raise a child or children solo, and time and money for legal recourse usually doesn't exist. The deadbeats have no problem losing $500 a week as a bad gambler, spending $50 a night on post-shift cocktails, stuffing a twenty down a stripper's g-string, or buying a $300 bag of buds and stems. Deadbeat dads don't think about their kids being ridiculed at school for wearing the same clothes day after day, being absent from the dentist chair for years, or not having a PC to do their school work on, which leaves them spun out in life's educational first turn. One rarely sees a mother with indifference to the welfare of her children—it's almost always the father. But Jody lived for his daughters; there was no sacrifice he wouldn't make for his girls, making him an exception to the rule.

When I left King Lear, Jody was a little misty-eyed. I was too. We had endured a lot together in six years of restaurant work, especially when that restaurant was located in a tooth-and-nail city like Washington. Gavin and Jody had made me their "go-to" man during service crunches and I worked hard to justify their faith in me. They made the often unbearable world of fine dining service a little more bearable. If I was right in my musings that people don't change, it's a good thing where great men like Gavin Taft and Jody Thibideaux are concerned, a tragedy with boys like Nesbie Rasmussen.

☞ The brave 36th has passed such an ordeal as would try the best veteran regiment in the service, and wide spread is the mourning for relatives and friends' who have laid down their lives in its ranks. The lists of wounded have been drifting by degrees to our northern firesides, as the regiment has fought time after time, but up to yesterday no familiar names had appeared in the list of killed. Warren, Rains, McCann, Ermatinger, wounded, reported, and friends were thankful it was no worse. But yesterday came the sad news that Lieut. Galloway, of Co. K, was among the killed.— Lieut. Galloway was one of the oldest residents of our village, and was well known from St. Louis up, as a prominent lumber dealer and manufacturer. By his energetic action in recruiting he obtained the 1st Lieutenantcy of Co. K, and in all the engagements the regiment has participated in, he has shown the best qualities of a soldier. His life, like the many thousands gone before, has been offered up for the cause of freedom, and wife, children and friends are left to mourn his loss, and mourn the trials of our country. May God comfort his bereaved family and help them in their great affliction.

Chapter 10

Military Men and War Heroes
(Col. David H. Hackworth [†] */ Cpl. Patrick Tillman, Jr.)*

*"We can't hold the hill, even if we take it,
but orders are orders."*

Lt. John A. Galloway, 3rd Division, 65th Infantry,
Fox Company, *U.S. News & World Report*,
February 29, 1952, page 24.

   I have served with and to so many who have served in the
military that my experiences require their own chapter.
   Colonel Lawrence LaSalle was a King Lear legend and
beloved regular who knew how to treat people and how to get
what he wanted. He was a seventy-six-year-old Texas oil baron
and lady lover with more cash than the combined cast of *Friends.*
LaSalle, like many regulars, had a specific table where he always
dined and a specific drink he always drank, Johnny Walker Blue
times two on ice in a brandy snifter. He hated smoke, wasn't a
rusher, and loved the garlic-basil sourdough bread that Castillo
would bake just for him. When he entered the restaurant, the
waiters stood at the doors and would all jokingly bow down to
the Colonel like allegiant Egyptian slaves in the presence of
Tutankhamen. Other times we would announce his entry into
the restaurant in fifteenth century Britannia fashion, complete
with the rotten tooth accent. "Ladies and gentlemen, all rise for
the Duke of Anacostia, the Prince of Pennsylvania Avenue, the
J Street Jester, Sir Lawrence of a labia LaSalle." The Colonel

---

[†] One of the most extraordinary soldiers in history, Colonel David H. Hackworth (1930-2005) fought
in WWII, Korea, and served 4 tours in Vietnam. His heroism earned him 8 Purple Hearts, 2 DSM's,
10 Silver Stars, 8 Bronze Stars, 12 foreign awards and 2 Merchant Marine decorations. A military
legend, it is widely speculated that Hackworth's outspokenness for the concerns of military personnel
cost him both general stars and the CMH.

would fake as if he were in the wrong restaurant, bluff a move to exit, and then proceed to his table in the upper room. On occasion he would bow himself and say to the penguins "those who are about to dine salute you!"

Most of the dining room patrons didn't recognize LaSalle, but knew he must have been someone of grand importance from all the bother the staff was making over him. When passing the bar, he would say hello to a few of the flies while reaching to shake Roosevelt's hand, a quarter-folded twenty between his thumb and index finger in gratitude for the extra few glug-glugs of JWB. From there it was straight to his table, a sniftered double Blue rocks waiting. LaSalle would wave over the busser who stood at tableside attention anticipating cash, ask the lad's name and spot him a twenty, too. His bread was fired at his first step into the restaurant and in front of him ten minutes later, at which time another double Blue was due.

From there it was a leisurely lunch with any of several highly polished women, all over fifty and not a dud in the lot, each having that Raquel Welch quality that makes a grown man's mind wander and imagine the sordid scenarios to follow once those school marm glasses were removed and the release pin was pulled allowing her amber locks to fall. On occasion, LaSalle dined with and suffered through some jamba-juiced yahoo trying to get a fistful of the Colonel's dollars. "Larry, just listen to this, Condos on Pluto, it'll be great. Sure materials, heating, and transportation will be pricey, especially at minus five hundred degrees Celsius, three hundred mph surface winds, and a nine year shuttle ride just to get there, but we'll have a complete monopoly on the Milky Way housing market. A modest investment of $44 billion cash gets the ball rolling and you in on the ground floor. How 'bout it there, Larry?" Had the Colonel snapped his fingers we would have converged on the putz like famished lions on a tackled Serengeti zebra. LaSalle's penguins ready to protect and serve.

Colonel LaSalle was also a man with a great sense of humor, always trying to outwit the staff. He called me over once and asked if I had any spare prophylactics, saying he was down to his last one as he pulled out a condom the size of a discus that looked more like a rolled up airport windsock. The waiters loved to return his fun, whether it was giving him a six-digit lunch check or serving him a salad that was composed of only a single leaf of watercress, half a cherry tomato and two pumpkin seeds. Once LaSalle ordered a three-pound Maine lobster and we served him a tiny half-ounce crayfish on a humongous white plate, insisting his lobster had shrunk during the cooking process. When it came time to pay, it was always a hard fifth of the total, a handshake, and crisp cash bonus twenty. Take a lesson from the master.

LaSalle's car was very much like him, a glossy silver Rolls Royce that the King Lear valets were quite protective of (they also scored a twenty). Verner, the captain of our excellent valet crew, was moving the Colonel's car across J Street to the parking garage when an older model Mercury Cougar roared out of nowhere and plowed into the Colonel's Rolls. Mortified, Verner jumped out of the car to confront the person who had wrongly broadsided the most cherished of the eighty cars entrusted to him that evening. At that instant, the Mercury peeled off and away into the night, a classic hit-and-run. Nesbie was notified and so too was LaSalle who came out to look at the damage. The Chief of Police, who was also a King Lear regular, came out to take a peek for himself.

Beside the smashed Rolls was the bumper from the hit and run Cougar, complete with a District license plate. The Chief reached in his pocket for his cell phone and dispatched a unit to the hit-and-runner's house. The cops knocked on the door and asked the answering man if he had been driving his Cougar that evening. The drunken man nervously said "No" and the cops said, "Well sir, your engine is warm and your bumper impacted the side of a Rolls Royce on J Street about twenty minutes ago. Why don't you come with us, and we'll get you a mint for your Thunderbird breath." The man was charged, LaSalle's car was fixed, and Verner aged ten years in twenty minutes. After the accident, Colonel LaSalle told Verner, "Don't ever fret over it, son. You're a good man, it wasn't your fault, and besides, it's just a car."

Colonel LaSalle was a West Point graduate who flew B-26 Martin Marauders during World War II, flying and surviving 103 bombing missions in the European Theatre of Operations, including three runs on D-Day at altitudes so low that shrapnel from one of his own bombs hit his plane. While the B-17 Flying Fortresses were flying at 15,000 feet and missing their targets badly because of overcast skies, LaSalle and the other Marauder pilots were flying within a wingspan of the German bunker line trying to help out the infantrymen who were getting cut down on the beach assaults. LaSalle survived one hundred and three missions, which is amazing considering that there was a fifty percent mortality rate in flying just twenty-five missions for the B-24 Liberator and B-17 Flying Fortress crews.

LaSalle named the plane he flew *Trafalgar* after the inspirational poem by Francis Turner Palgrave. One morning LaSalle and his four crewmembers were flying over German-occupied France en route to a bombing target. They were taking heavy Nazi flack, being rattled about the sky by fierce explosions as LaSalle descended his Marauder and turned for the final leg of the bombing approach. Suddenly there was a severe flack explosion off his right wing that shattered the canopy, disabled the starboard engine, and destroyed his instrument panel in a cloud of sparks and electrical smoke. He glanced to his copilot to find his friend had been decapitated from the flack burst. LaSalle kept his composure and continued the approach to target, dropping his ordnance and flying the crippled *Trafalgar* back to England, covered in the flesh and blood of his copilot.

He was awarded the Distinguished Flying Cross for a mission that would haunt him for many years to come. In the late 1960s, LaSalle was very ill and was comatose for over a month. While in the coma, he had a vision of the copilot who had been killed that fateful morning. The man appeared to him in a pinstriped suit and hat and told LaSalle that he was at peace and to stop punishing himself with feelings of guilt for having survived the mission. When LaSalle awoke from the coma, he told his doctors about his vision. They dismissed it as a hallucination, but LaSalle knew the vision was real.

Danny Kilpatrick was a man who forced me to muse that drinking too much booze is like getting too many tatoos – someday you'll regret both. He was the perfect personification of alcoholism. He showed me that heartless men don't stay true to their wedded high school sweethearts and forever changed my misguided visions about American soldiers in foreign wars. Danny didn't have any formal lesson plans or fireside fables with stark revelations, he just lived his life, and this teenaged boy looked on in lurid fascination.

Danny Kilpatrick was a career restaurant leprechaun who worked as a captain at the Uptown Club, an undiluted Irish genetic code and a career in fine dining service being a stone-etched promise for unadulterated alcoholism and unending adultery. For Danny, drinking, boinking, and drinking was the order of each day with occasional breaks for vomiting and spending quality time with the wife and kids. He was in his mid-thirties and not particularly handsome, his appearance taxed by the circumstances of spending half of each day hungover.

That this man was married was wrong. Wrong like Michael Jackson's wine club. How any woman tolerated this man was a baffling question with no logical answer. A few months into my term at the Uptown Club, I overheard Danny cussing with his teeth clenched as he prepped his captain's station. I asked him what was wrong and he said that his wife was itching again. Only seventeen and ignorant about sex, precautions, protection, infidelity and moving freckles, I said, "Big deal, she has an itch. Go to the pharmacy and get her something for it."

DK said, "Nah John, you don't understand. I gave my wife the crabs, again, and this is the third time in two years."

I told Danny to tell his wife to use Old Bay seasoning instead of talcum powder and everything would be fine.

Danny tried hard not to laugh but his lips wouldn't stay sealed, even if the laugh came at the expense of his crab-covered wife. Crabnester blurted out laughing, "Damn you, John! She'd definitely toss my ass out on the street if I told her that."

A piece of advice for men in the hospitality industry,

especially those with severe cases of roaming trouser trout: don't get married. And for the women—don't marry a drunken, Irish, puking pervert with flaring venereal disease. You can do so much better. I must remind you at this point that Danny Kilpatrick was a food server and while this text is very much pro-server, I must concede this argument to the customers. It's perfectly natural to want a waiter who doesn't have lice, mites, monkeypox, Lyme Disease, silverfish, rickets, ringworm, barn fleas, boll weevils, West Nile virus, rheumatic fever, athlete's foot, bryozoans, chiggers, spirochetes, scabies, rabies, or venereal crabs. In fact, you should insist on it.

DK was indeed a military man who had served as an army cook at a firebase just outside of Saigon. He was grateful to be ladling out chipped beef as a kitchen hound instead of out firing rounds into the jungle nebulae as an infantry cog, walking point, stepping on land mines, and scanning the tree line for his legs.[†] Though not a rifleman, Danny often risked life and limb in the ominous brothels of Saigon, a gold card whorehouse player who had contracted venereal disease with the frequency the average man gets shaving nicks, including syphilis, crotch crustaceans, and several cases of gonorrhea. DK had even contracted the dreaded bull-headed clap one time, and was proud to have done so. I don't know much about the bull-headed clap, only that the soldiers would rather have suffered Vietcong capture—one's jockstrap won't fit anymore and urinating becomes tantamount to scaling Everest, only with much more screaming.

When Danny's scepter was temporarily out of commission from previous bouts with VD, he found other ways to sow his oats. He told me that his most frightening experience during the war came when he and a mess buddy were occupied with a pair of Vietnamese rentals, Danny's escort being in the midst of that special time that only women must endure. Most people might have reconsidered the situation, life having left a boxcar full of indications for DK that wartime gratification in a Saigon whorehouse was not meant to be that night. But a malfunctioning wand, a menstruating minor, and the promise

[†] In the Vietnam War (1959-1975) 58, 229 American personnel were killed and 304,000 wounded. Of the wounded, 134,000 were severely wounded or permanently disabled. Agent Orange defoliant related deaths are estimated at .25 million and Veteran suicides in excess of 81,000.

of venereal disease did not deter the morally destitute Private Daniel Kilpatrick as he and his stew-stirring mess mate did what drunken skunks do with women for hire in coach-class houses of ill repute.

After the hoo-ha and in the foggy darkness of the morning, the two were awakened by mortar explosions and the sirens from the firebase that signaled the soldiers to grab their weapons, take cover, and for those off base to get their asses back to the base. DK jumped up, trying to find his pants, but the room was too dark. Even after his buddy had managed to turn on a light, Danny still couldn't see or even perform the relatively simple task of opening his eyelids, though not for lack of effort. His eyes had been glued shut with a most repulsive epoxy generated from his rented, menstruating minor (DK did not recount this moment with such delicate verbiage). Finally, like a stubborn clam, Danny was able to pry his right eye open as he and his cohort grabbed their boots and their pants and furiously sought the exit door.

The North Vietnamese mortar volley continued as the pair found the street and dashed for the base. Suddenly the hard-charging pair tripped over something in the road, both slamming face first into the ground. The cyclopean Danny looked back to see that they had been tripped by an anaconda, indifferent to the sirens and mortar barrage. Adrenaline at critical, the crazed pair jumped up and ran toward the guard gate frantically trying to identify themselves so as not to be shot by the paranoid sentries, shells still falling and the dark morning loud with the sounds of machine gun and rifle exchanges. A medic rushed over to the winded Danny, attempting to treat the brave soldier whose face was covered in dried blood, one eye still closed. DK pleaded to the medic that the blood on his face wasn't his own, when in fact he had cut his forehead on the ground after tripping over the anaconda, an itsy bitsy Kerry cut boo-boo that was fixed with a half inch Band-Aid. Danny altered the facts ever so slightly, reporting that it was a mortar fragment that had grazed his head, and he became the only man in the history of the United States military to be awarded commendation for a crimson face, service beneath contempt and not remotely related to the call of duty.

As an upscale waiter captain, Danny Kilpatrick was the best there was. His happy-get-lucky Irish nature and disarming grin won patrons over instantly. He had perfected the art of tableside service; his specialty was anything flamed. His favorite fired dish at the Uptown Club was flamed lobster, which required heavy cream, butter, brandy, and an unsuspecting, yet very much alive Maine lobster. People loved the showmanship, though it seemed to me that the lobsters suffered humiliating fiery public executions. When I saw the lobsters sitting on DK's guerdon, I felt sad knowing the condemned future that was in store for them. The same was true for Danny Kilpatrick with his binge alcoholism and depraved lechery, the only difference being that fate and commerce killed the lobster. Danny chose the path of demise and self-destruction, a hammered loser in the tug of war between free will and alcoholism.

Some people's images are synonymous with pain and suffering: Adolf Hitler, Tonya Harding, Pol Pot, Terrell Owens, Idi Amin, Saddam Hussein, Kim Jong-il, Clay Aiken, Osama bin Laden, Slobodan Milosevic, Charles Barkley, Pat Robertson, and Lyndie England. To the J Street brohams and helper minions, it was the ugly mugs of Brigadier General Quincy Brewster and his winged-monkey, I mean wife, Katie, one of the worst nightmare deuces in restaurant history. General Brewster was a blimpish, retired Army Intelligence officer and Mrs. Brewster was a frail and paled-faced moaner who could never be pleased and convinced the staff that God didn't exist. She was forever raving on about her precious companion, a little shih tzu. She preferred the company of a tiny dog because any other life form able to run away or negotiate a doorknob wouldn't have stood to be around her. The General only stayed because of her dowry. Both were in their mid-sixties (this applied to age and jacket size for the General), and I became their favorite waiter. I must have sinned in a previous life.

When they made reservations, they demanded a specific

table, which wasn't so bad, only they took almost four hours to eat. As you know, no table turn, less dinero, angry waiter. The Brewsters also refused to allow any waiter who wasn't a white, American-born, non-Jewish male to wait on them, cloaking their racist reasons with facades of displeasure with prior service and using their complaints as justification not to tip. They even had the audacity to complain when served by Sinclair Kahana, arguably the best waiter in Washington, and left him not one nickel on their $550 check.

No matter who served them, there was always a flaw in the meal, something that wrecked their evening, yet the Brewsters always returned, dining at King Lear every week and making the staff miserable. I lost all respect (actually the coffer was already empty) for Nesbie for letting this pair of fuckers back in the door, and he knew it. Hence, Nesbo made me the Brewster's regular waiter, though I was able to dodge the table some of the time with days off and other call parties. The fact that they didn't want a black, female, Jewish or any other non-WASP Yankee to wait on them made the collective staff furious, driving us to drink, more so. Where was Whoopi Goldberg when we needed her?

Bitchess Brewster ate nothing but lobster, but it had to be male. She claimed that male lobsters were more tender. I claimed that menopause had shoved this woman's sanity off the continental shelf. Her request required the waiters to run back to the lobster bin, reach in and find a male. I refused to do it, sneaking Jacques a couple Dos Equis in exchange for washing off the bright red roe. As for drinks, Mrs. Brewster sipped Champagne at a rate slower than room temperature evaporation and General Behemoth spent forty-five minutes nursing a single Boodles gimlet. The waiters could gulp a gimlet in the middle of a two-word sentence while whistling. As for wine, the Brew Crew drank nothing but Chateau Lafite Rothschild, four bones a bottle, but never tipped on it, the bastards. Waiting on the Brewsters was like waiting on three tables with the resulting income of one Diet Coke deuce. They had no clue how much they were despised by the staff. Military intelligence, my ass.

But the staff's salvation came thanks to our revered owner, Constantine Papandreas. Blimpy had ordered his usual bottle of Chateau Lafite and upon tasting it, said it was faintly sour. I tasted it and disagreed, and brought it to Roosevelt who was sitting at the bar with Earl Styles, two oenophiles whose wine knowledge was unrivaled in the District. Both tasted it, as did Preston and Angus, all agreeing that said wine was pure nectar. I asked General Brewster to try it again and he said "I'm sorry, but you boys aren't used to drinking the fine Bordeaux that I'm accustomed to and this one is no good." What did he mean by that? That King Lear's staff drank nothing but Mississippi outhouse moonshine on trailer park picnic tables? Perhaps this was true, but we could still tell if a snooty bottle of French grape squash had turned the corner or not.

Yet somehow, I ended up bringing General Brewster and Mrs. Battle-ax another bottle of $400 Rothschild, which he also quickly panned as unfit for his consumption, demanding a third bottle, chop-chop. Roosevelt and The Pearl were watching me serve the second bottle. I glanced to them and nodded my head once in consternation, letting Rosie know that the General had rejected another perfect bottle of Lafite. Roosevelt discretely informed Constantine and I excused myself from the Brewster's table, the two thinking I was off to get a third Rothschild. Constantine met me at the service bar and said, "John, what the hell's their problem?"

I said, "Well sir, the General says his wine palate is a little more sophisticated than ours and we can't recognize a flawed claret. But the truth is that they just want attention."

Constantine grabbed a wine glass and tasted the second bottle, shook his head in anger and said to Roosevelt, Nesbie, Preston, and me, "We'll give'em some attention. Nesbie, get their coats. Rosie, tell Verner to pull their car up. John and Preston, you're with me."

The three of us walked over to the table, Sinclair, Mitch, and Angus joining up with the lynch mob at the Brewster's table. Constantine said, "You folks will have to leave and are not welcome back. You've abused my staff for two years and it ends now. Here are your coats. Your car is blocking traffic. Now get the hell out of my restaurant!" Constantine then said to his penguins, "Boys, see the Brewsters out."

The two were lifted out of their chairs by the angry penguins. The General was speechless and Mrs. Brewster's objections were silenced by Mitch's finger in her face as he pointed and barked, "Shut your face, woman!"

Preston had both hands on the General's right arm as the parade marched toward the door. This was the time for Presto to speak, sotto voce, two inches from the terrified General's ear saying, "So the black man isn't good enough to serve you and your damn wife, huh? You think 'cause you're loud and you're rich and call yourself General that you're better than me? You're the worst kind of hypocrite there is and now the black man who isn't worthy of serving you is kicking you out of King Lear. You wanna spill my garbage, fat man? I'll give you a mess you can't believe!"

As the now ten-waiter rugby huddle marched the pitiful duo out the front door, the rest of the patrons looked on, frightened yet fascinated by the angry penguin parade. Once out the door, all hands came off the couple as if a crash cart nurse had yelled, "Clear!" The Brewsters made double time for their idling Crown Victoria, not looking back.

Outside, Mitch said loudly so the Brewsters could hear, "Hey Preston, what's that thing you say about women?" Preston crisply answered, "All women are whores, my man." Grinning, Mitch sarcastically asked, "Even Mrs. Brewster?" Not hesitating Preston responded in an authoritative tone that let all of Washington know, slamming the carnival sledge hammer hard on the second syllable, "Especially Mrs. Brewster!"

The Brew-two had created so much animosity at King Lear that they knew a return would never be possible. Constantine and Clay Papandreas were the most generous and likable restaurateurs in Washington; to exhaust their good will seemed impossible, but sure enough the Brewsters had managed to do it.

The penguin parade arrogantly strutted back into the restaurant feeling victorious, like superheroes who had just saved the planet by vanquishing a couple of dark villains. The diners looked at the returning penguins with momentary awe as we began resuming our duties, wanting to yell out, "Anyone else having a problem with their wine tonight? Nah, we didn't think so."

Funny how other diners become a tad more humble after witnessing an eviction. King Lear wasn't the only eatery to excommunicate the Brew crew. The Brewsters were banned from several other restaurants in the District, one because they made several disparaging remarks about the executive chef, who was female. You try hard to make people happy, but it is never acknowledged enough that **service is a two-way street. A pass thrown but not always caught, even when it's right on the numbers.** To put it in a military metaphor, you can't be a good soldier when you're fighting for the enemy.

After work that night, King Lear's penguins sat down at the bar and toasted the Brewster's permanent departure, doing so with a couple bottles of perfectly good Chateau Lafite Rothschild, though to get the Brewster deuce forever out of Dodge, we would have drunk Drano.

I have worked with many people who served in the Navy, most hating to spend time at sea. Topping that list was Jason Calcaveccio, a Gulf War veteran who served as a radioman on the missile cruiser USS *Dragonfly*. Navy life from day one was hard on Jason. During basic training, he had all four wisdom teeth removed and, post extraction, was sent to rejoin his training group for several hours of demanding PT (physical training). Still numbed by Novocain, face swollen, mouth full of gauze, and the oral surgeon's footprints fresh on his chest, he dizzily tried to keep up with his class. He recalled a pool of blood dripping from his mouth while doing push-ups, the drill instructor's heart having no compassion for the recruit who made Uncle Sam pay for pulling his teeth.

At sea, things only got worse. Every newby sailor did time in the "pot shack," a cramped steamy room full of dirty pots and pans whose numbers could not be diminished despite hours of scrubbing and scouring.

But for Jason, the most difficult task at sea was trying to sleep. On the *Dragonfly*, the enlisted men's berthing was located directly below the galley, and the primary slumber hindrance wasn't enemy fire or heat, but cockroaches. The *Dragonfly* had difficulties with severe roach infestations from the on-board foodstuffs and supplies. Daily sprayings and cleaning did little to decrease the roach count. The problem was so bad that Jason and the other enlisted men put cotton balls in their nostrils and ears so the cockroaches wouldn't crawl in their orifices as they slept. The heat of the Persian Gulf only worsened the roach invasion. Jason finally realized that the only places he hadn't seen roaches were in the air-conditioned compartments of the *Dragonfly*, and one such place was the radio room. He stashed a pillow and blanket behind the radio panels and was able to tame his exhaustion.

After his duty in the Persian Gulf, Jason Calcaveccio still had two years left on his enlistment, but was able to get a discharge from the Navy because of a tattoo picked up on leave in Newport. On the outside edge of his right hand Jason had FUCK YOU tattooed in bold blue ink so whenever Jason saluted a superior officer they would see the aforementioned profanity. "Captain, here comes the President!" "Don't let Calcaveccio salute him!" The Navy dumped Jason like rotten garbage. Prior to his tour at King Lear, his foxtrot yankee tat was removed, though not too thoroughly.

Perhaps one of the most unsung military men I ever worked with was Lyden Bolivar, the gifted pastry chef of Augustine's, a sixty-five-year-old man who was no stranger to the scourge of the invisible sharks. In the mid 1980s, his wife was killed in a restaurant fire that claimed over a hundred lives. Though it was 1997 when we first met, the grief of his wife's death was still very apparent in Lyden's eyes. He had managed to escape the blaze and at first was certain his wife had done the same. But she hadn't. Like Colonel LaSalle, Lyden was left to ponder the unanswerable question of why he had survived and another person had not.

As a pastry chef, Lyden had a short fuse. Most do. He would spend hours preparing various gourmet treats, that when demanded, had to be plated and out the door in a matter of minutes. With entrees, most chefs have anywhere from fifteen to forty-five minutes for preparation. With desserts, it's five minutes or less unless the patron preordered a souffle or special occasion confection. Lyden hated being rushed in setting up his artful treats but had no choice when swamped with orders. Since dessert is the final food course in the meal sequence, the pastry chef tends to be the last cook to go home. Lyden had to wait for the final dessert order or no dessert nod from the last table before he could leave.

Sometimes the waiters would forget to tell Lyden that the final table had declined desserts an hour ago and he had been waiting in the kitchen for nothing, well into his twelfth hour of work, every second of it standing up. That's a long damn day when you're twenty-five, let alone sixty-five, not to mention lifting fifty-pound sacks of flour, peeling six-dozen apples, or scooping rock hard ice cream with arthritic hands. Despite all of his aches and pains, Lyden never let up, even when he was hurting badly.

Lyden had several specialties, though perhaps the best was his kiwi-key lime pie with a chopped coconut and macadamia nut crust, referred to as regular old key lime pie by the staff and patrons, though there was nothing regular about it. A slice of this pie was plated ambrosia, so good that you would trade your children for a single bite.

Most dessert curious Florida women in the second half of their existence are incapable of producing original thought and inflict upon their servers predictable dialogue that tortures the hypothalamus. First was their justified question inquiring what I thought Augustine's best dessert was. After informing them that it was Lyden's key lime pie, I silently began to beg God in Heaven that these women would not say what I knew they were surely going to say. My prayers would always go unanswered and the women would blurt out that phrase that made me want to flip the table over in fury. "What color is it?"

"Excuse me while I kill myself."

Never go into a restaurant and ask what color the key lime pie is, it labels you as a blithering idiot, confirming the waiter's suspicions. It is analogous to asking if there is an "R" in the month so you can eat oysters. "Let's see, is there an 'R' in August? Give me a minute . . . concentrating . . . scanning . . . I'll say no, there is no 'R' in August." You're correct. There is no 'R' in August, but there are three 'R's in the phrase "You're very ignorant." Cold-water oysters, regardless of the month, tend to carry a reduced risk of bacterial botulism and, just as with people, color is not an indication of quality.

To answer the question of Augustine's key lime color, I would always say "canary." But the Florida women weren't through with their witticisms and would say, "Well, I make the best key lime pie in the world and there's no way your key lime pie is better than mine."

I would squash the Florida women's claims with one run-on sentence that left them silent, two seconds from a nervous breakdown. "Well ma'am, for the last five years, Augustine's key lime pie has been voted the United States' most outstanding key lime pie by the Key Lime Council, headquartered in Key Largo and the certificate is on display in the lobby of the State Courthouse in Tallahassee. If you have any questions, please call the good folks at the Key Lime Council."

The Florida women would wave the white flag, begrudgingly saying, "Just bring me a piece, damn it."

Lyden always checked the waiter's schedule to see when I was working because he knew I made his kiwi-key lime pies fly. When I left Augustine's, key lime pie sales plummeted and not long after, the Key Lime Council's headquarters was destroyed by the ferocious winds of Hurricane Zamora, never to be rebuilt.

For every place mankind has been, there was someone to go there first, be it crossing the ocean in a fragile wooden ship, flying into the stratosphere, swimming the English Channel, or spiking a flag into the frommage verte of the Moon. Lyden Bolivar was among this group of elite explorational firsts as a crewman aboard the USS *Nautilus,* America's first nuclear-powered submarine and the first vessel ever to sail under the North Pole.[†]

While serving aboard the *Nautilus,* each crewmember wore a small film badge that would show indication if exposed to a

---

[†]In 1958 the USS *Nautilus* (SSN-571) was the first submarine to sail beneath the North Pole. On March 17, 1959, the USS *Skate* (SSN-578) was the first submarine to surface at the North Pole.

certain level of radioactivity. The historic cruise beneath the North Pole was underway when an Electronic Laboratory Technician (ELT) determined that Lyden's film badge indicated a slight change. Lyden was pulled off duty and immediately put into a cramped walk-in cooler for isolation until the reason for the change could be determined. At that point, Lyden was the most isolated man in the world, locked away in a cramped cooler in a relatively small experimental submarine, submerged deep in dark frigid waters under the jagged ice cap of the North Pole, with only his thoughts to keep him company. Several hours later the change indication of his film badge was determined to be erroneous and he was released from his prison beneath the sea. The prison term that was the anguish of losing his wife in a restaurant fire was a sentence without parole.

Curtis McCrea was an Augustine's regular and retired carpenter who liked Sundays off. He had spent his life working Sundays, though none was quite as bad as one particular Sunday in Oahu in 1941. A gunner's mate second class, Curtis was working on the deck of the USS *Sharpsburg*, cleaning the ship's 44-mm anti-aircraft guns when he looked up to see a two-wave locust storm of 353 attacking aircraft that signaled the beginning of the war with Japan. For Curtis, there were so many firsts in a matter of seconds. Never had he seen a dead body, never had he seen a man killed, never had someone tried to kill him, never had he tried to kill someone else, and never had he heard so much noise in his life. The battle erupted like a volcano and after the 44-mms had spent their ammunition, Curtis picked up a rifle and began firing at a Zero flying a strafing run at the *Sharpsburg*. He had noticed that all the sailors who were diving for cover seemed to be getting hit, so he stood his ground, defenseless on the deck, firing as the Zero flew right at him. The enemy plane riddled the deck with bullets on both sides of Curtis, one of which cut the chinstrap of his helmet in two, whistling just under his ear.

Though he had survived the assault on Pearl Harbor, Curtis told me that there was one sound and one image he encountered during the war more troubling than the attack itself. The disturbing sound was the metallic knocking coming from the sunken remains of the battleship USS *West Virginia* (BB-48) up to **16 days** after the attack. The noise wasn't made by settling wreckage or loose machinery, but was made by the trapped sailors who could not be rescued banging on the pipes and walls of the *West Virginia*.

The disturbing sight was the image of a hand. The *Sharpsburg* was part of a carrier escort group in the Pacific that was attacked by several waves of Kamikaze planes. During one firefight, the carrier his ship was escorting, a quarter mile ahead in the formation, took a direct Kamikaze hit, and the concussion of the suicidal Zero's explosion was felt on the *Sharpsburg* five hundred yards behind. After the battle, Curtis and his shipmates inspected the *Sharpsburg* for damage, but thankfully there was little and no sailor aboard his ship had sustained any injuries. But, on the forecastle hatch of his ship, a severed hand was found. The crew's only conclusion was that the severed hand belonged to some unfortunate sailor who was on the flight deck of the carrier ahead when the Kamikaze exploded, and the hand was blown a quarter mile onto the bow of the *Sharpsburg*.[†] Curtis told me the image of that hand still bothers him, and not one day goes by without recalling the knocking from the USS *West Virginia*. I was proud to know Curtis McCrea, a gentleman carpenter and courageous sailor who had survived the attack on Pearl Harbor and served his country bravely in WWII.

If asked to name the worst person you've ever met, you'd probably have an answer. To answer that question, I would say Douglas Fontaine, a fixture figure and one of six men (referred to as "the boys") to whom I served an extended lunch every Wednesday at King Lear. When I say fixture, I mean fixture as in one of those hideous three-hundred-pound cement angels urinating into a pond that's been an eyesore in your great aunt's garden since 1947. Fontaine was a seventyish, short, little, impatient fuck with wiry silver hair and a bright red face, made so from too much Stolichnaya. Though French-Irish in his heritage, this vodka-soaked frog was a Confederate-Klan combination in his socialization, a man who could not possibly have spouted more

[†]The USS *Sharpsburg* was so named after the Civil War battle at Antietam Creek, September 17, 1862. The single bloodiest day in American history, 12,410 Union and 13,724 Confederate lives were lost. Post-amputation gangrenous infection would subsequently kill thousands more.

racial slurs, speaking an epithet for anyone unlike him. Any question posed about a well-known non-Caucasian could get him to cough up a slur. "It's sad the way Barry was set-up." "What? Why that crack-piped coon should have never been mayor!" "But you'll agree that Simpson was framed." "Jesus man! He's the guiltiest nigger on the whole plantation!" "Well, at least Judge Ito did his job." "Why that mu shu gook was on the take." "Hey, how about that Million Man March?" "Someone should tell Farrakhan to march his Uncle Ben convention back to Africa." "Is that Menachem Begin dining with Margaret Thatcher?" "All I see is a kike and a dyke." "What about our Olympic track team? I can't believe how fast those relay guys are." "Yeah, well, there was probably a cop chasing them. Were they carrying a baton or a stolen TV?"

As a businessman he had made his money by owning an insurance company, no doubt collecting premiums and evading his clients in their desperate hours of need. As a military man, Fontaine was an F-86 Saber Jet pilot who arrived in Korea just as the conflict ended in 1953, too late for combat. He was upset at never getting a chance to shoot down Soviet MIGs. The people who knew him were upset that Soviet MIGs never got a chance to shoot down Douglas Fontaine. Of all the condescending bastards who kept me gnashing my teeth, DF took top honors, the worst of the worst. If he had suffered a heart attack in King Lear, I would have written a letter to 911 instead of calling, postage due.

Hate-filled people are easy to figure out. The people they hate the most are themselves, hatred manifested in acts of unkindness toward others, cruel words, racial slurs, and self-destructive behaviors. Their common denominator is ignorance to the suppressed truth that the person they most despise resides within their own skin. Pick any miserable person you know and there stands your example. Fontaine was a hate-filled mongrel, whose cruel comments and unreasonable demands all tallied to make him an impossible customer to serve.

Once seated with the other boys for their Wednesday lunch, Fontaine was quick to bark for his hot bread. Castillo would fire a loaf just for the boys, but it took time to bake, obviously. I would greet the boys, see who wanted a cocktail and Fontaine would demand bread four times before I had even gotten a drink order. Everyone was on a first name basis and I was able to be extremely frank with all the boys. The conversation would go like this:

JG: "Gentlemen, good afternoon. May I . . ."
DF: "John, we need hot bread and butter right away!"
JG: "Doug, give me a little credit. It's working. I serve you and the boys every Wednesday and know that your bread is a priority. Roosevelt has picked out a couple bottles of Kidneestoane Zinfandel fo . . ."
DF: "No matter what you do, bring the bread first, and don't forget the butter!" (At this point he's embarrassing his tablemates and I'm wondering if anyone has a pistol I can borrow.)
JG: "Thanks for mentioning it, again, because I forgot after the first few thousand times you asked for it. *Doug wants hot bread. Bring Dougie hot bread. Hurry-quick with Doug's hot bread!* I'll be writing that on my suicide note."(A few of the boys would order a cocktail and as I started for the bar Fontaine would deliver another jab.)
DF: "Just don't forget the bread. And butter, too."

I would say nothing, simply stop in my tracks, fold my arms, turn and stare directly at Fontaine. Though a drunken fool, he was bright enough to deduce that unless I was in motion, no service or transportation of bread, butter, or drink could occur. In thirty seconds, he had exhausted my allotment of patience for the entire month.

The Other Boys: (In reprimand) "Jesus Doug, let the man be."
DF: (In a soft retreating voice, looking at me but speaking to his tablemates.) "Uhm, sorry. I know that John will bring the bread and butter the second it's ready, hopefully soon."

I would make a beeline for the bar, the first drink rung on their check being an iceless top shelfer that I drank myself, dropping to a knee for the chug.

Tolerating Fontaine could only be accomplished with acts of revenge, and the first tool with which to collect atonement was the bread itself. Fresh from a 550-degree convection oven, the loaf was untouchable, though still I tonged it into the commercial microwave for a Chernobyl mini-meltdown that heated it to within a half degree of spontaneous combustion. The basket and napkin were also heated, and I deliberately didn't slice the loaf so as to force Boy Wonder to use both hands to tear off a piece. Four seconds after the microwave's beep, the basket was square in front of Fontaine, who would rip into the bread basket as if he hadn't eaten in a week. The instant his mitts were on the bread, he would yelp in pain and often fumble the bread onto the floor, eliciting a five-voice reprimand from his displeased poker pals, each scold including profanity, disgust, and disdain for Fontaine. He would plead, "Well, that fuckin' shit is hot as hell. I burned my fingers!" And any one of the boys would retort, "You wanted it hot, you asshole!" I'd grin at whoever was first to say it.

Now Fontaine faced a dilemma—eat the bread that had just rolled on the dirty carpet or wait fifteen minutes for another loaf to be baked. For Fontaine that fifteen minutes would feel like a stretch of time longer than five consecutive showings of the movie *Gigli*. King Lear's carpet was clean as far as restaurants go, but still home to yet unnamed pathogens, hair from half a million people, and dried spills and fluids best not described. There was no hesitation in the choice. Fontaine could not endure the wait and would opt to eat the floor bread, picking it up with the basket napkin and dusting it off like a ranch hand might dust his wind-caught Stetson that had fallen on the Utah trail. At least once a month, Fontaine did the firebread fumble, so satisfying to watch it was painful.

Bread-fetcher Galloway found other ways to provide Fontaine with the service he so richly deserved. The Preston garlic Caesar trick worked well, but all the boys suffered on that one. "Please, John, no more garlic in my salad, my wife hasn't touched me in a month." As far as salad consumption was concerned, Fontaine was a sorry sight. He was, among his many endearing qualities, a chain smoker and master of the delicate art of smoking while consuming food, keeping his salad fork in one hand and his blazing death stick in the other.

The grape squash switch also worked well on Fontaine. While the other boys were drinking a delicate red I served Fontaine nothing but Wal-Mart wine, his nicotine-numbed palate never knowing better. DF was always spouting about the plates not being hot enough, which prompted Castillo to place Fontaine's entree plates under the broiler for a few minutes to acquire that space heater glow. When serving DF the plate, I would place it too far forward or an inch over the table's edge, forcing him to move it, burning his paws every time.

And every sixth week, when it was Fontaine's turn to pay, there was padding. I tracked the weeks and I knew when Fontaine's turn was up. I would serve him doubles all afternoon long, leaving him far too intoxicated to discern that his check had been padded. Constantine and Clay, though not privy to the chicanery, profited from the gouging of Fontaine to the tune of several thousand dollars during the four years or so I had served the boys.

My hatred for Fontaine was not just based on his diction and demeanor, but perhaps most of all on how he protested about guide dogs for the blind. It only happened four or five times over several years, but even once was unacceptable.

King Lear was always honored to serve anyone with a handicap, which included the blind and their seeing-eye dogs. King Lear's waiters even offered to walk these dogs while their owners enjoyed their meal, making a strange sight for the pedestrians of Washington. "That guy sure doesn't look like he's blind, and why'd he get dressed up in a tuxedo to watch his dog take a shit?" But back in the restaurant, Fontaine, upon seeing a guide dog, would not shut up with his endless complaints, attempting to be witty in his protests.

"Why does that dog have to be here? That dog has germs. That mutt drank half of my Stoli! There's a flea in my salad. Someone should tell that dog to get the hell outta here. Why do you guys allow mutts in King Lear?" He went on and on. I begged Fontaine not to protest, as did his tablemates, but he just raved on and my heart sank for the blind patrons who I knew could hear his cruel rantings. It was pathetic. How did Fontaine live this long without someone murdering him? And what about those poor dogs? They sat, unflinching, beside their masters while their acute sense of smell was tormented by the dense aromas of beef, veal, and lamb flying about the dining room. Those heroic animals were better behaved, better groomed, and more intelligent than any louse in the bar, had better vocabularies than all of the busboys, and were no less than a trillion times more likable than Fontaine. But hate-filled people hate themselves, and the doggie he despised most was named Fido Fontaine.

Poker was the game once the boys finished their lunch. Their table would be cleared of everything except drink glasses and ashtrays and the gaming would continue until their table was needed for pre-theatre dinner reservations. One Wednesday, the boys were in overtime and their table was needed for an early party waiting at the maître d's podium. I politely asked the boys if they could relocate to the bar, and drunken Fontaine, down three Ben Franks, barked back at me, "Hey John, we're in the middle of a game right now so you can just kiss my fuckin' ass!"

The other boys stood up as I pointed at Fontaine and said, "What the hell did you just say to me?"

He looked at me and said, "You heard me, just kiss my fuckin' ass!"

My adrenaline raced in anticipation of the butchery, for I was about to assault a customer. The dam that was the sum of my life's aggressions was about to break. Losing my job, being arrested and going to jail didn't matter. I was going to kill the most despicable man in Washington and make the world right again. Two of the boys grabbed me, calling over a few other waiters to help restrain me, one said, "Get Doug the hell out of here!"

The other three boys hustled Fontaine out of his chair and outside in record fashion, letting him know that he had crossed the line. I yelled at the boys and waiters holding me back saying, "What are you guys holding me for? Fontaine's the fucking antagonist here!" One of the waiters told me to calm down and I said, "No way, I don't want to calm down. Fontaine can't talk to me that way, fuck him!"

They walked me into the accountant's office to try and cool me down. Fontaine did not return that evening and after about an hour I was level-headed enough to work the dinner shift. The next day, Constantine called me over and told me what he decided to do about the situation. He said, "John, the other boys all backed you up and said Doug was way out of line. You're not in any trouble. I know you try hard and you're one of my best waiters. I'm banning Doug from the restaurant for a month, but I want you to always remember what I'm going to tell you now. That is, always avoid a confrontation if you can. Always. Fighting is for fools, and smart people always walk away. There may be a time in your life when you have no choice but to fight, and when you do, knock down the walls. But if you can, always avoid confrontation."

I acknowledged his wisdom and said, "Thank you, sir. I appreciate you looking out for me." Constantine gave me a smile and a pat on the back. After his suspension, Fontaine apologized for his outburst. But his tango with contrition was a fleeting condition and he was back to his bastard self later that same day. More proof for my theory. People don't change.

"Time heals all wounds" is just a Band-Aid aphorism with a Hallmark ring and no truth with regard to war and soldiers. When war ends, time does not heal all the wounds, or even lessen the pain inflicted on so many. The bleeding doesn't stop, the restless nights continue, and for the mutilated veterans and their families, the fiercest battles are yet to come. Such was the case with Victor Neal, a King Lear regular and master commodities trader who was paralyzed as a young soldier in Korea after stepping on a land mine. The injuries he sustained would leave him in a wheelchair for the rest of his life. They gave him a Purple Heart for his trouble.[†]

Despite not being able to use his legs and having only limited use of his left arm, Victor was very adept at getting around. He could travel very short distances with a special pair of crutches and never sat at a table in his wheelchair, but always in a regular seat. His wheelchair folded and the waiters would put it in the coatroom while Victor was eating. As a customer, Victor was like Earl Styles, with a zeal for fine wine. He knew every staffer by name and always had a pleasant disposition. Victor rightfully enjoyed celebrity status among King Lear's staff and all the penguins and busdogs would stop by Victor's table to say hello when he was in the house. As mentioned earlier, you can sum up a waiter's feelings about star regulars in one word. That word is "protective." It was certainly true with Victor.

Even for regulars, a seat in a crowded bar can be difficult to find, and King Lear's bar was no exception. Victor enjoyed a social drink, but never expected preferential treatment in the matter of getting a barstool. He would lift himself out of his wheelchair and sit on the stairs that lead to the upper dining room and enjoy his drink and conversation from the steps. This was when the waiters got mad, not at Victor, but at anyone owning a pair of functioning legs who wouldn't relinquish their barstool for Victor. Victor didn't expect to be given a seat at the bar, and to the staff's sheer amazement, very few would offer.

Everyone had their reasons. The rental girls weren't about to give up their seats, for them a barstool was business. A seat at King Lear's bar was what a deli case is to sliced pimento loaf. The impatient patrons weren't going to offer seats they had waited an entire ten minutes for, besides, it was King Lear's fault for not having enough barstools and making them wait for their reservations. And the barflies weren't about to budge. Their barstool was their island, upon which they were king.

[†]During the Korean War (1950-1953) 54,246 American GIs were killed and 103,284 wounded.

They had been there since the ink was still wet on that morning's *Washington Post* and had had their bladders surgically stretched so they could sit until closing and thus not lose their seats.

This left the waiters to solicit a seat for Victor. He hadn't asked, but it was our duty. This was one of the few things we did that carried some degree of honor. Being socially adept for the most part, I had no qualms in seat solicitation, targeting the younger males first. "Excuse me sir, could I possibly ask you to offer your seat to one of our handicapped patrons. It's for our friend Victor over there and it's painful for him to sit on the steps." The plea usually worked, but on occasion the affirmative response was conditional, "Yeah, he can have my seat, but you gotta buy me a drink first." I would not hesitate to speak my mind, jacking up the volume to evoke peripheral scorn. "You want the house to buy you a drink for offering a paralyzed veteran your barstool? What the hell's wrong with you?"

Immediately other seats would be volunteered and I would walk over to Victor and tell him a seat had just opened up. He was always surprised that there was a vacant stool in such a crowded bar. Victor would have relinquished his seat had any standing woman asked, though she'd be too busy rushing to the hospital after I broke her nose. Every staffer at King Lear felt as I did about Victor Neal. He was one of our own. But you can do more for disabled and paralyzed veterans than just offer them barstools. Much more.

The fittest of the fleet and the toughest of the recon are the men and women of the Marine Corps, from the maggot recruits to the star strewn generals. To argue otherwise shows you don't know much about the United States Marine Corps.

One fine example was a King Lear three-star star named Casper Rapaport, a shorter, sharp-shaven, V-shaped Marine Lieutenant General with more ribbons than a Nordstrom gift wrap booth, the extreme antithesis of the average King Lear sot. He was a lunch man only, and not only embodied the ideals of the Corps, but qualities of an ideal customer as well. Concise, polite, articulate, and a one-fifth tipper, this man wasn't about to be late for his reservation, slobber over an attractive woman, or get drunk and humiliate himself. This made LG Rapaport seem almost out of place at King Lear.

His presence awakened a great deal of subconscious jealousy among the career barflies. The flies were weak, tanked, fat, and unfit with lives that were crumbling down like imploded housing projects. Casper Rapaport was successful, stronger than a Brahma bull, and well respected in the military and political communities of Washington. But jealousy never takes a direct approach, always traversing an evasive course to its target, and such was the Lear flies' envy of LG Rapaport.

A few of the bar blobs would protest that it was unfair that the General was permitted to dine without wearing a jacket and tie; military uniforms were the only exception to King Lear's coat and tie rule. "Hey, he's not (pause for a lick of Knob Creek) wearing a coat and tie and you made me wear one, so damn it, he's gonna wear one. Tell him to put one on now." Explaining over and over again to the protesting flies that military personnel in uniform were dressed in accordance with King Lear's dress code were words thrown upon deaf ears. The flies were capable of hearing, but the explanation was just too painful to hear. The unconscious interpretation of the explanation was the voice in the back of their minds alerting them to the fact that they were doomed alcoholics, realized by looking at the successful and tie-less military hard-charger who was not a slobbering drunkard. The game which was a barfly's life was unwinnable, late in the fourth quarter, and down by five scores. All these feelings awakened by an officer in a military uniform, ringing loud like Pavlov's bell.

I knew exactly what this feeling was because it was halftime in my life and the scoreboard wasn't in my favor.

Since achievement in life, sobriety, and revocation of King Lear's coat and tie policy weren't possibilities, the act of not properly adhering to the King Lear's dress code was the protester's only course for personal fulfillment. There were several ploys employed.

The first was to enter the restaurant without a tie, be given a house tie, and then wear it like a scarf. This was a bad move and Constantine would be the first to render judgment saying, "Put your tie on correctly or I'll have a few of my waiters tie it on for you so tight that you'll be red 'til rapture."

The next stunt was to enter King Lear wearing a tie with some type of winter jacket or windbreaker. Here, too, public humiliation was the key. "What, I can't wear this? But it's a Patagonia!" "No sir. Although the fuzzy collar and mitten hooks are impressive, it does not constitute a men's dress jacket." And there were always the "dash-in" guys, hoping to get a drink and promising to put on a coat and tie "in a minute," using a few loud words to try and intimidate the staff. All Constantine or Clay had to do was snap and point, and any proximate penguins would converge and toss, the uncoated and tie-less knowing that resistance was futile.

Potatoes and pumpernickel aren't often regarded as terrifying objects, unless you've spent twenty months as a WWII prisoner of the Nazis. Such was the case with Bradford Whitaker, a B-17 Flying Fortress navigator, whose plane, *The She Devil*, was shot down over Stuttgart in 1943. He and his wife were regulars at King Lear with the curious, yet staunch, insistence that bread and potatoes never be set on their table. To my great fortune, I became the Whitaker's regular waiter and eventually learned the reason for this unusual request. Mrs. Whitaker told me that during her husband's incarceration, all he and his fellow prisoners were given to eat was dark bread and potatoes. The mere sight of either caused Mr. Whitaker to tremble. Mr. Whitaker loved King Lear with its giant slabs of beef, but avoiding these two specific foods in a power restaurant is difficult. Like Curtis McCrea with the image of a hand and the sound of metal knocking, the sights that awakened the painful memories of his time as a prisoner were bread and potatoes.

For some war survivors, even the image of beef is troubling. One of the last tables I served at King Lear was a group of ten people brought in as guests of the Red Cross. Six were Bosnian refugees who had been in the States for only a few days. When

I served one of the elder Bosnian women her steak, she looked at the gluttonous piece of beef and started crying. The Red Cross representative told me the Bosnian woman had seen too many of her family and friends starve to ever enjoy a meal again. Surely the most helpless feeling in life is the inability to go back in time and take away the pain from the people we loved.

Another customer who was a regular at the Coventry had fought as an infantryman in Europe during World War I. He was born in the year 1898, just thirty-three years after the end of the Civil War. I recognized his lapel pin from my grandfather's own medals, and the gentleman doughboy was honored that I knew so much about an almost forgotten war. The conflict had killed hundreds of thousands of soldiers and civilians. But one of my proudest links to American history came by way of a ship named after the city where I was born.

Angus the Shagger and I were able to get a private tour of the Smithsonian's storage facility in Anacostia. Among the many impressive pieces of historical hardware was a wingless *Enola Gay,* the very same B-29 Superfortress that had dropped the atomic bomb on Hiroshima. I pressed my hand against the fuselage for a few moments in acknowledgment of the horrors and sacrifices of World War II.

Yet another link to the *Enola Gay* would cross my path at King Lear. I had purchased and read the outstanding book *Fatal Voyage* by Dan Kurzman, the incredible true story about the sinking of the USS *Indianapolis,* the last American ship sunk in WWII.[†] The *Indianapolis* had delivered the internal mechanisms for the atomic bomb to the Pacific island of Tinian, the same bomb that was carried and dropped by the *Enola Gay.* After delivering the bomb parts and while en route to the Philippines, the unescorted *Indianapolis* was sunk by a Japanese submarine. Unable to transmit an acknowledged Mayday signal, the crew of the *Indianapolis* was left to die floating in shark-infested waters for five days. For the lack of food, fresh water, and lifeboats, while going insane with thirst and fear and slowly burning in the intense sunlight, the majority of the crew died unnoticed in the middle of the Pacific. The *Indianapolis'*

[†]The Fifth Fleet flagship USS *Indianapolis* (CA-35, a *Portland* Class heavy cruiser) was sunk in action on July 30, 1945, just two weeks before the end of WWII on August 14, 1945. 883 members of its crew were lost.

captain, Charles McVay, tried desperately to save his men, but only 316 of the crew of 1,199 survived the sinking and the horrific five days at sea. McVay, who had survived, was brought to trial and court-martialed as a Navy scapegoat, a hero blamed for the blunders of others. Wrongly convicted and badgered by angry calls and letters from the bitter families of his lost crewmen, Captain McVay committed suicide in 1968. He was exonerated by the Navy in 2001. But posthumous exculpation for a forsaken hero like Charles McVay doesn't even begin to acknowledge our nation's debt to this incredible man.

To my astonishment, one of the surviving crewmen, Eugene S. Pritchard, an electrician's mate, was a King Lear regular I had served several times. Seeing him brought the tragedy of the USS *Indianapolis* to life for me and touching the *Enola Gay* brought everything full circle. I never asked Pritchard about his horrible experience at sea, I just felt honored to shake his hand. In Kurzman's book there is an extremely moving passage about a sailor wounded during the sinking, while dying in another man's arms and delirious with thirst, with saltwater in his wounds and tormented by the screams of his shipmates being eaten by sharks. The man suddenly had a lucid moment seconds before his death, looked up at the sailor holding him afloat and said, "Tell my wife that I love her and that she should marry again."

There was another man I served who had also floated about the dangerous waters of the South Pacific during World War II. One of the youngest flyers ever in Naval aviation, he was a Grumman TBM-3E Avenger pilot based on the light carrier USS *San Jacinto*. During a bombing raid over the Japanese occupied island of Chichi Jima, his plane was badly shot up and his tail gunner killed by anti-aircraft fire. Though able to drop his ordinance before ditching his plane, he was injured during the bailout. His belly gunner, who had also managed to jump, was killed in the fall. Once in the sea, the wounded flyer was able to inflate his raft, but not before being stung by a Portuguese man-of-war.

From Chichi Jima, a Japanese patrol boat was dispatched to capture the downed aviator. Just moments earlier, the USS *Finback,* a submarine on coast watch for just such an emergency, surfaced and intercepted the young airman. The *Finback* then submerged and cruised away, sparing the pilot what would have been a hideous fate.

During WWII, American pilots were so despised for the destruction they caused that Japanese officers often cannibalized American airmen. Those not cannibalized were tortured and subjected to fatal medical experiments such as vivisection and transfusions with animal blood and seawater. The prisoner commandant on this particular island was notorious for eating the livers of captured airmen and was executed after the war along with nine hundred other Japanese officers on charges of war crimes and atrocities.

But the *Finback* saved this pilot from such horrific inhumanities, and he survived World War II to forge history himself. His many accomplishments included becoming Director of the CIA, helping to bring down the Berlin Wall, driving Iraq out of Kuwait, serving as U.S. Vice President for eight years, and becoming the forty-first President of the United States, as well as father to the forty-third. His name was George Herbert Walker Bush.

Forty-nine years later, President Bush had lunch at King Lear and JG got the call. It was just another December lunch shift and I came in a little before 10:00 a.m. when Gavin approached me and said that President Bush would be the guest and I would be the waiter. I was one of twenty-five waiters on staff, seventeen having more seniority, but Gavin chose me for the task and I felt honored to be deemed worthy of serving the leader of the free world. For the most part, seasoned waiters don't tend to enjoy serving high profile tables. One gaff and your goose is cooked. Food critics require wet-nurse levels of attention and arrogant congressional types tend to think they're pharaohs, but serving President Bush was something I would remember forever.

I was a little better acquainted with George and his family

than the average bear. I had served his gracious wife a few times at the Coventry, voted for him twice, played basketball with his son Marvin in Alexandria, and voted for Jeb in Florida and George W. for president twice after I moved to Nevada. That day, President Bush was part of a table of twelve. Barbara was not in attendance. Gavin told me President Bush would be my only table, and appointed to assist me if needed was the albino-haired, hash lad himself, Dustin Doobie-jay Vannoy, the worst possible choice for second chair.

At the same time Gavin was giving me the presidential nod, Vannoy was down in the parking garage, locked in his dark-windowed Fiat sucking on a mini travel pipe in preparation for the lunch shift. He would smell like Ricky Williams when he finally arrived, which was always late, and I didn't want President Bush to think that I, too, was a dope-dumbed, wine-snatching, mauve-eyed mandrill because of proximity to, association with, or similar attire to surfer boy Vannoy. I even thought about telling Vannoy that the Baltimore police department was auctioning off confiscated marijuana that morning, but the disappointment he would have felt at the police information desk would have devastated him. I had to take my chances with Harry Chronic Jr. close by.

I began setting up Bush's table in the upper room when a pair of burly Secret Service agents walked up and introduced themselves. They wanted to know a little about me, who else would be serving Bush's table, any tables nearby, and where the various exits were. As predicted, weed-whacked Vannoy posted with his catatonic disposition, though fortunately the Secret Service weren't downwind of DV.

Vannoy saw the agents, waved me over and said, "What if they brought bong-sniffing dogs?" I replied, "Dustin, it's *bomb*, not *bong*, and luckily for you, they didn't bring the smell hounds today."

The agents looked around the restaurant and then I walked them through the kitchen. At first, the kitchen Salvies thought the dark-suited buffalos were INS agents, but Castillo called out in Spanish that the strangers were presidential guards and not hombres de immigración.

We returned to the dining room and the agents looked for a suitable table where they could eat, have full view of Bush's table, and be able to spring into action if need be. The Secret Service men finished their screening of the restaurant, made a few phone calls, and soon after President Bush and his entourage arrived for lunch. The dozen-person parade headed for the upper room, led and trailed by several additional Secret Service agents, who glanced about like vigilant eagles, checking the way for potential harm. The time was a quarter 'til noon and the majority of the restaurant was still empty.

President Bush sat in the center of a long rectangular table, the "Jesus seat" as the waiters referred to it. On his immediate left was a three-star Army yes-man, and on his right an older woman who appeared to be a public relations executive. Once seated, I approached the table and greeted the President and his guests. President Bush looked me square in the eye and said, "So, I guess you drew the short straw." I thought for a second and replied, "Well, Mr. President, I think they checked the voting records of the waiters and that's why I was given the privilege of serving you today, sir." He grinned, the table chuckled, and the presidential ice was officially broken.

The truth was that if the penguin's voting records had been checked, it would have been revealed that I was one of only five waiters who did indeed vote for Bush. Of the twenty-five waiters, nine were registered and only eight voted. Most of the waiters were active drug users and wanted at least a glimmer of hope that illicit drugs might someday become legal, something that would never happen with a Republican in office. Dustin Vannoy would have forfeited his right to free speech in exchange for legalized marijuana, though the very thought of him increasing his already Rastafarian-level of pot consumption was inconceivable to the mortal mind. Even if locked away in a sealed bong condo where a dozen flueless chimneys incinerated endless mounds of the choicest cuts of *Cannabis sativa,* Vannoy could not have possibly inhaled more dioxed reefer aroma. Most of the waiters who didn't vote were just too lazy or lacked the foresight to register. The non-voting waiters protested with clichés. The most common was "It's a choice between two evils," though they didn't ponder evil when they were shooting black tar heroin with an underage prostitute on Christmas Eve.

I obtained the party's drink order. Only a few ordered alcohol, and the rest drank iced tea, juice, or bottled water. After serving the drinks, it was time to take the food order. I looked to the most senior female, the lady on Bush's right and said, "Ma'am, would you care to order now?"

General Honeysnuggle cut me down like a Cally redwood commanding, "President Bush will order first!"

Well children, write this one down and laminate it. I don't care if you're dining with the Pope, Elvis Presley (sorry Elvis) or the President of the United States, in fine dining in any country that doesn't use stoning as a method of execution, veil their females, lay slaughtered animal carcasses on their church altars, or require a magnetic compass to pray, **women always order first.** I didn't appreciate Bush's asskiss sidekick talking down to me, but President Bush wasn't about to correct his Doberman pinscher in public, so he smiled, winked at me and gave me his order. General Yesman may have been a brilliant military mind, perhaps even graduated from West Pointless, but he didn't know jack about fine dining etiquette. I then immediately returned my attention back to the woman, wondering if Honeysnuggle was going to cry again. He eyed me but held his tongue, while I pitied the soldiers in his command. Had he corrected me again, I would have suggested we set up a card table on the back porch for the women to dine at.

The party ordered, lunch was served on time, and everyone seemed quite content. One of the advantages of serving VIP tables is you get priority in the kitchen. Defying the General, I served the women their entrees first, still wondering if Cryboy was going to fire off a flare gun or have a couple of Secret Service agents tackle me or something. Maybe I was going to be sent to Leavenworth for gender service violations, but by that time General Objection's second Glenmorangie had taken effect and he was a calm puppy for the meal's duration.

Before long the presidential luncheon was over, the PR lady I had tried to serve first paid the check, a fifth and then some, $100 tipped on their $470 check. President Bush stood up, shook my hand, thanked me for the attentive service, actually taking a moment to chat with me. I had always been impressed with his accomplishments and character, and the exchange only further strengthened my positive opinion about this great man.

Only at his departure did the other patrons begin to notice that President Bush was in the house. The upstairs lunchers had noticed the President, though harbored the common sense and class to respect his privacy. As he exited past the bar, most of the drunken flies contorted themselves to glance upon the President as his entourage moved swiftly toward the front door. Word got around that I had served him and suddenly I was the celebrity, though I downplayed it all the way. I was just a person along the path, all reverence due belonged to President Bush.

We later learned that Gavin had been requested to give the penguin's files to the CIA for security screening. Odds were that I was picked to serve Bush because of my then recent NAOCS application and its related background clearances. We estimated that the escorting firepower there to protect Bush was around 35 persons, most being stationed outside the restaurant. In July of 2003, the post 9/11 elevations of caution were quite evident. Here in Las Vegas, while attending a private party that included Vice President Cheney, I counted sixty U.S. Marshalls and Secret Service personnel plus dog (Darby), eight doubled-manned metro police units plus two dogs (Mojo and Pumpkin), a squad of paramedics along with a leviathan-sized ambulance, and the PD ghetto bird (police helicopter) flying vigilant orbits at a thousand feet above patio. Of the dozens of Secret Service were five high & tight cut men sporting black Kevlar head to toe (it was 117 Fahrenheit and sunny that day), armed with one on the waist, another on the ankle, and two of the five men toting giant black canvas bags, surely containing some kind of heinous "pop n drop" delivery platform. Enough bang to stymie any eager-to-meet-Allah Al Jazeera misanthrope. The security tension was definitely there, obvious among the guests. People were holding their Magellan martinis with two hands, afraid that if they lost grip and their glass on smashed on the floor, they'd get perforated in a most unpleasant fashion. In May of 2004, there was an even larger conglomeration of security shooters and snoop dogs when, by special request, I was asked to serve First Lady Laura Welch Bush and building magnate Steve (Wynn Las Vegas Resort) Wynn.

But the war hero whose impression was indelible on many of the penguin's hearts was that of a retired forester from Duluth, Minnesota named Rune Peckenpaugh, a frequent dining companion of Colonel LaSalle. In WWII, Rune had endured atrocities and inhumanities approaching that of Holocaust victims. As a captured U.S. Army soldier in humid Corregidor in 1942, Rune had survived the storied Bataan Death March, three voyages in lightless cargo holds of Japanese transport vessels (known as "hell ships"), P.O.W. incarceration in the most inhospitable jungle conditions, and almost two years of bayonet-motivated slave labor working on the Burma-Siam railroad.

As you might imagine of someone subjected to prolonged starvation and the panoply of physical and mental insurrections spawned by severe malnutrition, Rune hated to see wasted food. It wasn't just a belief, preference or idiosyncrasy, but instead, a survival mechanism born of a desperate soldier pushed to the edge of human endurance, often forced to drink feculent water and eat the entomological refuse of the jungle floor. His experiences were something subsequent generations would never understand, but hopefully respect.

Rune and Colonel LaSalle had just finished dinner, and were having coffee. Their waiter was King Lear's answer to Lance Armstrong, the saintly Roland Lockheart. My station was next to Roland's, my hands full dealing with a Plumpjack on a four top, an executive whose life was being ruined because his 24-ounce veal chop wasn't the color of rare he had demanded. He wanted it Burgundy rare, not pink rare. I tried explaining to him that veal meat was more white meat than red meat and thus, a rare milk-fed veal chop would never be the same shade of New York sirloin rare. But Plumpjack wasn't about to get an education from me, a lowly waiter. All the time, LaSalle and Rune Peckenpaugh were taking in the exchanges, Rune increasingly tormented by such a brazen waste of edible food, the still water that was the pain of his past was being brought to a boil. Chef Jacques was none too pleased either, but his concerns were only in regard to his workload. A second chop was hurriedly prepared, ultra-blue rare, Hillary-cold, coagulated, and downright nasty. Even a famished timber wolf would have passed on this veal chop. He flippantly returned chop two.

The third time was no charm for Plumpjerk, livid that his three month calf chop wasn't the dark red color he desired. Retreating, I excused myself to call in Clay. I explained all the details to Clay, who went up to speak with the Plumpjack. But just before Clay made it to the man's table, Rune had gotten up to say something to the man. Three entrees wasted was more than Rune could stand.

Rune asked Plumpjack, "Excuse me sir?"

Annoyed, and curious, Plumpjack retorted, "What?"

Rune then fired with full inflection, saying "JUST EAT YOUR FUCKIN' CHOW! God Damn! Why do you keep wasting food? Don't you know that there are people starving out there? So many people starving. What the fuck is wrong with you?" Rune then stormed out, passing Clay who had just arrived at the table.

LaSalle went after Rune, as Plumpy sprang up out of his seat and said, "What the hell kind of restaurant is this? And what the fuck is that crazy old man's problem?"

Clay, who had tremendous knowledge and admiration for his military vet regulars, quickly responded, "You watch your mouth and show some respect for that man. He's been through things in his life that you would have NEVER survived. So just shut your mouth, finish your meal, and then get out. There's no check if you leave right now."

Plump and his mates quickly conferred, then left, saying nothing while being stared down by several mad penguins throughout the dining room. Roland was nowhere to be found. He had run outside after Rune and LaSalle, and about fifteen minutes later, the three returned after Rune had composed himself. Penguin word had gotten around quickly and all of the waiters went to the front door to shake Rune's hand, give him a hug or pat on the back as he returned. Room was made at the bar for the two, as Rune apologized to Clay for his outburst, feeling bad that he had created any additional commotion. Clay refused the apology, saying "Fuck that guy, Rune. This is your place, not his. Besides, if you didn't say something, me or one of my boys would have."

LaSalle bought a round for Clay and the penguins, and asked that we all raise a glass to Rune. LaSalle looked at his buddy and said, "To Rune Peckenpaugh. A gentleman, a scholar, and our friend." Clinking our glasses, we cheered for Rune, a touching and genuine moment.

Rune smiled as he looked around at the people and penguins standing about him, then humbly shook his head and said, "Thanks, guys. You're some damn fine people. Damn fine. I sure wished you boys could have been in my unit with me and my buddies back at Corregidor in '42. I'd serve with you guys anytime."

Roland, knowing what we were all thinking, stepped up and said, "Thank you, Mr. Peckenpaugh, sir. That means an awful lot to us. And just remember this, you're part of *our* unit now, brother. And we always look after our own."

In April of 2002, Rune became the last surviving soldier from his original Army infantry regiment. On May 29, 2004, a fading Rune proudly attended the National WWII Memorial Dedication Ceremony in Washington. Just one week later on June 5, 2004, on the eve of the 60th anniversary of the Normandy Invasion, and on the same somber day we lost Ronald Reagan, Sergeant Thomas Rune Peckenpaugh quietly left his earthly encampment to rejoin his Army regiment. He was 83.

S INCE THE END OF THE CIVIL WAR,
THE CONGRESSIONAL MEDAL OF HONOR
HAS BEEN AWARDED 1,338 TIMES.
OF THOSE, 583 WERE AWARDED
POSTHUMOUSLY.[†]

[†] Army Sgt. 1st Class Paul Ray Smith was posthumously awarded the CMH for his heroism
on April 4, 2003. Killed while single-handedly fighting over 100 Iraq combatants, Smith
provided supressing fire from an exposed position after ordering wounded U.S. soldiers be
evacutated to safety.

Chapter 11

Yesteryear's Celebrities

(*RIP Bob Keeshan, Captain Kangaroo*)

"But a thief can come knocking
Even with blood on the door
And drink up your fountain of youth
And throw your jewels and your crown on the floor."

John Mellencamp, "Suzanne and the Jewels,"
Human Wheels, Polygram Records, Inc., 1993

Into every restaurant, a few celebrities must fall. The finer the restaurant, the harder the downpour. One of the obvious signs that you're a seasoned hospitality veteran is the complete lack of fascination with high-profile people and the utter disgust with those who are fascinated. A front houser in a power hotel or restaurant gets to the point that, unless it's God himself, you don't care who you're serving or what they've done. "Eli Manning's here." "Wait a minute, I thought his dad didn't want him to go to this restaurant." "Jo-Jo Bounceball is here too." "And I should care?" "Well, he does lead the league in scoring, sires, domestic battery, and rape." [†]

The disdain stems from the way people devaluate themselves in the presence of celebrities, screaming like giddy schoolgirls on the banks of the red carpet or in the icy background of morning talk shows. Mick Jagger isn't Jesus (I'm pretty sure), the words "celebrity" and "hero" are not synonymous, and you'll never find a hero wearing a Vera Wang or threatening to

---

[†] While most stars tip appropriately, there are many celebrities who are notorious grat-shafters, some of the very worst being former and current professional athletes. Pay attention NBA.

move to Ottawa because his candidate of choice lost the election.

If you want to meet someone special, talk to a police officer, nurse, fireman, teacher or social worker. If you're looking for someone to admire, spend the afternoon with a forgotten senior citizen who has likely lived though harder times than you will ever know. And if you want to meet a hero, get yourself over to any veteran's hospital where they convalesce by the hundreds, or walk the grounds of Arlington National Cemetery, where they rest by the hundreds of thousands. If ever blessed with the opportunity, shake the hand of a war vet, or anyone in uniform who answered the call and does their duty.[†]

But amidst the cynicism, perhaps there is a shard of satisfaction in having encountered some of the world's more notable people. From Tua, Magua (Wes Studi), Hawk (Avery Brooks), and The Rock to Ricky Rudd, Ashley Judd and Roger Mudd, I've served too many megastars to count or remember, though a few stand out in the microfiche of my mind.

Outside the confines of a restaurant, I've had a few notable people cross my path. My paternal grandfather interviewed, among many famous world leaders, Juan Peron and Fidel Castro. Ronald and Nancy Reagan wrote my sister a get-well letter while she was in the hospital with leukemia, and a second letter to our family two days after she died. I met several of the undefeated 1972 Miami Dolphins in Indianapolis in 1973, and watched Emmylou Harris perform a concert in Virginia while seated with her parents. I have letters from wine pioneer Robert Mondavi and music phenom Bruce Hornsby. I've had drinks with Sylvester Stallone, and shaken the hands of Jim Kelley, Billy Graham and in mid-show, Master Magician Lance Burton. Lance then borrowed my nephew for a stage trick. I helped two-time New England Patriot's Super Bowl savior Adam Vinatieri move his kicking coach's motorized wheelchair down a flight of steps during a day-long blackout in Vero Beach. I've worked in homeless shelters with several Washington Redskins, and been given tennis instruction by Vitas Gerulaitus. I've met Sandy Koufax, Robert Urich, Charo, and congratulated Tony Curtis on his Lifetime Achievement award. Joe Torre wished

[†] On February 1, 2006, 14 year Las Vegas Metro police officer Sgt. Henry Prendes was shot and killed while responding to a domestic violence call. He was 37, and left a wife and two daughters. Sgt. Prendes' funeral, held on February 7, 2006, was the largest funeral in Nevada history, which included a several thousand vehicle motorcade and police helicopter formation flyover. Approximately 150 police officers are killed in the line of duty every year in the United States.

my father a happy birthday in December of 2003, and I was there. I've gotten a compunctious phone call from ESPN anchor Kenny Mayne in response to a letter I'd written, and have a Camden Yards foul tip last touched by the 7 Cy Young guy, Roger Clemens. I snagged a practice puck shot high by a different type of penguin, Mario Lemieux, and have signed photos from aviation bravehearts Chuck Yeager, Steve Fossett, Gabby Gabreski, John McCain, Robert K. Morgan (*Memphis Belle's* Captain), and Jimmy Doolittle's B-25 Mitchell raiders Ed Horton, William Bower, and Richard Cole. I have even had the extreme honor of speaking with stoic American hero and dauntless leader Commander Lloyd M. Bucher, captain of the USS *Pueblo*, just weeks before his death on January 28th, 2004. He graciously signed my copy of his book, *Bucher: My Story*, which details the wrongful North Korean attack and capture of the *Pueblo* in international waters in 1968, and the subsequent and brutal eleven month imprisonment of himself and crew.

But my first non-celestial star encounter as a restaurant lackey was some flash-in-the-pan actress named Rita Hayworth after she and a friend dined at the Uptown Club. She stepped into the kitchen to thank the boys in white for such a fine meal and everything came to a halt. I didn't know anything about her, only that she was dressed in black with meshy black stockings and seemed to have some kind of magical radiance about her. Only several years later did I appreciate the magnitude of her presence. Like a first kiss, celebrated Rita Hayworth was my first celebrity encounter as a hospie grinder.[†]

A few years later and halfway to Chicago, it was all about Dawn Wells during my college years in West Lafayette. While attending Purdue, I worked nights waiting tables at some long since defunct restaurant named Clemente's Reef when Mary Ann from *Gilligan's Island* stopped in with her theatre group for dinner. Clemente's Reef was one of the better places to eat in that dusty college town, though back then in West Lafayette, the Ponderosa was considered fine French cuisine, Dog 'N' Suds was the Hoosier version of Tavern on the Green, shoes were worn only in winter, and cloth napkins were strictly for

---

[†]During her Hollywood career, Margarita Carmen Cansino (Rita Hayworth) starred in 61 movies between 1935 and 1972. A 1964 Best Actress nominee for *Circus World*, Hayworth died of Alzheimer's Disease in 1987.

billionaires. When Dawn Wells came in, the patrons and staff almost couldn't contain themselves. They hadn't seen this much excitement since the miniature golf course installed a windmill and the campus fraternities were permitted to have trampolines. Meeting Mary Ann Summers would make their uneventful Lafayette lives complete.

The waiters all wanted to serve her, each staffer having agreed that she scored higher on the lust charts than fellow castaway Ginger Grant. The sole question that plagued our male minds was why Professor Roy Hinkley, Jonas Grumby (The Skipper) and Willy Gilligan weren't constantly trying to quell their throbbing, biological urges, cast away with two lusty wenches adorned in skintight clothing. Forget about twig gathering for the signal fire. Given enough time, even Mrs. Eunice Wentworth (Lovey) Howell would have rated consideration.

Though I don't recall who ended up serving Dawn Wells' table, it likely was the highlight of their college career. "Mom, Dad, I have good news and bad news. The bad news is I flunked out of Purdue, sold my car to pay for beer and bail money on spring break in Sarasota, have no idea how I got this Nirvana tattoo, and got this fifteen-year-old chick from Pescadores pregnant. We'll be living in the basement until the baby is old enough to work. She's a big fan of curry. The good news is I met Dawn Wells and she signed this placemat for me."

As a waiter at Charles Street Chop House, Roy Orbison was the grandest of all music moguls I ever served. When I first saw him, he looked like the chubby, near-sighted, kid brother of Elvis, his triple-thick black locks dominating his head. Roy's soft-spoken, sincere demeanor and kind smiles mirrored the heartfelt lyrics of his songs, his gentle disposition bordering on shy. Like Rita Hayworth, I didn't know much about Roy Orbison, only that I had seen him sing "Crying" on *Saturday Night Live*, and unlike Elvis, he remained stationary when performing. His dining companion and self-professed road manager was just the opposite of Orby—a nervous twitcher who acted more like a worrisome parent to Roy than a friend, employee, or dining companion. At the end of the meal, Twitch gave me a rolled up dollar, leaned over and said, "There you go, son. George is smilin'." I had no idea what the man meant, put the dollar in my pocket, and shook Twitchy's and Roy's hands in gratitude as they departed.

Afterwards, I went into the kitchen and unrolled the dollar to find a miniature mound of Colombian talcum. Perhaps George was smiling but the waiter wasn't, two hours of attention and the only gratuity left was a single buck and a tiny bit of blow. Since I wasn't a fan of Sizemore flour, the kitchen staff disposed of the powder for me, my popularity with the cooks never higher. The news of Roy's death later that year saddened me greatly.

Bob Hope may have been the best-known celebrity I have ever waited on. He and his bride were guests at the Coventry one afternoon. Very common with celebrities and their non-celebrity spouses or mates is the good cop/bad cop scenario. The renowned celebrity is the pleasant, jocular, and limelight-friendly one, while the non-star mate is the claws of the couple, the protector of the better half who fends off the public and authoritatively barks when something needs attention. Mrs. Hope did all of the talking, bordering on unpleasant, though the reasons for her unhappiness soon became apparent.

Of the hundred plus people sharing the dining room with the Hopes, no less than a dozen pair of eyes were on the couple at any one moment. Even worse were the pointers who look and point at celebrities like tourists on paparazzi safari after spotting a cheetah in the brush, hoping not to spook it. "Shh, honey, over there, it's Bob Hope. He's about to eat a squab, see where I'm pointing. Uh-oh, he's looking up, don't stare, he's knows we're here now. Act like you didn't see him. If he gets up to use the restroom, I'll go, too."

The chasm downside of fame is having every public move you make scrutinized by people who should be made into organ donors. The Hopes were gracious and at the meal's conclusion, Bob gave me an appreciative thank you. From that point on, I always went out of my way not to recognize celebrities; they had enough to worry about with the gawkers.

One of the pilots training with me in Vero was John F. Kennedy, Jr., but before I met the Camelot kid on the tarmac, I had met John at King Lear. No one person's presence in the restaurant ever caused more of an estrogen stir than when JFK, Jr. came in to dine. The women went blithering nuts, most making fools of themselves or reaffirming the established fact. John had been in a few times and was one of the classiest celebrities I ever encountered. This was the case the first time he ever dined at King Lear.

John came in without a tie, and not even for the saluting son of our assassinated thirty-fifth president could we break King Lear's dress code. We informed John about our dress code and offered him a house tie, but he opted to dash over to Garfinkel's and pick up a Perry Ellis. He never protested the rule and was the epitome of grace, despite the pointers' frenzy approaching critical. We would hide Camelot's son at a corner table and post a penguin guard to deflect the teary-eyed women seeking his autograph. Often the pathetic pouters would enlist their husbands or boyfriends to do the deed, tearing a page from the wine list or grabbing a dessert card, lining up to ask John for a signature. When the penguin sentry would tell the panting stargazers that Mr. Kennedy and guests should be allowed to enjoy their dinner uninterrupted, the news was never taken well. Some cried when turned away. One rebuffed female fly never spoke to me again after I squashed her dreams of kneeling beside JFK, Jr.

John did sign a couple of autographs after his meal for some of the more persistent female pests. One woman who had gotten his signature told her husband, "I want a divorce! I plan to start a new life together with John F. Kennedy, Jr.'s autograph. We love each other and even though he's just a scribbling on a cocktail napkin, I think we can make it work."

And for the men who gawk, howl, stop, drop, and roll when a beautiful female celebrity comes into the restaurant, please note the following: That hot woman spends her nights banging her personal trainer and then mocking your mindless mating calls after the lovin'. Despite all of her beer commercials and pornographic pictorials that make you think otherwise, your drooling adoration and total absence of intellect frightens her to the point she carries a Glock in her purse. So stop embarrassing yourself, watch much less television, read a few books written before 1950, hit the gym, and start acting like a self-respecting man and not a downloading, mumbling, organ-grinding, libido-possessed, self-devaluating degenerate.

The most important person in any restaurant you're in is *you*. And for the autograph seekers, just remember that the crayon picture on your refrigerator that your five-year-old drew is worth about a million times more than any autograph you may get. And just how much are those Barry Bonds juice balls worth now anyway?

Senator George McGovern, presidential candidate and distinguished WWII Liberator pilot, was another King Lear regular who never expected preferential treatment. He wouldn't identify himself when calling to make a reservation, which almost got him squeezed out of the mix on more than one occasion. The answerbitches would be screening calls and just when we were about to tell the unknown caller that there wasn't room in the manger, we would recognize his voice and ask, "Is this Senator McGovern?" He would confess. "Senator, please let us know it's you. We were about to tell you to try Dixie Pig."

Most of the senators and congressional figurines were just the opposite, veritable vanity fairies. One congressman, unlike Senator McGovern, was in for lunch at the Coventry with four young male lackeys and one lackette in a situation similar to that of President Bush and General Admission. I asked the young lady if she cared to order and one of Hitler's Youth, not a day over twenty, brusquely interrupted me and said, "Waiter, Congressman Pimpslap should order first!" Congo Pimpslap stepped right in and ordered, not missing a beat. He enjoyed the Koresh-like adoration, and, no doubt felt he should order first, gender having nothing to do with the matter. He was a powerful congressman who ate lots of fiber. Everyone else around him were just pawns, prawns, and puppets. After the meal, a team of Percheron stallions was required to remove the young shitwit from the congressman's ass.

David Brinkley was a class customer from start to finish and much like Senator McGovern in that he made all the right moves, none of the wrong, and expected absolutely no special treatment. This made the penguins want to look after him all the more. He, too, was a regular King man who liked rail vodka on the rocks and his New York sirloin a skosh over medium. But if he had wanted Lo Mein made in Sante Fe, you can bet your loganberries that we would have gotten it for him and that's no exaggeration.

One evening Mr. Brinkley and his two guests were being served by a probationary period waiter, Andrew, who was at the bar getting their drinks. Andrew ordered two glasses of Pommard and a Ketel One on the rocks. Omar and I were standing in line behind Andrew and knew he was getting Brinkley's drinks. Omar asked if DB had changed from our house vodka, which was Smirnoff, to Ketel One, which was a dollar more. Andrew said "No, he just asked for vodka on the rocks, but I'm sure a guy like David Brinkley can afford Ketel One." In surround sound, Omar and I read Andrew the riot act, "Damn it Andrew, you fucking moron. The reason a guy like Brinkley comes in here is so he won't get jerked around by the waiters. It doesn't matter how much money you think someone has, it's not your call!" Omar took the table from that moment on and Andrew was fired the next day.

The fact that David Brinkley was a high-profile celebrity didn't matter. The fact that he was a genuine human being who treated the staff well is what made us want to look out for him. I had waited on Mr. Brinkley eight or nine times and of all the power people I had served, he and Jean Dixon were my favorites.

The first time I saw Jean Dixon, I didn't even recognize her. She was a frail thing, well-decorated in expensive jewelry which was all the camouflage she needed to blend in with the Israeli busload of Jewish matriarchs that filled the finer seats of

King Lear on any given night. The first time I met her, she held my hand with both of hers and said, "You have a good soul." To another waiter she said, "You have no soul." To another five penguins she said, "You have no liver!" An amazing woman, truly.

She would dine with her family and was a lamb devotee, though had only the appetite to eat about a third of a portion. The rest we would wrap for her to take home. She was gracious and never demanding, a star customer if ever there was one, giving me inside information on the next day's horoscope that she wrote for the *Washington Post*. I loved talking with her and listening to her wisdom.

When Jean Dixon was ill and hospitalized at Georgetown University Hospital, she called up Clay and asked if she could get a meal delivered. Clay obliged, on the house, and knowing that I was her regular waiter, asked me to make the arrangements. I abandoned my station and packed up a lamb chop dinner with all the trimmings, jumped in a cab and hustled over to Reservoir Road to serve Jean Dixon at her hospital bed.

In the hospital, the tall tuxedoed man with a Sunkist Lemon box got his share of odd looks from the medical staff. "That's right, I just left my bride at the altar and came here to cure the scurvy epidemic." I reheated her food in the nurses' station microwave and plated each item as if it were being served inside King Lear. I was proud to be Jean Dixon's butler, if only for an hour. After she finished her meal, I packed everything up and she gave me a kiss on the cheek to say thank you for such gallantry. Gallantry that was second nature when serving people like her.

You didn't have to be a celebrity to be treated like a star by the staff of King Lear. Most of the food delivered from King Lear went to former staffers afflicted with AIDS. Though we did so with a song in our hearts, it was troubling in that there never seemed to be a time when someone wasn't dying young.

There were also a few older regulars who had frequented King Lear since its opening during the Carter administration who had difficulty making it to the restaurant. For these special people we would deliver whatever they wanted. One such couple was Vance and Jackie Parsons who lived in the nearby Watergate. The Parsons had been lunch regulars from day one, but both were sick, and just to visit King Lear even once a month was a journey for them. Mobility is something people don't tend to appreciate until it's gone or compromised. Mr. Parsons looked just like Dwight Eisenhower and Mrs. Parsons had an unfathomable collection of dress hats, so many that some of the waiters helped her catalog and store her off-season hats in the basement of the Watergate. The waiters would even set-up and decorate a Christmas tree every December in the Parson's living room with an ornament bearing each of the front houser's names. When the Parsons did make it into King Lear, it was as if no other customers existed. We were all like sons and daughters to them. Every waiter, no matter how busy, would stop by the Parsons' table and chat for a while. If you were in a rush to catch a flight and the Parsons were in the house, you had no chance of making your flight with a bellyful of King Lear cuisine. The Parsons gave the penguins a sense of pride in a mostly prideless profession, a kind and gentle couple who are immortal in the hearts of all the King's men.

One time, a lunch quartet of well-dressed men came into King Lear and ordered a bottle of wine. "We'd like a bottle of Fess Parker Riesling." I served the suits the requested wine. "Uhmmm. We love this Fess Parker Riesling. Nothing tops Fess Parker Riesling. Taste the wet, minerally, stone, citrus hues in this delicious bottle of Fess Parker Riesling. By George, this Fess Parker Riesling is the finest bottle of Fess Parker Riesling Fess Parker has ever produced. We confess that Fess is the professor when it comes to quality Fess Parker Riesling."

"Jesus boys, I'm just the waiter here and it's only been two minutes since we met, but if you say Fess Parker Riesling one more time, I swear I'm gonna lose my mind."

"Just tell us this. What do you think of Fess Parker Riesling?"

"Well, I really like red wines much more than whites and in my opinion Fess Parker Riesling is a festering bottle of . . . You're Fess Parker, aren't you?"

"That's me."

"I demand that Fess Parker Riesling become the national drink of the United States of America and that school children be forced to drink a bottle of this delicious Fess Parker Riesling every morning prior to the Pledge of Allegiance and if all the rivers of North America flowed with Fess Parker Riesling, the world would be a better place to live."

"Calm down son, you're okay."

Not recognizing Fess, I had put my foot where a couple swallows of Fess Parker Riesling should have been. How often does a waiter get grilled about a wine by the vintner himself, a vintner who was also a famous actor?

Fess was too cool for school. He knew he and his business companions had blindsided me and all he could do was laugh. The man who had portrayed Daniel Boone and Davey Crockett told me he envied the fact that I got to wear a tuxedo to work everyday.

Fess then explained that when he and fellow woodsman actor Buddy Ebsen were invited to snooty Hollywood cocktail parties, the studio executives all got to wear Italian tuxedos while he and buddy Buddy were ordered to wear their Daniel Boone duds, including powder horn, musket in tow, and coonskin cap for chapeau.

I never served Frank Sinatra, but I did stand behind the living legend when he froze King Lear with a few of his songs. He had come in to eat with some guests and did an impromptu set that blew everyone away. There were only three people moving in the King Lear at the time. Frank was singing, Marcel, the pianist, was pecking, and Wally (Wally Gator) the bassist, was plucking his six-foot violin. Everyone else in the crowded dining room and bar were just wax figures in the museum room display titled "Consumption Junction." Sinclair ended up serving the Chairman of the Board, the coolest rat of the pack. It was clear that he didn't want to sign autographs or shake strangers' hands and had already served the entire restaurant by singing a few songs, but still some of the selfish, trashy stargazers missed the obvious visual cues.

I've served two separate celebrities named Haley in my life.

Number ninety-four, a man with five Super Bowl rings, Dallas Cowboy defensive end and San Francisco 49er linebacker Charles Haley was one. *Roots* author and Malcolm X biographer Alex Haley was the other. I have no intriguing anecdotes about either man, only the observation that both men are American legends in different ways. Charles was a man it took three men to block, a man who could knock down the Washington Monument with his tackle slap.

Alex was the author of one of the most inspirational books and television miniseries of the twentieth century. Alex Haley served in the United States Coast Guard starting as a mess cook during WWII but was promoted to Chief Journalist in 1959. A few years after his death in 1992, a refurbished medium-sized cutter was named after this great man, The USCGC *Alex Haley.* It's just a shame that the Coast Guard doesn't have aircraft carriers.

When Chris Farley came to dine one busy winter night, all the decent tables were filled and no one had intentions of vacating their seats anytime soon. Morris and I were sharing the maître d' duties, angry that a few of the patrons were dragging out their meals. Chris and his lady friend didn't have a reservation and the only two tables available were the worst tables in the house. Every restaurant has a lousy table; King Lear had two.

The first bad table was a four-topper by the front door, known as the "Doorfour" that experienced an Antarctican blast of frigid air from the frozen District streets each time the front door was opened in winter. During the frostier nights, you could see the breath of the patrons who were seated on the Doorfour. The only advantage to sitting at the Doorfour was the guarantee of having a chilled salad fork, so cold that it would stick to your tongue.

King Lear's other nightmare table was perhaps the worst table on the eastern seaboard, an emergency do-or-die deuce set up across from the restrooms just outside the kitchen doors known as the dreaded "Toilet Table." Located along the waiter and bus bastard highway, the Toilet Table was as close as one could eat to a restroom without actually dining in the can itself. Audible to anyone on the Toilet Table was the rush of water each time a urinal or commode was flushed, sounding like jets taking off at

Chicago O'Hare. When patrons perched at T2 inhaled a lot, they'd breathe in a few airborne Colombian molecules that failed to be vacuumed up the noses of the women who were snorting lines off of the ladies' room Tampax dispensers. "You know, I thought I needed a cup of coffee to get me going, but hey, I'm ready to get moving now."

One man who was condemned to the Toilet Table said he thought a guest in the restroom was ill because he was moaning so much. Bored T2 diners could monitor just what percentage of patrons washed their hands after nature's call and any extra sensory olfactory ability was not a virtuous trait to those remanded to the Toilet Table.

If the stench of fresh sewage wasn't enough to kill even a starving man's appetite, the English and Spanish profanity flying about the kitchen would. The dishwashing station was located just inside the kitchen door where King Lear's chief dishwasher, Angelo Compose, was forever cussing at the waiters. Angelo hated waiters, Americans, and most of all the seething breed that were American penguins. We would answer his unkind curses by calling him Tangelo, Jello, Antelope, Tangelo Composte, or just plain "Fuck You Chancho." In rageful retort, Antelope would respond by saying "Tu Fuck You," (*tu* being the pronoun for "you" in Spanish).

Imitating auctioneers, we would complete the verbal exchange by noting he had incorrectly used pronouns from two separate languages in one phrase. "All right I have two fuck you's, do I hear three God damns? Looking for four kiss my asses, I've got five motherfuckers. Do I hear six eat shits? In the corner I have seven stinking bastards, going once, going twice, sold to the wife-slapping, tick-picking, malt-liquored Spanish resident alien greaseball for seven stinking bastards! Congratulations to you and your burro."

So, to effectively dine at the Toilet Table required a deaf patron dining alone, with absolutely no sense of smell or propensity for claustrophobia. If we offered free food and drink to a street person so long as they dined at T2, they would have refused. "Naw man, I can't eat here. All dat flushin' 'n' shittin'. Fuck no. And tell those amigos to shut the hell up!"

Chris Farley and date took the drafty Doorfour by the podium and drank Irish coffees until a primo table opened up. They had nothing but compliments regarding the food and service. Had Chris been a waiter, he would have been a perfect fit on the penguin roster. I felt a distinct emptiness when I learned of his death.

NBA Hall of Famer Wilt Chamberlain was a sporadic Lear regular, an impeccably dressed, quiet giant with the perfect Vandyke beard. And he was excessively generous as Nesbie learned. The first time he came in, he slipped Nesbie a few bills and asked for a nice table. Nesbie stuffed the loot in his tux thinking that two dollars was a pretty cheap toss from a man wearing ten grand worth of bling and dressed in a two thousand dollar suit. Nesbie, needing all the cash he could get to quietly pay off his legal bills from his troubles on Necro-night, checked off Wilt's name and showed the party to their table, a borderline four top not far from the Toilet Table. After closing, locking the doors, and completing that evening's wench-rogering and disposal (referred to as "lock-up, knock-up, and bitch ditch" by the waiters), Nesbie emptied his tux jacket to find Wilt had tipped him not two dollars, but two hundred. The letch about fell over. Even worse was that he hadn't been particularly gracious with Wilt and his guests, giving them a marginal table at best. Nesbo felt like shit and could only make amends with WC if he came back to King Lear.

Wilt did, and Nesbie was all over the hundred point man, too much so as judged by the penguins. Wilt was even quoted as saying, "I've never been kissed by a white man before." Each time he returned, Wilt threw Nesbie two hundred cash and was the recipient of the finest tables and promptest seating in King Lear history. But WC's generosity wasn't limited to slithering, deceitful, dirtbag maître d's.

Wilt's favorite and therefore regular waiter was Ty, the shortest of D.C.'s short waiters who had upgraded his booze status since starting at King Lear from alcoholic junior grade to full-fish booze-hound. Ty drank no more than the average penguin, but at just over four feet tall and a hundred pounds lighter than the other waiters, the same amount of juice had less internal distance to travel, which got Ty cooked quicker. Friction with his wife who had just graduated law school didn't serve to diminish his thirst either, nor hinder his reservations about drug use.

But all was roses when serving Wilt, who was taller sitting down than Ty was standing up. WC gave Ty five hundred cash every time he dined no matter what the check or how many guests, loving the ICU levels of attention given to him by Ty and Nesbie. The first time Wilt gave little Orr the fast cash five hundred Ty's eyes lit up, and in a Tiny Tim tone, the fifty-one inch lanternless lawn jockey told the Gotham titan, "God bless you, sir."

It was the wrong thing to say. We gave Ty so much grief for saying that, mocking the miniature man monthly by quoting the phrase with a hard cockney accent. We would even throw in an "ever so much" with the Piccadilly mockery for an extra twist on the mental thumbscrew. But a little grief from his fellow waiters was nothing compared to the hurt and hard times coming up fast for King Lear's tiniest penguin.

But the one person I never met or served, but wish I had, was Vice Admiral James B. Stockdale. A 1976 Medal of Honor recipient, Stockdale didn't get the respect he deserved in 1992. A fraction of his tremendous accomplishments include being a Naval test pilot flight instructor, squadron commander, and carrier-based fighter/attack pilot with 26 combat decorations. In 1965, Stockdale's A-4E Skyraider was shot down over North Vietnam where he was imprisoned for eight years, four of those years in complete darkness, two years in leg irons, tortured and beaten throughout his execrable incarceration. Though already starving, he organized a hunger strike when a fellow prisoner was denied medical care. The recurrent theme of Stockdale's many postwar writings is how man can rise in dignity and prevail in the face of adversity. Such are the thoughts of a hero we should celebrate, a person of austere fortitude who deserves our unconditional respect.

And before you ridicule a man for turning off his hearing aid, perhaps you should first find out how he lost his hearing. You might then be more respectful.[†]

[†] On July 5th, 2005, Admiral Stockdale died at the age of 81. He had spent a tenth of his life as a prisoner of war, a life that was dedicated to the service of America. A ship will be named after Admiral Stockdale, but in truth, the Navy should name the entire fleet after him. RIP, Admiral.

7 SIGNS OF A PATHY SPORTS GAMBI:

1. BETS ON MORE THAN 10 EVENTS A WEEK

2. CONSTANTLY MAKES PARLAY WAGERS, AND BETS EXCESSIVELY ON NCAA BASKETBALL

3. WAS DISTRESSED AFTER 9/11/01 BECAUSE OF THE INDEFINITE CANCELLATION OF SPORTING EVENTS

4. BETS ON EVERY MARQUEE SPORTING EVENT AND ALL NFL SUNDAY NIGHT AND MONDAY NIGHT GAMES

5. DOESN'T HAVE A 401K, CHILDREN'S COLLEGE FUND, SAVINGS ACCOUNT, OR POSSESS A CREDIT CARD WITH A ZERO BALANCE

6. BRAGS ABOUT VICTORIES, LIES ABOUT LOSSES, AND DOESN'T KEEP A BETTING LEDGER

7. MOODINESS AND DENIAL

Chapter 12

Wings of a Boxer
(*The Tarhe*)

*"With a load of iron ore — 26,000 tons more
than the Edmund Fitzgerald weighed empty.
That good ship and (crew) was a bone to be chewed
when the gales of November came early."*

*"Does anyone know where the love of God goes
when the waves turn the minutes to hours?
The searchers all say they'd have made Whitefish Bay
if they'd put fifteen more miles behind her."*

Gordon Lightfoot
"The Wreck of the Edmund Fitzgerald,"
Summertime Dream, Reprise, 1976

Two thousand dollars was the price for getting hired as a waiter at King Lear. Like most businesses, other than religion and prostitution, you have to spend money to make money and this was the case with becoming a King Lear server. Topping the shopping list were three or four single breasted, single-vented, notched tuxedos. A dozen high-collar pleated tuxedo shirts, black ties, cufflinks, studs, wine tools, cigar cutters, lighters, dress socks, cummerbunds, and at least two pair of high-gloss dress shoes completed the list.

There was a specific strategy in everything purchased. The tuxedos had to be a wool blend for longevity and ease for cleaning accidents, sauce splotches, and enduring a weekly tuxedo avalanche floor fall. Pure cotton shirts were cooler and looked better when starched, but poly-blends could better withstand three hundred bleachings and starchings. King Lear's penguins bought their shoes a size larger because we wore two pairs of socks. The inner layer were thick white athletic socks to absorb shock and give ease to the knees; the outer layer were black nylon over-the-calf stockings to keep those damn gam veins suppressed. Most of the waiters wore gel insoles and knee braces when time between cortisone shots and ligament scopings ran long. Your cufflinks, studs, cigar cutters and wine keys had to be something aesthetically pleasing but not painful when sticky-mitted. "Forever borrowed without consent" was the penguin's phrase for items stolen or pawned.

Textbooks were also required to pass a series of written tests administered by Gavin and Roosevelt on topics ranging from meats, single malts, and the history of cigars to every *Vitas vinifera* known to mankind. We learned what varietals comprised a traditional Chateauneuf-du-Pape and the differences between Somalis and sommeliers, a piece of cod and a codpiece, Caesars and cesareans, Bach and baklava, LSD and LDS, polenta and placenta, metaphors and petits fours, merkins and gherkins, Rodin and Rodan, Halibut and Halle Berry's butt. We even had to purchase and read *The Tragedy of King Lear,* William Shakespeare's stage script of an imprudent British king who dies of a broken heart. He was the father of three daughters, the youngest being the wisest, and the elder two conniving and in dire need of some Ike Turner-style attention.

If you were doing double duty as a waiter and dealer, more hardware and software was required, including a pager, cell phone, gram scale, portable freebase kit, travel meth lab, coke cutters, horizontal mini-mirrors, sniff tools, battlefield bong parts and fittings, suck hoses, pipe cleaners, vials, Visine, zip-lock bags, police officer excuse lists, a .38 Special for the big traders, and a miniature Jimi Hendrix and/or Bob Marley poster to be proudly displayed on the inside door of your tattered locker. Before you served one porterhouse as a fetch monkey at thundering King Lear, you had reduced your available MasterCard credit by two thousand clams.

Outfitted and underway, my probationary period learning processes began, and like familiarizing yourself with a new neighborhood, mine was the task of learning about all the restaurant's regulars. The expendable regulars didn't get much nevermind, nor did the fencers, but the top regular doggies were must-know names.

One such man was a former professional boxer named Rudolf Valentino Faust, named after his mother's favorite silver screener, otherwise known as Val to the waiters. RVF was a nice piece of genetic work, six-foot even, thick dark hair, a Burt Lancaster-ish face, and hard cheekbones. Though in the second half of his forties, he was more handsome than most men are at any point in their lives, stronger than any five combined. His boxing days were long since over, but the business he owned wasn't much different. He moved giant objects.

You name it, he moved it. If a ten-ton asteroid landed on your lawn, he could relocate it. If you wanted your Jersey shore beach house moved to the Outer Banks, Val was your man. When your mother-in-law visited for Thanksgiving and never left, RVF could help. If you needed White House furniture discretely put on a moving truck, V. Faust was the man to call. And while he looked as if he could move anything with his bare hands and raw strength, Val owned an arsenal of equipment to help him get the job done, including a gorgeous Sikorsky CH-54B Skycrane helicopter that only he and a second stick spotter would pilot.[†] When he wasn't flying his Polish chopper or curling iron, Val was enjoying himself at King Lear. Though a flyboy, he wasn't a barfly, making RVF all the more likable. We never knew who could lift more—Val or his helicopter.

Mitch Morehouse was RVF's friend and regular waiter, and the two were close friends inside and outside of King Lear. The monthly rumor was that Mitch was going to leave Lear and break free of the restaurant doldrums to work for Val, but moving industry layoffs and lean economic times prevented

---

[†]The official nickname of the Sikorsky CH-54B is the *Tarhe*, also referred to as the "flying crane."

RVF from ever making it happen. When Mitch was off or on vacation, I got the nod to serve RVF, my aviation fascination helping to secure the duty. As a customer, Val, like Earl Styles, was relaxed, classy, and excessively generous. Often joining him were two other men, always there to eat and drink but never motioning to grab the tab. Though it was a given that Val would tip large when he paid, it angered the staff in that we thought his generous nature was being taken advantage of by these imposters trying to be like the legend himself. Neither of these table chumps ever once offered to pick up a check, even when financial times were hard for Val and he was perilously close to losing his business. Protective is the word. There wasn't anything we wouldn't do for RVF.

When I first started working at King Lear, Mitch noticed that I had spent the spree, bought and stowed all the goods and gear in the locker room. I had only served Val one time previously, but knew he was a star regular just by talking to him. Mitch pulled me aside one afternoon and said, "John, Val's got a problem and needs your help."

"Valentino wants me to take the Skycrane off of his hands? Tell him I'll do it, but he'd better top off the tanks on that bad boy."

"No, not exactly. Val just got a call from his wife and he's supposed to dine at the White House tonight for some kind of fund-raiser, but doesn't have a tuxedo. You're about his size and I thought he could borrow one of your spares."

I said, "Hell yes, I just hope it fits. I don't have those Herculean shoulders he does."

So like a couple of haberdashers, Mitch and I escorted Val to the grimy locker that doubled as the Salvie shit house. It was three hours past noon, which meant it was Lupe Santana stench hour.

Like the bells of Notre Dame, 3:00 p.m. was the time when Lupe, our mumbling pot washer, was also in the business of moving. Lupe had a sad story. He was a man who had lost seven family members. They were killed instantly when their van collided head-on with a tractor-trailer outside of Amarillo in 1984. Lupe had since crawled in a bottle and no one could blame him. The staff always snuck him hooch whenever possible, but booze aside, the offensive odor Lupe produced made tear gas seem like Chanel No. 5. When Lupe finished his stall work that afternoon, Mitch and I cleared the locker room like a SWAT team, entering stiff-armed with lighters blazing in both hands. Then, while I was fogging the room with disinfectant, Mitch laid pages from the *Washington Times* classified section on the floor so Val's feet wouldn't make direct contact with germ central.

We waved RVF in, his eyes watered and his first and only word was "Jeez!" Finally though, we were able to address the task of getting him dressed and though my coat was a little snug and long on the muscled man, he looked Oscar night dapper, although if he had flexed he would have turned my tux into Hulk rags.

On the way back to the dining room, Val stopped me, thanked me, and gave me a hundred, which I begged him to take back, but he refused. The next day he returned the tux with an additional fifty that he said was for dry cleaning. I refused to take it but he shoved the Grant in my jacket pocket and said, "Hey, just take it. Now I know where to get my tux for the inaugural ball, right?"

I said, "Damn straight. Anytime, anywhere. And if you so much as think about giving me even a penny next time, I'll loosen the screws on your Skycrane."

Like any true Washingtonian, Val was a devout Redskins fan, always on the emotional roller coaster as the team won and lost. He was a season ticket holder, and no matter what the weather, he and family could be found at every home game. On occasion, Val and family would even journey up to Philadelphia and New Jersey for road games against the Eagles and Giants.

On one November Monday, the District was happy because the Redskins had just defeated Cleveland the day before, but Val Faust was sporting a severe black eye. What man was suicidal enough to punch RVF in the face? Val told us he had been mugged the previous day.

He, his wife, and two children had gone to watch the Redskins and left the game early in the second half because his daughter wasn't feeling well. On the way to their car parked outside of RFK, he was jumped by a couple of young crims. The delinquents had likely thought that the Faust family would be an easy score. All they saw was a man, a woman and two children about to get into a late model Jaguar, seemingly well-off and without much defense. But the mugger's defense assessment was incorrect. The biggest of the four was a retired professional boxer with a night-night right hook that could puppet-drop a hippopotamus. Hence, this particular mugging would prove more costly for the gangsters than the vics.

Both men jumped Val with one landing a clean blow beneath Val's eye, though Val said he didn't recall feeling the punch at the time. He was too preoccupied with finding his old form. Val must have found it, hard elbowing one of the men who was trying to head lock him, pretty sure the punk suffered a fractured rib. Crim two, who was facing Val, swung again and missed badly, our boy answering the hitter's compromised stance with a Predator punch to the lower third of the man's face. Later, he told the penguins, "I'm sure I broke that fucker's jaw clean. I hit him full blow square and could feel his jawbone collapse against my knuckles."

The two injured hitters ran off, one with both hands on his jaw and the other holding his side in agony as if he had just suffered a burst appendix.

Though the fight lasted less than ten seconds, Val's wife and kids were terrified. Instead of looking for the police, who were probably concentrating on the game anyway, Val hustled his family into the car and hurried home, calling the cops while en route. The muggers were never apprehended, though their pummeled corpses might have turned up somewhere had they dared to touch Val's wife or children. Though his family was frightened and upset, the only visible damage from the mugging was the black eye. Val knew he was lucky that neither thug was carrying hardware, uncommon with District hood's rougher rap sheeters. The King's men were just glad our boy and his family were all right.

Rudolf Valentino Faust continued to be one of King Lear's all time favorite customers, his presence lending the restaurant an aura of power and exclusivity. He wasn't just a customer, he was like a big brother to the front housers, someone you wanted to please. Val was our friend, and no day was a perfect one unless he made it in. But God takes the great ones early, and Val Faust was no exception.

During his boxing days, Val was shot by an angler for not taking a canvass dive. Though he survived the bullet, he was given hepatitis-contaminated blood in a transfusion that would claim his life twenty-eight years later. He was only 49. No person's passing could have been more painful to the penguins; no one wanted to accept that he was gone. At the graveside funeral in Norfolk, Mitch read a favorite poem of Val's by William Butler Yeats from which a few lines read:

> *"My country is Kiltartan Cross,*
> *My countrymen Kiltartan's poor,*
> *No likely end would bring them loss,*
> *Or leave them happier than before."*

But Val, you were wrong. The end that was your passing left us hurting badly, dispirited and hollow, like a part of us was missing. God damn those invisible sharks.

NEVER SAY THE FOLLOWING:

1. I KNOW THE OWNER! *Remind me to spit in your food two times.*

2. DO YOU KNOW WHO I AM? *Ah, Mr. Floorsteak, Welcome. And no, that's not herb-crusted.*

3. WE WANT A QUIET TABLE. *None of our tables have ever made any noise. It's the 300 surrounding people that make the noise. Do you see where I'm going?*

4. (AFTER A CREDIT CARD IS DECLINED) RUN IT AGAIN! *Sir, I can run your card a million times more but it will come up DECLINED every time. Your only hope is that by swiping your credit card over and over again the credit card machine somehow turns into a time machine, so we can go back to a point in time when you did have credit.*

5. IS THE _____ FRESH? *Everything is fresh. Everything. You name it, it's fresh. The Dodo eggs-they're fresh. The Tasmanian wolf, yes I know it's extinct, but it's fresh. The T-Rex flank steak, the just-picked Tahitian guava juice, James Carvell's haircut, the Mars river water, it's all fresh.*

6. ARE THERE ANY CELEBRITIES HERE? *Did you get lost from your Japanese tourist group? Because that's what I'm thinking. Hey, look over there, it's Godzilla! He's about to step on those power lines. Oh-no, EEEEEEEEE!!!!*

7. I DON'T WANT TO MAKE THE CHEF MAD. *Wow, are you way late on that one. That ship left harbor decades ago. You adding to his anger pile is like chucking a sparkler on a raging forest fire.*

8. I'LL HAVE A VODKA TONIC <u>WITH A LIME</u>. *Really? A lime? Because we normally serve our vodka tonics with fish heads.*

Chapter 13

Heart Attack and Heimlich

(anaphylaxis and myocardial infarction)

". . . my religion is a natural religion,
and the first law of nature is self-preservation."

El-Hajj Malik El-Shabazz [Malcolm X] (1925–1965)
Speech, Prospects for Freedom, New York [1965]

You can't defy the odds, nor hide from probability. When you spend so many thousands of hours in a restaurant, you're going to see a few people have medical emergencies. Spend enough time in a restaurant and that emergency just might be you. This is true with too much time spent anywhere. Spend enough time as an air traffic controller and you'll see a plane crash. Call 800 numbers enough and you'll find that every customer service job in America has been outsourced to the Calcutta Curry Stirrer's Union. Drive drunk often enough and you will get caught. Watch enough NASCAR and you'll see a driver make his bayou bride a wealthy widow. Become a rodeo clown and you'll witness a bareback rider getting a fast hoof in the face. Skip enough rocks off of Scottish lochs and someday you'll see Nessie. Live long enough in America and watch the Amigos embroider a sombrero wearing Chihuahua on Old Glory while singing the Mexican-Mangled Banner. Watch enough sports and you'll see Shaq leave Jack, Phil come back, Tampa win Lord Stanely's Cup, and the Expos' time in Montreal expire. Go hunting enough with the VP and someday he'll bust a cap in your ass.

This is much more than Miami matriarchs claiming their

242   John Galloway

husbands are diabetic so they can get a table in a crowded restaurant without waiting. Or diners burning their fingertips on their entree plates despite four warnings, two table tents, and a three-hour Tony Robbins seminar dedicated solely to the fact that their plates were hot. This is about life and death: heart attacks, strokes, choking, lacerations, broken bones, allergic reactions, and food poisoning, not to mention all the physical trauma caused by the reckless behavior inherent to any place where booze is dispensed, political theory is exchanged, and sexual gratification carries the tiniest degree of likelihood.

The first time you witness a customer having a heart attack, you're almost in more shock than he is. You look at the downed man and wonder if he'll ever see sunshine again. The third or fourth time, you don't think much about it, you just dial 911. Everyone else seems surprised when a medical emergency occurs in a restaurant, but in truth they shouldn't be. Restaurants, and especially bars, are simply unhealthy places to be—physically, ethically, mentally, literally, spiritually, and historically.

The worst choking case I ever witnessed was during a weekday lunch at the Coventry. Two middle-aged men were dining at a window deuce when one of the boys stood up with a bright red face and arms held out like some kind of scarecrow describing the catfish he'd caught. The abruptness with which he up stood caused his chair to fall over and the sharp clinking of his silverware hitting his plate alerted half of the dining room that something was out of order in this otherwise calm lunch scenario. The frozen and panicked expression on this patron's face concurred; he was choking badly and couldn't breathe and it looked as if Saint Peter had just pulled his file.

This is where you find out who has moxie and who doesn't. The pointers don't have moxie, they never will. All they do is point. Pointing only helps if you're trying to park a jumbo jet or helping a drunkard find the sun. The mouth coverers don't help either. This group of non-action people are exclusively women and are shocked by any event, great or small. Why couldn't they have covered their mouths when they made that comment about street people needing to get jobs? There is even the hideous crossbreed of pointer/mouth coverer, but still nothing is getting done and a choking man swelling with carbon dioxide is about to die because no one has the donut holes to jump up and shake the trees.

To the great fortune of the choking scarecrow, Troy, maître d' that afternoon, knew what to do and did it. Standing about twenty feet away at his podium, he calmly walked over to the red choker, locked his fists under the man's sternum and executed a perfect two-thrust Heimlich. Normally when Troy stood behind a stranger and locked his hands it had nothing to do with Heimlich maneuvers. The red scarecrow gave up a deep "hoiw" and up came an untoothed ring box-sized square of Mahi Mahi, the fish so nice they named it twice. He spat it far enough to get the first down, and the waiters were amazed at how perfectly intact this piece of fish was. We even considered bringing it back to Zach for a reheat, resauce, replate, and re-serve to help lower food costs, but we had to see if the choker wanted to attempt an immediate floor-to-face rechew. No wonder this guy choked; this piece of poisson was huge.

The instant Scarecrow coughed up the fish, he leaned over with both hands on the window sill, breathing as if he had just legged out a triple, knowing he had taken oxygen for granted up to this point in his life. He wiped his mouth, turned to Troy and thanked him gratefully, apologizing for disrupting the dining room. Troy handed him a glass of water and asked the scarecrow if he wanted him to call the paramedics or be taken to the hospital or something. The man declined, seeming eager to resume his lunch and somehow get the pointers and mouth coverers to gawk at something else. It wasn't going to happen. He was the feature attraction that day and unless the White House caught fire, he was the show.

After the scarecrow and guest finished their meal, paid, and got up to leave, the staff looked on in anticipation to see what this man's life was worth. Apparently nothing. The scarecrow walked by Troy, shook his hand a second time but gave him not one cherry-red cent. A hundred dollars and a sloppy kiss certainly seemed due, but Helen-of got nothing. Troy vowed that the next time a customer gagged on a piece of fish, he wouldn't help. "Yes sir, I see you waving over there with a whole grouper stuck in your lung but the phone's ringing right now so just excuse me for a minute and then I'll be right over."

Much more distressing than a choking customer is a falling customer. A choking victim is usually some hurried stock trader who can be saved by a good Heimlich, and if not, the world is a happier place with him dead. Plus, it's hard to pity someone who's smart enough to graduate magna cum laude from Barbazon Obispo Polytechnic but too stupid to chew his coq au vin. However, falling happens often in restaurants and with women who suffer osteoporosis broken bones often result. Yet another valid argument for carpeting over hard flooring.

There is no distress in seeing a bar patron fall over in his or her barstool. In fact, it's almost funny in some macabre way and is a clear indication to the tender of when to end someone's bender. If you wake up stuck on the floor, glued in state from the remnants of other drinks and all the barstool legs look like trees in the Black Forest of liver damage, then you drank too much that night. Plus, a barstool fall, like choking, is the result of something self-inflicted.

But seeing any person fall, especially a senior citizen, is a disturbing image. During yuletide at King Lear, festive decorations dominated the dining room, including a picturesque plethora of potted poinsettias. Set on the two steps that led to the upper room were a pair of Ty-sized poinsettias, whose leaves intertwined with the brass handrails in clandestine fashion. Some patrons would grab the top of the poinsettias instead of the handrails, always resulting in a fall. The leaves were far too delicate to offer support. Several times even the nimble Oso Blanco had grabbed a fistful of poinsettias and tripped, though I was usually agile enough to regain my balance. I still bellowed out a profanity inappropriate for the season that celebrated the birth of God's son, swearing vengeance upon the entire decorative horticulture industry.

I hated those bastard poinsettias, though my disdain was not shared by my fellow penguins. Most of the waiters were fond of small plants, especially those grown in the secrecy of an over-lit walk-in closet, whose harvested leaves, once dried, chopped, rolled and smoked, or brownie-battered, baked and bitten, brought tranquility, additional appetite, compromised judgment, diminished cerebral capability, and possible incarceration. Homegrown herbal supplements notwithstanding, I caught a half-dozen damsels and two or three knights when not falling myself.

The final straw, or last red leaf in this case, came when a ninety-year-old woman took a fall and no penguins or bussers were near enough to save her. Though the sweet old woman survived the trip uninjured, I abducted the plants and retreated to the kitchen, dismembering them like a tabby in need of exorcism. The distress of seeing an older person fall becomes a permanent disturbing recollection in your mind. In that instant, you regard every victim as if that person were your own mother, father, or grandparent whose pain you'd rather bear yourself than see them hurt or injured.

Heart attacks are more of a personal thing, with nutritional socialization, genetic predisposition, demographic origin, and sedentary disposition factoring in heavily. Why I didn't see more hearts explode at King Lear, I'll never know.

It was a normal roaring Thursday night and I was teamed with Nesbie for maître d' duty. Every table was filled, the bar was three deep, and a dozen parties were stacked on the waiting list. Marcel and Wally Gator were filling the air with Como and Sinatra while Roosevelt and Jody were turning liquor bottles upside down as fast as gravity could empty them. In the dining room, fifteen of the District's finest waiters were serving a couple hundred diners the finest food in Washington. All pistons were firing on a finely tuned engine, cruising all ahead full into well-traveled waters. Sound collision! The evening was about to run aground.

At Table 97, a corner table in the upper room that overlooked the three-walled private dining room (PDR) was a trio of Atlanta business types eating migs (filet mignons) and drinking Rinkelphaise Pinot Noir (a fetching red) when one of the WASPs turned blue, grabbed his shirt pocket, and fell over in his chair. Having just seated a nearby table, I heard the tink of his wine glass tipping over, walked over, glanced down, and saw a well-dressed man quaking on the floor with a swollen blue face and distressed eyes. Dashing for the podium phone, I fullbacked to the front with full authority to plow down anyone in my way. I dialed 911 and told the operator that we had a downed man having a heart attack, stroke, or vivid Cindy Crawford fantasy. The operator immediately dispatched an ambulance, and after throwing the facts at Nesbie I went outside and told Verner, who cleared the front curb of all customer cars. But in D.C., a fire truck always accompanies an ambulance, and in this case it was a hook and ladder, one of only two functioning hook and ladders in the District at the time. Since King Lear was a favorite place of the Police Chief, three cruisers listening in on the frequency also joined the party. Besides, checking out the action at King Lear was much more fun than busting crack addicts for breaking into cars looking for change. Inside, Little Boy Blue wasn't doing any better. Only a third of the dining room knew that something was wrong and the bar sheep were oblivious to everything except whether or not their glasses were half full or half empty and the thoracic contours of some of the bustier rental rogerettes.

Marcel and Wally kept playing, knowing that something was going on from the speed at which I ran to the front. Wally Gator was sharp as could be and looked at me while plucking his bass with curious eyes. I banged my chest once like a territorial gorilla and pointed up to Table 97. He nodded, knowing that either someone had just gotten their check or that Dick Cheney was in the house, and leaned over to inform Marcel. The two would extend their musical set until the paramedics had come and gone. I looked at my watch and not even three minutes later I heard the first of the protect-and-serve parade sirens that would jam the traffic on J Street. Within the next minute, an ambulance, hook and ladder, and three cop cars were parked in front of King Lear, with all their lights spinning and radios squawking. The emergency vehicles and cruisers also prevented Verner and his subordinate valets from retrieving any customer's vehicle, but no one wanted to miss the show anyway. All this commotion caused by a blue-faced, yellow-bellied, red-necked white boy from Blackshear, Georgia.

I waved to the EMTs and they grabbed their toolboxes and followed me in as we hastily marched up to Table 97. To my surprise, Blue Boy wasn't blue anymore, but a normal white boy color, as he had started to regain consciousness on his own. He was able to speak and it appeared as if he had shaken off the heart attack all by his lonesome. Joining the paramedics at Table 97 were four firemen with enough equipment to battle a lava flood at the base of Mt. Vesuvius, all in full gear including helmets, masks, oxygen tanks, rubber boots, coats with straps and buckles everywhere, and live radios transmitting static above the clatter.

One of the firemen even had an ax. What was this man planning to do with an ax? Was there a woman trapped in one of the ladies room stalls? Was there a customer having difficulty slicing his entrecôte? Had one of the penguins laid out a line of blow so big that it required a fire ax to cut it? We knew it was inevitable. Another firemen had a huge stretch of hose looped around his shoulder. Either there was a fire close by or someone was about to get a monster high colonic.

At this point Blue Boy was back to normal, conversing with the EMTs who had his shirt open as they checked his vitals. All this time the pointing and mouth-covering had been gaining momentum like an Ann Arbor stadium wave the third time around. The waiters were still attempting to serve food, but the EMTs, firemen, and warehouse full of equipment blocked all the critical lanes.

During the heart attack and subsequent attention, Blue Boy's tablemates just sat and drank their Rinkelphaise. Somehow this seemed wrong to me. "Wow, Myron had a heart attack. Umm, taste the gentle tannins, clues of pneumatic pressing, and suggestion of eucalyptus in this macerated masterpiece Pinot

Noir." At the same time, the bar train kept chugging on, no distraction aside from the absence of additional alcohol deterring the hardcore bar mongrels. There could have been a nuclear blast across the street and they would have kept on partying. "You know, I heard a blast and my face just melted, but what the fuck, I think I'll have another drink."

The best view of the action was had by the patrons in the private dining room, especially a table of twelve, six on a side, all twelve with a down-the-throat view of Blue Boy and the emergency personnel. There were two other tables of four in the PDR and those who could see were narrating for those who could not.

What was going to happen next? One would think that the EMTs would have plopped Boy Blue on a gurney, shoved his ass in the back of their ambulance, and sped off and away into the night. I'm afraid not. Doing so would have made far too much sense. An argument ensued between the paramedics and the kid with the exhausted heart.

EMT: "Sir, we can't force you to go to the hospital, but we strongly advise you to do so. Your vitals are stable, but you have an arrhythmia that needs to be checked out at the appropriate facilities."

Blue: "Nah, I'll see my doctor when I get back home."

EMT: "Sir, I think that's a bad decision given that you've just suffered a minor heart attack. We'd be happy to take you to the hospital as a precautionary measure."

Blue: "No, no. I'll be fine. I'm going directly to my hotel after dinner here and will catch the first plane to Atlanta in the morning."

Buds: "C'mon now, Myron, you should really do like the man says."

EMT: "Your friends are absolutely right. It's just for the night and we'll take you there. Sir, please, do the right thing here."

Blue: "No, No, No. I am just fine. I appreciate your concern but I'll be fine now and will see my doctor tomorrow back in Georgia."

The verbal tug-of-war only took a few minutes, but seemed like hours. The staff just wanted a decision made. Pick a course of action and do it. Go or don't go, stay and die, leave and live, live and die, eat and die later, drink and stay, sit and spin, just pick a fate and go with it and take Ancel Ax and Horatio Hosehelper with you.

The EMTs made Blue Boy sign some kind of release stating that he had been advised to go to the hospital and had refused. After another five minutes of packing and clacking, the emergency crew finally moseyed through the dining room and out the door to stow their gear in their trucks. Nesbie thanked the crews for coming, and as restaurant people should always do, invited them to stop in for a drink sometime. The commotion was almost over. Marcel and Wally got to rest their digits, the diners went back to dining, and even the frenzy of pointing and mouth covering almost disappeared. Unfortunately, the game wasn't over; it was only halftime.

The train was about to get moving again. The emergency crews were poised to unclog J Street and King Lear was climbing back to cruise altitude. The bar had never broken stride, though rumor surfaced that something had happened in the back room. So long as the door to the auxiliary liquor storage room wasn't blocked, all would be fine. Nothing ever slowed down King Lear's bar. If the Second Coming occurred during a full bar blitz, the flies would have said, "Can you tell Christ to wait? I mean, it's been two thousand years and all of a sudden now he shows up and expects me to leave my spot here at the bar. God damn, the guy gets crucified and thinks he owns the world."

Meanwhile, the faint-hearted man on Table 97 apparently had not gotten enough attention that evening, despite a dozen men and five vehicles answering the call when he first turned blue. The EMTs were just about to drive away. They had done their duty, run to a dying man's side, and begged him to go to the hospital. But he said no, he was fine, no medical care or hospital stays for this man, no way. Bad choice. *Heartache of the Gorgeous Georgian* was such a great movie, we were about to rewind it and watch it again. Angus the Shagger, Table 97's waiter, ran up to

Nesbie and said, "The bloke's having another heart attack!"

Nesbie burst out the front doors and ran beside the ambulance that was just about to roll away and said, "Hold on guys, the man's down again!" The head EMT pounded the dashboard with his fist before climbing out. He yelled out to Hoser and Question Axer and said, "Grab that fuckin' gurney, this motherfucker's going to the hospital even if I have to sedate his ass!"

Back into the restaurant came the paramedic parade, including firemen helpers with their gear, straps, buckles, restless radios, and yes, colonic hose and giant ax. I had visions that waiters should all carry axes. "This gratuity is unacceptable and you have three seconds to double it before I go Chuckie Manson on your wife. Capiche?"

Just as the EMTs and Axen Hosers made their return to Table 97, Blue Boy went from cobalt to ivory and was coming around again, shaking off his second heart attack in ten minutes. It mattered not. Even if Blue had pummeled Apollo Creed and cried out "Adrian," his ass was still leaving the restaurant en route to either a morgue, a hospital, or a dark alleyway. If the EMTs didn't do it, the staff would have. Watching the second wave of commotion were the private dining room patrons, still poised on the sidelines looking to see what would happen next. The EMTs again didn't need to perform CPR, though rechecked Blue's vitals just in case. The EMTs told Blue they were taking him to George Washington Hospital, only a few minutes from King Lear. Blue Boy was able to get in two syllables of objection that the head EMT refuted like a Saudi King scolding one of his harem who had barked out the Prince of Bahrain's name during passion's joust. "I don't . . ."

EMT: (Speaking at amphitheater volume in case Blue Boy's hearing ability was impaired by his twice faltering heart) "You have no choice this time! You're being taken to George Washington and that's the way it is."

The head EMT's eyes of stone let Blue know that if he argued the matter further, he'd be stabbed with a fat syringe of sodium pentothal. Blue Boy's fellow Rinkelphaise chums just kept on watching and drinking, reaffirming the waiter's theory that nothing combats chaos like a liquid pacifier. But Blue's tablemates were taking calm to an extreme. Either the heart-attacked man was an arch rival competitor in business or had a wife that looked like Faith Hill back at the hotel who would need a lot of comforting.

The firemen positioned the gurney next to Blue's table, lowered it and hoisted the man onboard. The upper half of the gurney was elevated so Blue Boy was sitting upright for the most part. The EMTs and firemen covered the man with a blanket, belted him in, and walked the gurney down the two steps to the main floor like Egyptians carrying a litter upon which Cleopatra was perched, except Cleo needed a shave and chest wax, and had been sweating from his fibrillating heart.

The situation was almost over, or so I thought. At the bottom of the two steps in front of the PDR, one of the EMTs paused to grab his toolbox. Blue Boy, looking at the table of twelve in the private dining room from his upright position, looked down, looked up, and after a momentary swelling of his cheeks, expelled his dinner. The PDR patrons, in unison, voiced a perfectly synchronized onomatopoetic cacophony of disgust, the puked projectiles of steak and mesclun clinging to Blue's blanket like ornaments on some kind of hideous Christmas tree.

The sight sealed the deal that I would never endeavor to be a paramedic and left me furious that Blue was too stubborn to go with the paramedics the first time around. Why couldn't this man have puked in the ambulance or hospital? Like a Frenchwoman's armpit, this night was getting hairier by the minute. No one cared what happened to this man, his twin heart attacks, stubborn southern attitude, and projectile vomiting having stymied any compassion previously held in the healthy hearts of all the other people at King Lear that night.

The head EMT was now full-gone livid, turning a furious red faster than the guy on the gurney had twice turned blue. One of the firemen unbuckled the gurney seatbelt while another rolled up the emulsion-soiled wrap and looked for a staff lateral. I motioned one of the busmen to grab it, and the disgusted busser scowled at me before taking the hand-off. The busser first headed to the pantry garbage can, then thought the matter through and zipped outside to pitch the enzyme-engulfed blankie into the dumpster.

As Blue Boy was wheeled through the dining room, he was eyeballed by all he passed. Nesbie, again, thanked the EMTs for their efforts as we held open the doors to hasten the heart attacker's departure. The next inclination Nesbie and I had was to chug a cocktail, but order had to be restored to this little western town. Evicting the troublemaker was a good start.

All the staff, with the exception of the musicians, were now buried in anxious diners and their back-logged dinners. The kitchen had an avalanche of orders already plated and in desperate need of serving. The paramedical roadblock had dammed the waiter highway, plus, smart penguins don't tell oversized firemen with axes to "get the fuck outta the way." In the kitchen, waiting steaks and chops were now overcooked from being held so long and would have to be tossed and redone, only adding to the stress levels. The bar had been maintaining its own, as it always did, just as long as it stayed stocked.

Constantine's command post was a prime seat at the bar and Nesbie had kept him advised of all the events during *Heartstop and Sputter, Parts I* and *II.* Our revered owner told Nesbie to bring the private dining room patrons a few bottles of wine to ease their vomit trauma, which he did—four bottles of Sailor's Choice Syrah, the preferred wine of Tacoma slumlords and blind Biloxi jazz musicians, a month older in vintage than the Wal-Mart wine.

The worst of the buried employees were the valets, still waiting for the hook and ladder to unclog the street so they could retrieve the two-dozen cars now demanded from patrons who had finished their meals, saw the show, and were ready to go. Incoming calls had overwhelmed King Lear's switchboard, forcing Nesbie to put all five telephone lines on hold.

We often did this when inundated with calls from the lifeless bastards who call amidst the dinner rushes. One reason for doing so was to force the callers to ponder why the phones were busy during the dinner jam. Think. Concentrate. I know you can get this one. Why do you keep getting a busy signal at King Lear when you call during the dinner rush? Think some more, I just gave you the answer in the previous sentence. Still don't know? My God you're pathetic, I'm calling social services to have your children and pets removed from your home.

When callers did connect, we would never say that there had just been a medical emergency or that the Virgin Mary had just been spotted in the bottom of a V.O. Rob Roy, we would simply say it was busy. The unwritten rule when working as the answer-bitch/matrix was never to dispense information, only to collect it. If you did dispense information, you gave out erroneous information. This rule applied to our in-house patrons and out-house pedestrians, too.

On this night there were many outside onlookers who were curious as to what was going on and Nesbie told a few of them that a doctor had just performed an emergency appendectomy on top of the Steinway.

On any given night, the most common question asked was whether any celebrities were present, to which we would always say that some legend had just left. "Yeah, Yul Brynner just finished his meal at the table next to you." "Wait a minute, he died a long time ago." "Yeah, well, that's what he wants people to think so they won't hassle him so much. He left to go drink with a guy named Benny, who used to work here." "Wow, did you hear that Enid? Yul Brynner!"

Slowly though, the staff was climbing out of the weeds and King Lear was getting back to normal ops. The business chums kept drinking, now on their third bottle of Pinot Noir, unaffected by the removal of their twice attacked and once removed tablemate. Much wine makes for a brave face, however melty.

An hour or so later, many of the departing patrons inquired as to how Blue Boy had fared; fine and dandy, we later learned. In the upper corner of the dining room was a woman who had hosted a party and demanded free dinner for herself and guests. "We shouldn't have to pay for this meal because of all the nonsense with the paramedics and such ruining the atmosphere!" Her table was situated at the opposite end of the upper room from Table 97, and they had received their entrees before Blue Boy's first color change. Incredulous, I said, "Excuse me, Mrs. Dooshawitz.

A man suffers a heart attack and you want a free meal?" Where's that ax? A chronic problem with some spoiled regulars in privately owned restaurants is that they feel they are owed something for being consistent regulars and are constantly searching for something for free. Constantine refused to comp any part of the whining matriarch's bill, though she retaliated nonetheless by tipping Sinclair only a fifty on her six hundred dollar check. But that's the way some people operate, and Sinclair said he was surprised she left him that. All you can do is live, learn, and endure.

That was the third of three strikes against Mavis Dooshawitz. Once she had insisted that a dining room patron not drink his beer direct from the bottle, as he was doing. She demanded "Go tell that man to pour his beer in a glass! How awfully rude." The penguins refused, instead offering the man free wine and hookers if he drank direct from a wine bottle in front of Dooshie. Then there was the glengarry spat. There was an older regular customer, Dewey Zorn, who often dined at King Lear wearing an Orioles baseball cap. The penguins knew why, but such information was privileged. If in King Lear concurrently, Mrs. Dooshawitz went nuts, telling the waiters to have Mr. Zorn remove his hat when in the dining room. We refused, and finally Mavis sprang up, marched over to Mr. Zorn and insisted he take his hat off, saying that his hat-wearing ways insulted all the other diners. Dewey fish-eyed Mavis, then removed his hat, revealing spotty patches of hair loss indicative of intense chemotherapy. He said, "I'm sorry ma'am, but I have lymphoma and the treatments are making my hair fall out. So if you don't mind, I'd rather keep the cap on, if that's okay with you." Dooshawitz, shocked, apologized to Dewey, and then deflected all the blame on the waiters, trying to vilify the penguins for her misdeeds. "You should have told me! Why didn't you tell me?" Mitch, her waiter that evening, responded, "I'm afraid that's not our place to say. And I'm damn certain it's none your business anyhow. And it's obvious you've made Mr. Zorn feel bad. And he already has enough bad feelings to worry about without your little comments. If you have any complaints, about me or Mr. Zorn, you can go talk to Clay or Constantine." Mitch was never shy about speaking his mind.

And finally are those in restaurants who get burned. Kitchen crew hourly hounds don't count because they get burned so often they hardly blink, using more burn gel than deodorant (well, actually, they use more frankincense than deodorant, but that's another matter). And in the dining room you have finger-singed customers and toupee flambè mishaps, the fires further fueled by the hens who sloshed on White Diamonds like hurricane seawater. **Note:** *King Lear's training manual stated that Bananas Foster was so-named because the children of the first man to attempt making this flaming dessert inferno ended up orphaned and in foster care.* But the worst burning witnessed as a manservant happened to me when myself and a few other waiters were figuratively burned after making an assumption.

Five guys, 35-65, came in for dinner at Romeo Charlie's with a lone, *muy caliente* woman, a dirty blonde chambermaiden, drinking red apple martinis at a pledge bet clip, and wearing, of all things, a screaming, snare-drum-tight Hustler tee shirt that barely covered the twins. There was no doubt to the staff, this was a hired ride. (Escorts are quickly spotted, especially when, an hour into the meal, the man asks, "Now what's your name again?" After the lovin', the renters are quickly spotted too, usually with STD lesions). Partying like a lotto winner, the entire dining room noticed the Hustler girl, while in the prep station, we waiters cast our judgments. "Those gamecocks are gonna pile on her like jack cheese on nachos!" "Oh yeah, those boys are gonna enter her like the Holy Land." "They're goin' tap that ass like the first keg of Oktoberfest." "There's a party in her pants and everyone's invited!" "They goin' go Kobe on that thing." And even me, so sure, saying "No doubt, gentlemen. Those dudes are going to pass her around like cranberry sauce at Christmas dinner. And yes, there will be seconds!" But we couldn't have been more wrong. When I dropped the check, Hustler girl whipped out an Amex Platinum card, for as it turned out, she was the owner of a lucrative Lamborghini dealership in southern Cal, and the five doting boys were her employees. We had all been burned by assumption; a sucker-punch helping of humble pie for the entire staff, though we ate it with a smile.

DATE 8o

TO: John

FROM: Laura

☐ NOTE AND RETURN   ☐ FOR YOUR APPROVAL
☒ NOTE AND SEE ME   ☒ FOR YOUR INFORMATION
☐ NOTE AND FILE/DISCARD   ☐ FOR YOUR SIGNATURE
☐ NOTE AND FORWARD   ☒ PLEASE ANSWER
☒ INVESTIGATE AND REPORT   ☐ PREPARE REPLY FOR ME
☐ PER YOUR REQUEST   ☒ GET MORE DETAILS
☐ TAKE APPROPRIATE ACTION ☐ PER OUR CONVERSATION
☐ ....   ☐ ....

COMMENTS:

you won't
play bar with
me! ☹

09 DM 9078 PRINTED IN U.S.A. NOV 71—TRANSMITTAL

Chapter 14

Bivouac at the Bar
(remember Victoria Snelgrove)

"Now John at the bar is a friend of mine
He gets me my drinks for free
And he's quick with a joke or to light up your smoke
But there's someplace that he'd rather be."

Billy Joel, "Piano Man," *Piano Man,*
Sony Music Entertainment, 1973

The over-quoted proverb "whatever doesn't kill you makes you stronger" has no applicability to bars and the hermits who dwell in them. A more fitting adage would be "whatever doesn't kill you or leave you unconscious allows you to drink some more and kiss away your money and allotted days on planet earth." A bar is a poor man's club where people can retreat into their darker desires and collectively fix their fixes. Excessive drinking, chain smoking, runaway gambling, drug abuse, and infidelity are just a few of the vices that thrive inside the moldy Petri dish that is the confines of a bar.

Perhaps the primary sin is wasted time, whose party tally is recorded by the trench lines on your face. There was so much more you could have done with your life while you sat and fermented at your favorite watering hole. You could have worked a few extra hours to reduce your debts. You could have spent some time at the gym so that you might live past fifty-five. You could have visited your father, who is completing his life's journey alone because you can't tear yourself away from that cocktail. You could have taken flowers to your mother's grave, picked the weeds, dusted off the marker, and closed your eyes in grateful reflection of the woman whose sacrifice is the reason you exist. You could have played catch with your son or helped your daughter with her algebra, or vice versa. You could have made dinner for your wife, who, unlike you, is working late trying hard to make things better. You could have gone hiking with your dog and stopped along the trail to admire the magnificence of a sparrow's nest. You could have donated the clothing you'll never fit into again to a local church or worked a few hours in a soup kitchen. You could have even watched the news. But no. You elected to sit and get plastered.

After your third drink, you suddenly have the answers to everything in life. You are the authority on all things great and small, the bar's very own Friedrich Nietzsche of knowledge and your brethren drunkards around you are forced to listen to your musings because they don't want to abandon their drink or barstool. Besides, they'll have ample time to spout their own answers to the universe once you pause to sip or signal the tender for another. Another fiber that will come together to form the rope that is your three-decade-long suicide lasso. The sober truth is you don't know *any*thing about everything. If you were as intelligent and disciplined as you claim, you'd realize that your liver is the size of a doormat, and the only exercise you get is when you stumble to the head to piss away the fifth of Drambuie you just drank. The entire staff hates you and no one gives a shit about anything you have to say. It's all a lie and your life is a colossal waste.

Nothing good happens in a bar. It's only a haven for people who are cowards when it comes to the matter of life itself. Maybe a drink or two is fine here and there, but you spend ten hours a week or better in bars. You look like Joe Cocker and drive like Toonces, and your life is messier than a Wal-Mart parking lot.

Charles Street's bar was a Plexiglass square surrounded by wooden seats that curved upward on both ends to make falling off less likely. This wasn't a guarantee that people wouldn't fall off of their barstools, but it reduced the numbers. The dayflies of historic Old Town would walk to Charles Street, which was commendable. Once drunk, or drunker, these patrons could walk home and possibly spare a few lives by not having tried to operate an automobile. If all of the world's flies did their drinking within foot or public transportation distance of their homes, coroners and cops would find their workloads greatly reduced. The Charles Street dayflies would spend noon to six drinking Hefeweizens and eating fried oyster sandwiches, then migrate home to pass out watching prime time television. As for how they earned an income, I have no idea. Either they had a successful sibling, moved back in with their parents, or won a malpractice settlement when their dentist drilled the wrong chomper.

At night, the rookie drinkers took to Charles Street's tavern, a yuppie menagerie. The Alexandria males were very stereo-typical, practice squad players from the Abercrombie and Finch farm club, all wearing pleated J. Crew khaki pants with cuffed hems, brown woven belts, blue button-down Tommy Hilfie shirts, penny loafers with coins, combed back mousse-abused hair, and Achilles' dipped in lethal amounts of CK stinkwater. The lads would lean on something, suck a Sam Adams and scope the prairie for gullible girls with tight asses.

The women were equally predictable. Mostly blondes (some forced, some natural), with triple-pierced ears, excessive make-up, high cheekbones, and blouses opened up just enough to get the testosterone flowing. Most chewed gum and all smoked cigarettes. Since the girls wouldn't eat, or stuffed their index fingers down their throats when they did, they needed something to suppress their hunger. That something was invariably a carton of Marlboro Lights. They would stop into Charles Street with just enough money for one drink, their second round provided compliments of any male with whom they made suggestive eye contact. Additional rounds would be bought and consumed at Chadwick's over biographical discourse, though usually the women would tease the lads just enough to make them think they had a chance and then collectively fake a visit to the restroom and bolt for the door, off to an all-night District mosh pit where the male patrons could offer them more to titillate their senses than just Marlboros and Fat Tire Amber Ale.

The most amazing event I ever witnessed at Charles Street Chop House's bar happened when a couple of ripped cavemen got into a heated verbal exchange. At the zenith of the debate, one of the arguers proclaimed, "I bet $100 I can knock you out with one punch." The unknown puncher was making a bad bet. The taker of the bet was Clark Carrolton, a stocky, Lagerfeld-abusing contractor from the Bronx that no man could knock out even if he had allowed an unabated blow with a four-foot iron ingot. Carrolton retorted, "You're on, fucker!" Both threw down a Francois and marched outside in the rain to answer the question that has baffled scientists for ten centuries—could one toasted dolt knock out another with a single punch?

Word spread like wildfire and suddenly two stories of dining came to a standstill, all of Charles Street's windows fogged with the breath of pressed faces struggling to watch the donnybrook. Only the contenders were outside in the rain.

Carrolton stood at attention ready to take the hurt, jaws locked and lips tightly clenched to protect his teeth as his now drenched head swayed back and forth from his beer buzz. The puncher stood at limb's length, drawing back his arm like a bow, ready to deliver the punch. A split second before striking, the hitter noticed that Carry had his eyes firmly shut. Rethinking his punch approach, the hit man hastily retreated twenty feet then took a straight-armed mad dash at Carrolton's face. The puncher's silhouette looked like an ATF battering ram about to crash a Compton crack factory. The hitter struck Carrolton's ugly mug with full authority, knocking him down, but not out.

The force of the blow caused Carry to forget the agreed upon rules of engagement and he sprang up from the bricks to return the hurt. The two fought and struggled in the rain until a couple of Alexandria's finest handcuffed both without question and carted them away for a night in the gulag. The only winner of the argument was the bartender, who made a quick $200 minus the cost of a pair of unpaid bar tabs.

The Coventry may have had one of the more civilized bars in Washington, though the aforementioned adjective and noun are rarely seen in the same sentence. There was just too much direct sunlight flooding the Coventry's main bar to attract any career drinkers. The Coventry didn't have any regular lush customers, or larcenous pourboys who made lushes want to drink their fixes there. The Coventry's bar wasn't comfortable, nor did it offer concealment, the most important attributes sought by professional alcoholics. Every aspect of the Coventry somehow pertained to aesthetics; its bar was highly visible and overlit, making it no place to be clandestine. Binge drinkers are like sleazy southern preachers. The physical qualities they demand in a bar are the same ones a Bible Belt Baptist bellower looks for in a motel when seeking the proper place to defile a trusting choirgirl. No black-belted whiskeyfish ever floundered long at the Coventry.

At the other end of the spectrum was King Lear's bar, an ever-changing enigma of thirst, lust, powder, smoke, power, deception, and debauchery. No innocence here, only iniquity. King Lear's bar was an alcoholic's Mecca, with more flies than a fresh prairie pie, because it had all the qualities an all-pro booze-hound looks for in a second home.

First, it was dark and windowless. You never want too much light in a bar. The things you see might frighten you: blood shot eyes, jaundiced teeth, grooved crow's feet, nicotine-dried skin, and a groggen gang of obliterated desperados who are hard-pressed to remember their mother's maiden names. A bar isn't a health spa, but instead, in fact, a death-accelerating chamber. The boozer's idea of healthy is the celery stalk in his fifth Bloody Mary.

Second on the bar checklist is comfort, and King Lear's bar was comfortable. There were brass railings along the top of the bar, which reduced the number of spilled drinks, and black leather stools around three sides of a giant rectangle so all the King's sots could park their mushy asses and inspect one another as they sipped, sat, and slobbered. Some of the leather stools had brass nameplates on the back in memory of fellow flies who had either passed on or drank enough bourbon to float a Carnival Cruise ship. Is it not disturbing to think that a person's most-remembered life accomplishment was their twenty-year tenure intoxicated on a barstool?

Third on the tavern checklist was secrecy, and King Lear's bar offered its fish the utmost secrecy and refuge. Suspicious wives were constantly calling in search of their AWOL husbands who hadn't been to work in days. "No, ma'am, haven't seen your husband in quite some time. Yul Brynner is here, but your husband ain't." The truth was her work-missing mate was right in front of us, drunk out of his mind, touting his gridiron losers, and pondering a rental-rogering. But, the penguins weren't about to give up a regular no matter how repulsed. He enabled us to pay our rent; the inquiring wife just wasted our time. If you think your husband is blind-blitzed and chasing strange tang, then surely he is and you could have better spent your change calling a lawyer and locksmith instead of the restaurant, wasting everybody's time.

Familiarity is yet another vital factor in bar desirability. The King's penguins and tenders knew everything about their cavalcade of gin kittens, from their pill habits and annual tax frauds to the countless times they begged the owner's girlfriend to meet them at the Willard, and we aren't talking cribbage and chamomile tea in the courtyard. Setting the best examples of customer familiarity for both fly and diner regulars were Constantine and Clay. They could meet you once, and three months later would recall your name and greet you like a college classmate. This alone made people want to run back to King Lear, being chummed by two such dynamic men who were legends of Washington commerce and hospitality.

But truly, the single most important aspect to any place of social gathering is the presence of women. Women make any undesirable place desirable, be it hospitals and grocery check-out lines or courtrooms and sporting events. King Lear offered the gamut as far as female regulars, and no lonely pony need drink alone when lapping from the liquor trough at the King

Lear corral.

King Lear's most beautiful woman was Melissa Simmons, Constantine's long-time girlfriend and absolute favorite dame of everyone. Melissa was the complete package and nothing short of stunning, absolutely drink-dropping fine. Intimidatingly tall and Claudia Schiffer-ish in appearance, Melissa was a retired model who had gotten her start after becoming the original Allegheny Beer girl. When she entered King Lear, all heads turned as this glowing Amazon goddess lit up the room. All she needed was a spear and an attitude. Though many years younger than Constantine, the two made for a very sharp Park Avenue-looking couple. Melissa, as well as being exceptionally attractive, was also gregarious and sharp-witted, making her all the more attractive. But, in the presence of a beautiful woman, men tend to show their true colors, none of which are found in a rainbow. Some of the pathetic regulars were weasels, constantly hitting on Melissa behind Constantine's back, thinking that no one knew about their attempted passes and propositions. The fact that Constantine had been a noble friend to these louses and was always picking up their dinner tabs and buying drinks didn't matter. To them Melissa was irresistible and they just had to try and put their hands in the cookie jar.

It's only a matter of fact that some men have no sense of right, wrong, trust, honor, or ethics, and listen only to their pleading libidos whose argument becomes more convincing with every sip of Mojito. Even Nesbie had put a full-court press on Melissa, his own boss' girlfriend, betraying one of the finest men in Washington and jeopardizing his own family, home, and livelihood.

To Melissa's credit, she gracefully endured and deflected the advances made by the lower orders. And to all those bad boys out there who thought that Constantine didn't know about your backstabbing ways, you were wrong. He knew, along with all the other wretched details of your miserable existences. The penguins knew, too, even voting on whether or not to bash your asses into oblivion. Although Constantine had always said to avoid confrontation, there are some things in life you hate yourself for not doing.

The second finest siren of King Lear was Maye Stallworth, wife of Congressional printing kingpin Paul Stallworth. Maye was a gorgeous, ample-bosomed bombshell with Nordic cheeks and light brown hair. Like Melissa, she turned every head in the room and even caused Marcel and Wally to miss a few notes. Paul, like Constantine, was also a well-polished gentleman and with Maye, made for the marquee couple of King Lear. The Stallworths were exactly the type of couple Clay and Constantine wanted in their bar: attractive, successful, stylish, and intelligent. Of all the wedded pairs who spent happy hours at King Lear, the Stallworths were the undisputed favorites.

Like Melissa, Maye had many male admirers, the most notorious being Jamie Turk, a crude-mouthed mutant who owned a construction company. He was better known from his days as collegiate guard for the Nebraska Cornhuskers twenty years earlier. Turk liked to drink and yak in Georgetown, but did some of his quenching and gazing at King Lear, along with a few fellow cavemen. One of his favorite directions to look was any magnetic heading in the way of Maye, which he did like a hungry leopard, waiting for the right time to jump a gemsbok. One night Turk voiced his desires, swaggering up to Maye with a proposition that resulted in Paul shoving the woolly mammoth without considering the ten inches, hundred pounds, and eighty-four notches of ugly in Turk's favor. Avoiding any further confrontation, Turk retreated to his ape entourage, though he smiled back at Paul and opened up his jacket just enough to show the Stallworths that he had a gun tucked under his belt. Though terrified, the Stallworths calmly elected not to leave the bar until Turk and his posse departed, thinking that he wouldn't fire a gun in the middle of a crowed bar.

Turk and his mates soon did leave, and it was the last time he would ever set foot in King Lear. Turk was killed three nights later, shot in the face at a local club after propositioning another man's wife. A man who also had a gun. The court's ruling was self-defense.

Catherine Cullen Bryant was yet another ravishing fawn,

though far too refined and articulate to be appreciated by the flies. This was because the average sot was much like a dog and regarded women in the same fashion. They didn't care about your pedigree, who walked you, if you could speak, or even if you had your shots; all they wanted was to smell your ass and possibly lick themselves. Catherine was a descendant of famous author William Cullen Bryant and proud member of DAR, Daughters of the American Revolution. She was extremely attractive in a subtle way with fair skin, light blond hair, and delicate swept-back features. She always dressed in conservative business attire. She worked days as a paralegal and would enjoy a couple glasses of Viognier before catching the Orange Line home to Falls Church. Her grace and elegance left her out of place in King Lear's bar. She never used profanity nor considered playing ribald damsel for free kibble.

This wasn't true with most of the bar's lookers and hookers. Lear's bar hags tended to be the worst offenders when it came to the art of El Paso trucker mouth, and as for a fine meal, most wouldn't think twice about playing lay-down Sally.

Catherine was also a favorite of the Mob and union heads, to whom King Lear was a second home. The zooters knew the rules with Catherine and invited her to dinner for the sake of having an attractive and cerebral woman at their table, not as concubine for a repugnant, under-laid hitter. She wasn't a fish to sleep with and didn't care to know who was sleeping with the fishes.

Another of Catherine's alluring attributes was that she wasn't a loquacious Cathy, unlike the majority of the verbose lady flies who just wouldn't clam-up no matter how much you begged and pleaded. They couldn't help it. After you've had eight Cosmopolitans and stuffed your nose with a half-dime of District dust, you're going to tend to yak like Nicole Richie on a Red Bull high.

The possibility for companionship abounds in a bar and King Lear's community speakeasy was no exception. This was true for both penguins and patrons. I wasn't inclined to taste any of the over-handled fruit. Many of the casabas had really been passed around, and often suffered from social phylloxera, dropped, bruised, kicked, or half-eaten. But Catherine wasn't a blabbing, weathered alcoholic, but instead, was conservative, shy, and never out of control. She wasn't married and not seeing anyone at the time, so I quietly asked her out and discretely we began dating.

I kept things quiet because when a penguin started seeing a new woman, the other staffers just wanted to know one thing. Did you take her to Poke Town and how long before she let you? It was locker room talk at its lowest level and if you dated a woman too long before getting the goods, you'd be mocked as some kind of hideous failure. "What, two dinners and you still ain't had that juicy fruit? Damn, pimp. What the hell is wrong with you? You should be working on the break-up by now." Guys like Preston, Mason, and Dante only made matters worse by forever boasting how quickly and maliciously they could copulate with a new woman, a game of numbers with bonus points awarded for efficiency, corporal punishment, and additional personnel tagged during the same session. Points were deducted for daffodils and back rubs. So unbeknownst to anyone, Catherine and I went on seeing one another, no penguin or patron ever the wiser. But before long, and in a single sentence, Catherine and I were history. I was over at her house one evening and noticed that she had a battery-operated female sex toy in her nightstand drawer. "Why do you have a Sonicare toothbrush in your night stand? And there's no brush attachment. Oh, never mind." I asked her if DAR women received group discounts on such items. Her last two words to me were, "Get out!" I guess I struck an oversensitive erogenous nerve. She never called me again and I wasn't about to apologize for my playful remark.

A December-May relationship is a sorry sight. A powerful and wealthy man with a young and beautiful woman. If the man doesn't have money or the woman doesn't have youth and looks, the deal doesn't fly. Methuselah could be repulsively ugly with halitosis that could kill livestock and the lady could be as stupid as a sack of dead chipmunks, but so long as each played their role, all worked out well. Or so they thought. It's a type of long-term prostitution agreement with many sad aspects.

First is the salacious old geezer, afraid to confront his own mortality and haunted by the guilt of a life full of selfish misconduct. He jettisoned his loving wife of thirty years to be with a girl he has nothing in common with, a child bride younger than his own kids. He was born the same year Calvin Coolidge became president, and she crawled out of the womb the same year Elvis passed on. Though obvious, the aged fellow refuses to recognize the facts of the matter. His grand-daughter bride has to chew Valiums just to tolerate his touch; youthwife is secretly grinding on a Terrapin sophomore five times a week, has Glad Bags of Crosby twigs hidden all over the house, and tokes up post-thrust with her Maryland second-year while Cash Daddyo is out searching for the golf ball he sliced into next month.

The girl has mastered the science of usury, and is smart enough to know that if she fakes her orgasms, makes coffee in the nude, and tells her cash cow that fat, stinking, dirtbag, wretched old captains of industry like him make her mop-up moist, then all of her monetary dreams will come true.

The fieriest of the King Lear's December-Mays was the twelve-five of Krista Cabot and Brooks McClellan. McClellan was a sixty-eight-year-old control freak who had made his millions installing and fixing hydraulic autolifts throughout the Washington area. McClellan refused to get a divorce and sell the house for fear of the financial flogging he would have taken. A clean break would have even cost him his business. He had four children, all with children themselves, all opposed to his betrayal of their mother for a girl who could have mathematically been his granddaughter. Or his great granddaughter if calculated through King Lear busboy procreative ages. Krista was twenty-four and was a gorgeous, black-haired, porcelain-skinned, Sofia Coppola clone who lived in a magnificent Pentagon City penthouse apartment compliments of McClellan, who spent two nights a week there huffing and puffing.

The two frequented King Lear on a weekly basis, drinking at the bar for a few hours so the old man could show off his trophy. After a few elixirs and facades at the bar, the two would embark on a leisurely dinner, a meal that would start with civility and end in hostility. The penguins had never seen Mrs. McClellan, but had heard thousands of angry references to her. The most common was an irritated Krista demanding to McClellan, "Divorce your wife and marry me!" The old man was forever trying to calm Krista down, usually with success, but not until half the dining room was privy to McClellan's infidelity. Krista had barked out "Divorce your wife and marry me" so many times that it became a running joke with the waiters and maître d's. Just as *"You are the sunshine of my life"* identifies Steveland Judkins Hardaway from Saginaw, Michigan, "Divorce your wife and marry me" was the phrase that identified Krista and the money fogey.

McClellan wasn't about to divorce his wife and say au revoir to his money, chateau, and business, but he was going to keep eating his cake so long as Krista wanted the three-thousand-square-foot penthouse rent-free roof over her head. The two kept fighting with great predictability and the staff stayed amused. Krista even struck McClellan on several occasions, once with a pay phone receiver that gave the old man a cut that required several sutures to close. The waiters speculated that when she delivered the Ma Bell blow, Krista said something like, "Brooks, the phone's for you." (Wham!)

Another time the two came in with all the windows broken on Father Time's Maserati. McClellan claimed someone had tried to steal his car. Perhaps it was the most indecisive thief in grand theft auto history.

Not long after the window-bashing incident, Krista asked me out to lunch, taking me by surprise to say the least. I had served the demonstrative duo on several occasions. I accepted her invitation. We cabbed it over to the Red Sage and a light lunch turned into a two-bottle afternoon. We taxied back to King Lear and just before I hopped out of the car, Krista gave me a Casablanca kiss that left me speechless, the foreword of a *9 1/2 Weeks*-esque Penthouse letter. I wasn't complaining. No man not living in the Bay Area would have. I had been commissioned Roman Tub Commodore of her rubber ducky fleet. No one could know, most of all my penguin brethren. If I told two, then they'd tell two friends, and they'd tell two friends, and so on and so forth until by the end of the week some stranger would call me from Azerbaijan to ask how the tryst with Krista was going.

Though uninformed, my fellow waiters had their suspicions. The fixed grin on my otherwise serious countenance filled them full of wonder. McClellan could never find out. He was an angry NRA hardware carrier without the added mental angst of the thought of someone else hammering his glockenspiel, his jealous senility on permanent simmer.

When they were at King Lear, he never let Krista out of his sight, only using the litter box when she did, so as not to leave his thunderkitten unattended at the bar, defenseless among the tanked encroachers. When out of town on business, he called Krista with cuckoo frequency, trying to keep tabs on his Bo Peep, who was taking the call in a compromised position, a vision that would have made him swallow his bridgework. Though secretive in my actions, I didn't feel I was wrong to see Krista; all encounters, calls, and areola tuning occurred outside the confines of King Lear. I was single, as was she. I was only six years older than Krista, unlike the grey goat whose age was a few orbits shy of a half-century-older. But it mattered not, untrusting McClellan suspected his princess of something and hired a private detective to confirm his hunches. This made undetected encounters with Krista even more difficult.

Unable to catch his cat on the moon fence, McClellan finally gave Krista an above average beating, resulting in several vivid dark bruises on her lily fair skin. Krista insisted no lapse in fidelity and never mentioned my name, but Daddy Bankbook didn't buy it. Krista was also smiling more than usual. She refused to go the police to have her golden boy locked up, and I could see the ugly conclusion of this sordid triangle had I persisted in seeing Krista.

In life, intelligent people look down future's road to see how a situation unfolds. Everyone has the ability to do it, though few have the courage, and even fewer possess the spine to change. Deadbeats will never pay their child support, dopeheads will always fire up the magic, and desperate lovers hoping for their mates to change will die unfulfilled, their only recourse being the Madison County walk.

In this situation, the task of changing fell upon me, as it was clear that Krista and McClellan would keep on living as they had, one with unlikely hopes, the other with a cauldron full of insecurity, paranoia, and increasing distress at the thought of his ever-nearing mortality. Overcome with a sense of sensibility, I ended my classified run with Krista, the stealaway sessions not worth McClellan's further physical venting or the increasing likelihood of firearm discharge. Krista and I remained quiet friends for a while, but we lost touch after I left for flight training. She stayed with her old man, hoping against the odds that McClellan would cut the cord with his wife and betroth her, something that wouldn't happen.

There was another woman that most all of the penguins had seen naked on a regular basis. She was a tall, brown-eyed, black-haired stripper named Zeauie Morrison who shed her threads daily at *See Biscuits,* a sticky-floored tavern where the noon drunkards gathered to imbibe and drivel. Zeauie's husband, Lenny Morrison, was an older, wiry, introverted nicotine fitter, fresh from a five-year stint at Sing Sing. He had taken the fall for a politician's misdeeds, and in exchange for being a mop bucket swabbie for five to ten, received a seven-figure briefcase full of redirected, unreformed campaign finance funds. The hard time of doing hard time was very apparent on Lenny's face. Though only fifty-seven, he looked seventy-seven. Despite the difficult incarceration he had just endured, he was a pleasant man to serve: quiet, polite, and extremely likable. Zeauie was also likable, even when clothed, and extremely shy. Shyness is an uncommon trait among exotic dancers. Most civilized rules of society don't apply to strippers and the chimpanzees who admire them. You can pretty much do or say anything to an exotic dancer so long as the price is right and the terms are mutually agreed upon or pimp arbitrated.

This was not the case with Zeauie, she was a stripper and stripper only, and any and all extracurricular activities were strictly forbidden by Lenny. No rubbing, no lap dances, no copping a feel and blaming the Jim Beam, no thousand dollar pleas to fellate all five groomsmen. Look but don't touch; that's the way it was.

But there were many naughty chaps drinking at King Lear who had seen naked, shaking Zeauie a few hours earlier down the street. Seeing Mrs. Morrison having a drink at King Lear, these blitzed boys would invariably try to buy some satisfaction. To such uninformed mooks, Lenny would offer one clear and concise warning, any further persistence being met with resistance by one or both of Lenny's oversized prison pals, Terrel and Sammy, who always drank with the Morrisons. Most of the men endeavoring to prostitute Zeauie got the message on the first take, though I recall three who did not. One fine gentleman was escorted to the coatroom by Sammy where mere words convinced him to rethink his impropriety. This frightened lad even apologized to Zeauie. Another, a greasy, pig-mannered, penguin-despised Russian with AFLAC goose verbal acuity, shoved Lenny over in his barstool. Lenny's head missed the piano by inches, and the hard surface would have surely caved in Lenny's skull. The Bolshevik bastard was jumped by several waiters and customers, battering-rammed against and out the front door and promised extensive pain and injury should he show his face again in King Lear. The third lad propositioned Zeauie when Lenny stepped away to buy a pack of Viceroys. Terrel put his hand on the man's shoulder and said, "Leave the lady alone, that's my friend's wife." The man ignorantly replied, "Get your hands off of me, nigger!" The entire bar hushed and all looked around for the foolish mouth that had uttered such a dangerous phrase. Even more dangerous was to whom it had been uttered—a racially sensitive gentleman who had spent the last ten years doing crunches, curls, and bench presses. In a tranquil and collected tone, Terrel asked the offender to step outside, and the man agreed. No one dared follow, and a minute later only Terrel returned. Verner saw the outside exchange and told the penguins that after a few more inflammatory phrases, the aggressor shoved Terrel. Terrel answered the uncalled-for epithets and shoving with a single right jab to the man's abdomen. It was a Holyfield-style punch so intense it dropped the man to his knees, made his tongue protrude, and most probably ruptured his spleen and collapsed a lung or two. He was never seen again.

But most eager dicks with dinero could find a rental ride somewhere on King Lear's used car lot. What you drove depended on how much you wanted to spend.

The older models were cheaper, roomier, less responsive, and poorly maintained, some with a few missing screws and torn pink slips, and all had bottomless tanks forever in need of filling. Each required an air freshener and you could bet they'd be smoking after the ride. The vintage models also tended to be noisier, both on and off the lot, and everyone would know if you had been in a jalopy the night before. But even the low-end rentals made the fuzzy dice swing.

The mid-range models hadn't been driven as much and needed less body work, though all still had dents and scratches from reckless renters. They cost more money and needed higher octane to make them run smoothly, but their performance justified the expenditure. There was one Bavarian model in particular that liked to be driven on the opposite side of the road that no man could seem to turn on. But the unknown is often quite arousing, and even hard-to-start rentals were fun to ride once you got them turned over.

The top of the line was like Bordeaux wine, velvet to the touch and smooth like a Stylistics' song. They would take only premium and the payment would be huge, but their engines ran hot, and the ride would be unforgettable. And your wife would never know you'd been around the beltway.

The Penguin's favorite low-rent platypus was Mary Oakley, referred to by the staff as Typhoid Mary, best friend of Dawn Ho, the mouthy maiden who couldn't pay for her drinks unless kneeling. You didn't have to be an NTSB investigator to inspect her black box. You could ride through her tunnel of love for pocket change or a medium-sized bag of pistachios. She was the kind of woman who could weather a longshoremen gang-bang and still be hungry for more lovin'. "Aren't there any real men on this dock?" Her primary source of income production was satisfying the mildly perverse requests of the blurry-visioned out-of-town business low rollers. Though unappealing to a sober man, Mary hoisted her goods around as if she were Cytherea incarnate. This puzzled the penguins because the phrase that entered our minds when pondering a rendezvous with Typhoid Mary was "coyote gnaw." Had she been shipwrecked with Robinson Crusoe, Robbie would have asked nothing of her except coconut cracking and berry collecting. Her perfume, like her personality, was loud and excessive, as was her make-up. Still, Mary was able to collar some frugal Motel 6er every night, underscoring the fact that alcohol is a bad thing. When not faking orgasms for hairy-backed sales hustlers from Birmingham, she was moaning as a vulgar-mouthed wench for some 1-900-Bad-Lad phone service. Mary did market herself well, and never behaved as a blithering drunkette. The waiters had seen her drink for hours on end and never once had she shown even the slightest signs of intoxication. The penguins even counted her drinks on several different evenings, double digits and nary a buzz. Maybe she was a witch. I retract every unkind or judgmental word previously said about Typhoid Mary.

Among the mid-rangers was a King Lear regular named Paula Murdoch, a late thirties vagabond vamp with hazel eyes, brown hair, and curvaceous body. She was definitely doable so long as you didn't mind rolling the venereal disease dice. Her lusty package included three distinctive traits. First were her long muscular legs that left even the most hardened and horny lumberjack pleading for mercy. It was even rumored that she had used her legs to perform a Heimlich maneuver on a choking Clydesdale. Second was her mouth, which was much larger than a normal woman's mouth, able to make even the

longest Zulu warrior smile. Finally, and most noticeably, were
Paula's round, unjobbed, firm, larger than normal, mesmer-
izing breasts that were always on display, jiggling a hypnotic
spell that planted a petrified forest, begging the barflies to
reach out and touch, causing them to forget about their wives,
the church, and their once proud mothers. I can attest to their
firmness because Paula must have spent a collective month
rubbing her partons against me, trying to convince me to lease.
Though always sweating and tempted, I would gracefully
decline her advances and job offers, a statement that fourteen
of the other twenty-five penguins could not truthfully make.
That's right, fifty-six percent of my tuxedoed coworkers had
been through Paula's garden. That alone snuffed any thoughts
I may have previously harbored about a romp with Breasty
Murdoch. Forget about the fact that she had satisfied 4,700
strangers, some who would pay a bonus nickel to go sheathless.
It was my fellow penguins' questionable pasts that frightened
me. "You've been with a King Lear waiter? Damn girl, get that
infectious fjord away from me!"

Paula had an interesting story with a conclusion certain to
be tragic. She had grown up in a wealthy Washington family,
but became an exotic dancer in defiance of her overbearing
parents. Her claim to fame as a stripper was that she could
make a malt liquor tall boy disappear and did things with a
harmonica hopefully not taught at Juilliard. During her peeling
days, she became engaged to a prominent District political
figure who ended their engagement after Paula refused to
stop using drugs as he had begged her to do. He wanted
Paula to stop stripping and dry out, and even offered to pay
for detox. But her addictions were stronger than her emotions.

Not long after that her drug intake increased even more, and
to pay for her habit she opted to hook exclusively since it was
more profitable to be a flesh-renter than stripper. With her
debts mounting and her drug consumption redlining, Paula
was evicted from her Capitol Hill townhouse in 1994. It was
the last time she ever owned or rented a permanent roof of her
own. She didn't have a car, and for shelter crashed with her

nightly renters or stayed at any of several dozen friends' homes with whom she had personal possessions stashed. Some of the male friends required more than just a thank you and cheek peck for the favor. Paula enjoyed her new nomadic state, existing with no mailing address, credit cards, bank accounts, or health insurance, and toting around her life in a giant handbag stuffed with her essential daily possessions. Her debts could not be enforced and her vocation paid in cash, which kept her eyes dilated and income untaxable. Retirement wasn't a concern. Unless she made the decision to detox, continued use would kill her before her time.

The priciest car on the lot was Toriko Akazaki, a stunning, Asian, Stanford MBA graduate vixen that few could afford. Tori worked hard to be fine and with great success. She was of average height, silky black hair, angelic dark eyes, medium chested, with beautiful smooth skin and long hot legs, the kind that made ZZ Top want to sing. She spent two hours a day, every day, in the gym, and an additional two days a week in the salon, further polishing her package. "No" was not a word she ever heard. Not only was she fit and cerebral, but well-read and invested, and not one to powder her nose every half hour like the rest of the rentals and the majority of the posers. If you wanted to be Adam to Tori's apple-munching, snake-beguiled Eve, the price would be stellar and negotiated over an exorbitant dinner at King Lear.

The waiters knew the drill with Tori and her prospective clients, loving the scene because we knew the deuce check would be astronomical. Dom Perignon, Caspian caviar, a teenaged bottle of Chateau Margaux, Louie Tres, and a Maine lobster the size of an Airbust A380 were all mandatory items when price-fixing with Tori. The man just wanted to lock his legs around this angel, quell his fever and run. But when a dinner check bigger than his Charlotte mortgage payment arrived, many disbelieving boys would simply flip out. "Sir, let me help you find your eyeballs." "My sons can't go to college now!" Once Tori had set the price for dessert, the cash-light client would scurry up to the maître d's stand and demand to know where to find the nearest ATM. Tori only took hard green on the barrelhead. Her price varied, a William McKinley or more based on what she thought her infidelity boy could afford.[†] Once the check and romp cash was paid, the man just wanted to race back to the hotel and bump uglies, near madness in a sexually-frenzied state. By now, he had endured drinks at the bar, sipping Champagne, the rubbing of his thigh under the table, three bites of a Guinness Book lobster, the swirling of her finger around his Louie snifter in a seductive fashion that almost made him spike the ball on the thirty-yard line, and then got a dinner check that he would never be able to explain to his overdrawn spouse. He just wanted to leave and get laid. "Let's go! Walk faster! Oil your own self up, I'm about to have a misfire!"

Tori had always been very sweet to me, quite aware that I found her perspicacity as alluring as her looks and mannerisms. I was the only King Lear squire to whom she ever offered a gratis, savory slice of Asian yum-yum. She was stunning and I was willing, but somehow I was always able to decline, not wanting to become what I despised. We flirted like crazy though, mostly physically, her seductive spell bordering on cruel and inhuman. How I was able to pass on her fine self, I'll never know. But like me, Tori was able to beat the odds and escape King Lear for a better life. She took the money she had made from drunken louses laid, and opened a bed and breakfast with her mother somewhere in northern New England. I hope I can find it someday in the not-too-distant future and see if there was an expiration date on Tori's offer. Maybe next week sometime, early Monday morning at the latest. Is it Monday yet? Note to Tori: We're going Dutch on the dinner check.

The majority of the bar blobs were lost white males over forty in chronological age, one hundred and two according to the carbon dating of their kidneys. They all were similar in appearance. Most noticeable were their sickly Jacko pale complexions as the result of spending their lives bellied up at the bar. They whiled their days away drinking like fish and their nights trying to keep their cars between the light posts,

[†] William McKinley, the 25th U.S. President, is on the $500 Bill. Grover Cleveland, the 22nd *and* 24th U.S. President, is on the $1,000 Bill. Both men died in office.

pulling in well after the wife had been sand-manned in an effort to avoid explanations, accusations, and spawning. Vampires living in caves on the dark side of the moon, blind-folded and double zipped inside burlap body bags, saw more sunlight than our whiskeyfish.

The next similarity was obesity, each barfly being a fat blob. A motionless state and daily diet of five thousand calories, 89.722 percent of which were empty and from kidney-disinte-grating, brain-biting juniper juice, tended to make for one corpulent corpse. Being immobile and fat made them more depressed, which demanded solace alcohol, bringing on more obesity, more depression, and more internal organ damage, until the entire stage set just falls over and the school play is canceled. Even if a fly had lost weight, the accomplishment would be celebrated with alcohol and it was back to circle one. Any food they did eat was unhealthy. The only fresh fruit consumed was an accidentally-swallowed lemon twist or a piece of lime flesh from tequila shooters shot when knocking glasses with a band of Georgetown Law commencers. The only green vegetable consumed were Roquefort-stuffed olives that had soaked in a repulsive brine touched by the unwashed fingers of half the staff. The only thing close to fiber was a miniature plastic saber accidentally swallowed when they thought the gibson onions were conjoined twins. The intestinally-lodged cocktail sword gave the first year med students a much-needed laugh during their Intro to Autopsy class. As for protein, the bar nut bowl would have to suffice, though the nuts were so laden with salt that any deer not killed by Omar on his way to work could be found in the dry storage room licking the nut box. As for water, the only water consumed was in the form of melted ice cubes, formerly solid and adrift in their Gentleman Jacks.

As for grooming, that was only for horses and show dogs. Men locked away in bars tend not to fret over matters such as haircuts, shoeshines and manicures. Visits to the dentist to obliterate the ten-year's worth of tooth decay or address the Oklahoma Sooner levels of gum disease was considered an act of pure narcissism and, therefore, never occurred. Going to the gym was less likely than time travel, plus they'd get winded just from filling out the health club questionnaire and they refused to drink Gatorade unless it was amply diluted with Absolut Kurant. To them, Pilates was something you ate with Baba Ganoush. It was not uncommon to see a fly wearing the same suit, shirt, and tie combination three or four consecutive days, same shoes and crusty socks indefinitely. Less dry cleaning meant less discarded plastic and fewer wire hangers. One could argue that the environment benefited, so long as you didn't factor in the glass menagerie worth of bottles their unquenchable thirsts emptied.

Cars were yet another indicator of fly status. If their car was filthy and unwashed, with dirt-filled floorboards, missing hubcaps, and DOT salt deposits on the windshield from a winter six months past, it likely belonged to a fly. Car washes and Armour All were only detractors of time and money, both of which could be better spent putting a half-nelson on a Famous Grouse neat. Plus the boys at the car wash said the puke smell could not be removed.

Not every sot had a car, and those who did often forgot where they had left it twelve hours earlier. Flies would frantically call King Lear in hopes of locating their missing autos, having no memory of the previous evening's rum regatta. The three questions asked, in order, were "Was I in there last night?" "Was I driving my car?" "Did you forget to give me my car?" The answers, respectively, were yes, yes, no. Yes, you were here for five hours yesterday. Yes, you gave your car to the valets. No, Verner did not forget to give you your car. We merely concluded that a man unable to successfully dismount from his barstool without both palms touching the floor was far too intoxicated to operate a motor vehicle without killing a half dozen people. The valets had stuffed the drunken fly into a cab for the ride home. Though able to wake, dial, and locate his withheld auto, the drunky would still require ten more hours and several venti cups of Arabian Mocha Java before his blood alcohol level was within legal limits, in the unlikely event he didn't use a handful of dog hair to ease his throbbing hangover.

But the easiest way to determine whether or not a bar patron was a fly was simply to ask him how he felt about the movie *Leaving Las Vegas*. If he said it was a disturbing portrayal of the brutal realities of alcoholism or something to that effect, the answer was no. If, however, he said the movie was pointless, uninteresting, and overly dramatic, or commented on how much he liked the scene with Nicolas Cage and the Flying Elvi, then he was indeed a full-fledged fly, on readiness-to-drink alert, drifting out to sea to the island of vomit and misery.

And in this giant sea of inequity that is any bar in America, only one question baffled the mind. How did these witless and wasted souls perform any occupation, let alone one which allowed them to stay parked on a barstool all day and pay for the Manitobian lake worth of alcohol they drank each week?

Old money was one answer to the question, though many blobs were watching their inherited monies disappear faster than Lake Mead's water level and shore line. Since none were clever enough to invent anything beyond a larger cocktail glass, scams would be the plotted course, and the scummiest of King Lear's bar scamsters was Craig "King Con" Trudeau, a Hindenberg-sized zeppelin who could bilk a gypsy clan out of their own ill-gotten gains.

Trudeau was a self-professed Vietnam war hero, a Special Forces officer who touted nineteen confirmed kills: three VC, four Cambodians, two Laotian monks, a pair of water buffalo, a Peace Corps volunteer from Boise, the battalion dog—a Jack Russell terrier named Yikes that he accidentally ran over, one Praying Mantis, and five Vietnamese mothers who just wouldn't stop crying after a napalm strike incinerated their children, village, and ancestral burial grounds. Supposedly, Trudeau was one of the most decorated officers of the war, though historians must have collectively called in sick on the day they were scheduled to write about him. The only historical documents that bore his name were IOUs for his bar tabs; a stack of papers so large that, when compiled, ran longer than the *Iliad* translated into Esperanto. King Con referred to himself as an investment counselor, though financial Houdini would have been a more appropriate title. Investment money thrown his way disappeared faster than the Brazilian rain forest. He would boast about a lock stock pick that would double daily for the next five years, but no money given to Trudeau was ever seen again. He had taken hundreds of thousands from foolish King Lear customers, declared their investments unsuccessful and never indicated any feeling of guilt, remorse, or awkwardness toward those he had scammed. The money was never invested, but instead was used to keep overdue bartenders, bookies, ex-wives, and attorneys at bay. Trudeau was a crook, but the greatest crime belonged to those who wrote him checks. Investing money with a confident drunkard who spent forty hours a week plopped on a barstool, had no office, no tangible credentials, food stains on his clothing from two days ago, and whose business cards had a P.O. Box for an address and a disconnected phone number, yet still proclaimed to have more financial wisdom than J. Paul Getty. What the hell were you thinking?

Howie Sullivan was another abrasive, vocal, unlikable Lear fly who drank his body weight in booze every three days and had definitive answers to every question and subject in life. He was the most opinionated lush at King Lear, and believed that everything and everyone around him existed solely for his pleasure. Originally from Alabama, he had a southern yelp and Cable Guy mannerisms that made you wonder why he wasn't selling cotton candy at a demolition derby. He didn't think much of women, wine with a cork, clothing made in the absence of polyester, or subscribe to any modern theories of etiquette. Amazingly, Sullivan was an extremely successful vice president for a brokerage firm on East Capitol Street, electing to do most of his work via cell phone from King Lear's bar.

When he wasn't getting blotto at Chez Cirrhosis while making crucial investment picks, Sullivan was a hunting devotee, blowing away unsuspecting animals to help him get in touch with his manhood. His idea of sport was to dress in camouflage, spray a two acre patch of Fairfax woods with a few gallons of deer urine, and then, when a curious, confused, starving, and displaced whitetail wandered into the area wondering why it hadn't heard the several thousand other whitetails that had apparently just marked their territory, he would riddle the buck from a different time zone with a laser-targeting rifle. Sully was a regular at the taxidermy shop, carrying pictures of his larger slaughters in his wallet where another man might have pictures of his wife or children. Many of the King Lear inhousers took offense at Sullivan's hunting exploits and related braggings, to which he would reply, "God put animals on earth for man to use."

But why had God put Sullivan on earth? Was it to make drunken whimsical decisions with other people's life savings in between sips at King Lear? Was it to shoot deer and moose that were selfishly consuming the world's clover reserves and then hang their guillotined heads about his home in Annandale? Was it to drive home drunk every afternoon to keep school kids agile? Was it to get blown in the parking garage by a crack whore, yet give soapbox sermons about the District's increasing drug problems? Was it to toast a fellow fly's birthday while not recalling the day his daughter was born, despite witnessing the event and owning a recollection copy on VHS? Was it to share his opinion that women existed only for cooking, sexing, and childbearing? Was it to mercilessly inflict his banjo-plucking, freak show ticket selling personality on King Lear's staff to the point that we wanted to spike yet another heroin needle in our forearms? I wonder.

Every bar has a bad marriage, a couple that comes in and does their fighting in full view of the other flies. Of the several pairs of nuptialed battlebots who scored zero on *The Newlywed Game,* Hugh and Shannon Gilespie took top honors. A lobbyist and office manager respectively, the two locked horns in verbal fury twice weekly at King Lear.

Shannon was in her forties, stocky, vocal, shorthaired, and harbored a tomboy trait that made her attractive in a cameo-bang way. The kind of woman a guy wants to spend one night with, plotting his escape during the countdown, knowing that the nearest exit may be behind him, promising to call her back while not asking for her phone number or knowing her last name, and hoping she doesn't know where he works or lives.

Hugh was also in his forties, a misfit Democrat in a Republican bar. When Clinton defeated Bush in 1992, Hugh loudly sang *Happy Days Are Here Again* so many times that some of the King's crime lords threatened to dislocate his shoulders if he didn't shut his song hole. As predictable as TV prime-time plot resolutions five minutes before the hour, Hugh and Shannon would enter as a happy couple, have a round or two, and not long after would begin arguing over the most ridiculous subjects. Additional drinks only further turned up the tension dial as the insult phase commenced, all full-toothed, generic, and audible all the way to Appomattox. "You're an asshole." "Stupid bitch, what's wrong with you?" "You don't know what the hell you're talking about." "I knew you'd say that!" "You're crazy." "You must be havin' one of those heavy days." "Don't push me or I'll walk right outta here." "That's so typical of you." "Stop acting like a jackass." "Your sister's the smart one!" The final insult was always the same, ending the heated exchange like an anvil falling from the sky and crashing on concrete. It had the same effect as saying "cease fire," "strike three," or asking a woman who isn't pregnant when her baby is due. That phrase was "Shut the fuck up!"

Whoever said it first would be the victor of that night's argument, the loser retreating to the opposite side of the bar to recruit supporters for his or her side of the argument. The recruitment process began and ended with buying cocktails for the new drinking mates. The only price of accepting the drink was to agree with Hugh or Shannon's side of the argument. "You're absolutely right, Hugh, school children should carry firearms." Then the harsh glances phase began until the "Shut the fuck up" sayer would walk over and evasively apologize. Soon after the two would depart, not to be seen again until a few days later when they would reappear and argue all over again about whether or not Serena Williams has Venus envy, or if in fact Soylent Green is people. Note to the Gilespies: "Shut the fuck up, times infinity!"

Rats are everywhere in Washington, and King Lear's bar was

no exception. Not the Camembert-chewing, sewer-slithering shrews of the genus *Rattus,* but the grimy decapods of the ethicsless phylum *Lawyeris slimiest.*

Being a lawyer was an excellent occupation when doubling as a fly. So long as you had an aggressive legal assistant and a few scapegoat associates, you could get the day's legal trees chopped by eleven and yourself planted in the bar before noon. If, by chance, a court session conflicted with bar time, you could ask the judge for a continuance or move to subpoena a surprise witness in Vladivostokavia. If forced to attend a court session during prime hooch-lick hours, you could settle the case out of court or forego the cross examinations and expert witnesses, or simply allow the ass-smooching, index card-carrying associate trying to make partner to handle the case. Your closing argument could be done by quoting a few lines of Henry David Thoreau while throwing incredulous looks the jury's way. And if that still didn't make the gavel slam fast enough, you could put vodka in your water glass (no olive, it would raise suspicion) or simply blurt out a chorus of schizo-phrenic prejudices and epithets that forced an instant mistrial. Whether or not you won the case didn't matter, you were still going to collect all those billable hours, even though most of them were spent on a bender at King Lear. If your client went to prison because of your negligence, at least he wouldn't have to worry about paying his mortgage or finding companionship. In fact, you were probably doing him a favor. If you hit the jackpot and represented a client who spilled scalding hot drive-thru coffee on her labia majora, you could stay cooked for years.

Of the 117,000 lawyers who work and reside in and around Washington, no less than a hundred esquires traded theory and threw back happy juice at King Lear on any given day. One law firm had a half dozen regulars who never missed a lunch, eating and tanking their afternoons away at the bar. Unlike the other flies who endeavored to earn an income blabbing from their barstools, these sewer rats rose early, trained to work by 6:00 a.m., worked until lunch, abused their livers from noon to four, then Blue Lined it home, sauced, safe, and pissed only about the lack of a place to piss on the train. The wives took care of everything on the home front, their only concern, though never acknowledged, was the certainty of their husbands croaking via stroke or myocardial infarction before they ever saw their own daughters graduate law school. Hell's Sports Book had posted nine-to-one odds on these litigating whiskeyfishes buying the farm by 2007, with no available wager on the certainty that their wives had never missed a life insurance payment.

Doctors were no strangers to the King Lear's barland. Drinking in a dank bar offered several advantages over a day spent golfing. Primarily a shoe change wasn't necessary and you wouldn't work up a sweat unless you played doctor with a rental at the Landry, and even then you could keep your Florsheims on because your chosen wench of ill repute would be doing all the moving and gyrating. Sunburn was about as likely as a Washington Wizard NBA title, and for caddies, you had a battalion of penguins ready and willing to fetch your drink, debone your Dover Sole, and lie to your wife.[†] Although most of the fly physicians were tolerable, it was troubling to see medical men and women withering away at the bar twenty hours a week. Twenty hours that would require forty hours for detoxification, not even factoring in whatever trail mix worth of mind altering pharmaceutical candy they had prescribed for themselves (no secret there either, Doc). Some even smoked, apparently still waiting for more conclusive evidence on whether or not smoking is detrimental to one's health. Shouldn't these Hippocratic oafs have been dry and reading medical journals or learning the latest techniques, equipment, and technologies? The penguins put red asterisks in the phone book beside the names of some of the saucier doctors.

Carl Silverman was the favorite doc on the block, an orthopedic surgeon and team physician for King Lear's server corps; not a fish but, indeed, an outstanding cutter. Carl was considered the best in town at his trade, an opinion never

[†] When Washington's NBA team name was changed in 1997, the penguins submitted a name reflective of the city's essence: The **Washington Drive-by Shooters** (logo: a cartoon hoopster shooting a jump shot from the passenger side of a speeding white van). We also proposed that Florida's NHL team be called the **Miami Ice Cubans**.

disavowed by any of the penguins he had treated. King Lear's tuxers, like all the other high-intensity servers in the city, had chronically aching feet and knees. When the pain reached critical, the penguins paid Carl a visit. Many of the waiters had their knees scoped or bone fragments removed, but the most common request was for kneecap cortisone injections for some of the higher mileage penguins, without which a few of the staffers couldn't walk without grimacing. "Doc I need a shot." "But your knees and feet are fine. Why would you want a . . ? Hey, wait a minute. Get outta here!" Carl knew that the aching waiters couldn't afford to take three months off convalescing after knee surgery, so he did what he could to keep us moving, always at a fraction of his normal fee. In return his wine glass was never empty.

Yancy Marshall was a regular docfly, a gynecologist who had inspected the loins of many of the King's women, and treated most of the rentals when that southern itch turned out to be more than just a mosquito bite. Though a lush, he never violated his patients or their confidentiality. The other flies begged him to spill the news on the clap trappings of King Lear's call girls, but no matter how sauced, he kept his lips sealed. Doc Marshall was notorious for his colossal intake of Budweiser, drinking almost two cases a week, not including what he drank outside of King Lear or at the clinic. At fifty beers a week, or 2,500 beers a year, Doc Marshall drank over 230 gallons of Budweiser each year. Few people drink that much water a year, let alone beer, let alone a doctor. Prodigious drinkers who didn't behave like stumbling drunks despite drinking waves of alcohol were well liked by the staff. Yancy Marshall was something of an icon, an honorary inner-circle knight of King Lear's round table.

The wettest fish on the tuna boat was a Canadian named Leslie Walters, a red-haired, early forties, hall-of-shame drinker and chain smoker who supposedly was a cosmetic surgeon specializing in breast augmentation, though no penguin or customer could believe it. Most of the time, she was too blitzed to even hold her own steak knife, slurring her speech, and on a few isolated occasions she had even passed out at her table. Her cerebral quotient was as questionable as her social dexterity. She was the kind of person who thought the Khmer Rouge was the latest make-up line from Max Factor and that *Band of Brothers* was the Earth, Wind and Fire *Behind the Music* story.

Waiters tend to be skeptics when it comes to a customer's claims of fame and intelligence, and it was never more true than with Leslie Walters. There were customers who claimed to be war heroes who ate moose meat and watched hockey during the Vietnam draft. There were many people who claimed to be preponderant congressmen and senators, however puzzling. You had countless patrons always babbling on and on about their enormous wealth whose secured credit cards were declined when they tried to pay for a two-course meal. And finally, there were the frauds who claimed to be medical pioneers.

With Dr. Walters there was no doubt. This cosmetic Klondike was lying through her lip implants. There was no way on a sunny day in Nanoose Bay this woman could ever be sober enough to hold a steady scalpel and cut into another human being. But to our incredible dismay, Dr. Winnipeg Walters was indeed a cosmetic surgeon specializing in breast augmentation. Mitch found a full-page advertisement in an old Potomac Magazine with an airbrushed picture of her, apparently taken on her prom night. Overwhelmed with disillusionment, we got the phone book and made another red asterisk. A giant red, coaster-sized asterisk.

But the one man of no trade, who epitomized the tragedy of any bar, was Dax Fabini. One of the saddest men on earth, living only to sit at King Lear's bar, with no money, no job, no aspirations, debts beyond debts, and living at other fly's homes when not on the street, in a car, or at the YMCA. Quite simply, a dead man in a live man's body, trapped by his thirst like one of those pearl divers in a black-and-white picture whose ankle is caught in the mouth of an oversized oyster. He owed money to everyone, including penguins and tenders, but had a quiet, wounded puppy dog expression that made you want to help him out. He would gladly pay you Tuesday for a Van Hoo and tonic today.

Fabini would come in, sit at the bar and order a cup of coffee, but it wasn't long until he had a drink in front of him. Any of the other couple dozen flies felt guilty that Dax wasn't also getting lit, so invariably another bar blob would buy him a drink. Since he lived at the bar, Dax was present when some regular won a lawsuit, football pool, or had his wife whacked and bought a round or two for all the fishes in celebration of no more alimony payments. Dax was never seen eating and was more sedentary than a Heisman trophy, sitting so still for so long that rigor mortis seemed certain. He even limited his blinking so as to not overexert himself.

His vapid way angered those he owed money, for he was also motionless in the matter of seeking employment. Dax had never once pondered finding a job and wasn't about to do anything that required him to leave the bar or do more than speak in solicitation of additional alcohol funding. His life's priority was to stay intoxicated and parked on a barstool, and his feel-sorry-for-me approach earned him just enough pity cash to remain in his self-induced coma, a half-notch above vagrancy, a quarter-notch above death.

The insanity of working in a restaurant with a bar was perfectly demonstrated by Dax Fabini. You had a man tragically and irrevocably consumed by his vice, swept away by the white water river current of alcoholism. And those who benefited from his self-destruction were the owners, barmen, waiters, and busboys of King Lear, making us no better than the drug predators who rule the tougher streets of the world. We simply disguised our playing field. Our crack alley was a shining brass and leather appointed bar, and if you had money and a thirst, we'd be your dealer. No questions asked.

TEST YOUR RESTAURANT IQ:

QUESTION: WHICH OF THE FOLLOWING IS MOST ESSENTIAL TO OPERATIONS AT AN UPSCALE POWER RESTAURANT?

A. THE COMPUTER SYSTEM

B. THE GLASS/DISHWASHING MACHINE

C. THE EMPLOYEES

D. THE CREDIT CARD APPROVAL SYSTEM

E. THE HOOD EXHAUST FAN

Answer A is incorrect. Restaurant computers crash all day long, most often because the middle-aged, high-trousered, Sierra Mist sipping virgin who created the programs never worked a day of his life in an actual restaurant. Unable to bench press more than 10 pounds, he'd be a lousy employee anyway. Answer B is incorrect. Who needs a dishwasher? Dirty dishes, glasses and flatware can be chucked into bus tubs and washed next month, or taken home and washed, never to return. Or just plain chucked if the owner is a **classhole** (First Class Asshole). And often, the water in the dishwasher hasn't been changed in days, making it a grime rinsing/spincah leaf speckling device anyhow. The blind patrons thought everything was Brailled. Answer C is incorrect. Restaurants that normally march with 25 employees can run with 5. That's what adrenaline and management girlfriends are for, and why most managers are alcoholics. Answer D is incorrect. When the credit card approval system is down, direct calls to the credit card companies can be made. If that takes too long, waiters and managers have lists of impostor approval codes they use for off-line author-izations. Answer E is correct. Without a hood fan to suck away the fumes from ovens, ranges, and fryers, no restaurant can function. You can try, but soon the kitchen staff will be coughing, half blind, and the production line will look and sound like a smoky version of *Gorillas in the Mist*.

Chapter 15

Christmas Cards from the Mob

(*compensation hysteria*)

*"The superior man is modest in his speech,
but exceeds in his actions."*

Confucius (551–479 BC)

Most people have negative stereotypes about the boys of organized crime. People envision burly wops, stratospherically-interested loan sharks, point-shaving, unshaven Yonkers bookies, and contract hitters tossing a rug-wrapped, lead-headed snitch into the surreptitious depths of the Monogahela, a kind of carp-chewed human hasbeen Tootsie Roll or pig that had squealed in a blanket washing up on the shores of a Baton Rouge crab cannery ten months and many miles down the line. People think of mobmolls sporting all the refinement and mental savvy of Kahoka, Mizzou mud wrestlers, wearing skin-tight leopard dresses, Air-Sea Rescue red lipstick, and chewing gum like only a woodchuck could if a woodchuck would and could chew gum. People think of zoot suits and drug distribution, tax evasion, asphalt dermabrasion, political corruption, village protection, and football fields where forever unfound sopranos fertilize the dandelions. Most people think badly about the Mob, but not waiters. Mobsters, racketeers, and union leaders are the greatest fine dining customers in the world. That is, so long as they aren't extorting your restaurant.

The Coventry wasn't a crime lord's kind of restaurant. Eating a four-bite, two-ounce finch garnished with a quarter pomegranate and three asparagus tips served by a high-voiced dreamboat transvestite who thought the Tampa Bay Buccaneers was a dance troupe and suffered from a severe case of penis envy despite having one himself just wasn't the Mob's style. King Lear was, however.

King Lear was big, dark, powerful, and semi-private with an army of penguins and tuxed tenders who treated them like aristocracy. As customers, the mobbies were the masters, making all the right moves and none of the wrong. They weren't going to take ten minutes to order and then have every dressing, sauce, and seasoning served on the side, or moan on about their allergies, aversions, or dietetic speed bumps. Nor would they drink iced tea, split an entree, and then convulse like a tadpole in metamorphosis about the split charge. You would never hear them say "not raw!" when requesting a rare steak, ask if the pterodactyl was fresh, or be gullible enough to buy the lie when we said the South Pacific catch of the day was caught only hours earlier. The mobbies wouldn't bring their own wine and pass kidney stones over the corkage fee, or offer terrorist threats to their waiter if the java wasn't decaf. They weren't going to cautiously sniff each oyster, pick the raisins out of their bread pudding or hiss when an item was eighty-sixed. "I'm so sorry Mrs. Punchbuggy, but we ran out of the free-range duck because they all flew away."

The zooters wouldn't complain that the dining room was too cold or too loud, order a single dessert for the entire neighborhood along with a river barge full of silverware, or hand the waiter a fistful of credit cards to pay for one check. They wouldn't spend a half hour swirling a glass of Beaujolais, napkin-blot their word holes after each bleeding bite of steak, or eat their meals so slowly that a handful of well-motivated bacteria could have broken down the entree faster. The crimies weren't going to make their waiter three-trip for a single round of drinks or address him in a condescending tone when he returned. The big men weren't going to call or get called on their cell phones or plop their laptops on the tabletop while in the restaurant like the fucking bastard, insecure pretenders do, wrecking the dining atmosphere in a pleading cry for attention and chainsaw dismemberment. The crime kings didn't behave like intolerable, arrogant, insidious Antoinettes.

Topping the Mob's dining attribute list was their friendly disposition toward the staff. They knew that King Lear's waiters were the Navy Seals of Washington's waiter corps and when push came to shove the needs of the Mob would always take priority. The Mob and union heads went out of their way to get to know the penguins. They knew our names, first and last, where we were from, if we were married or had cubs, and always greeted us with a genuine salutation, handshake, or hug before they sat down. To be treated like a son or brother of such powerful men made us feel important, a rare feeling for a restaurant dot. Never did we speculate or even care about what these guys did outside the restaurant, because when inside King Lear, or outside for that matter, they were our kings, our boys, and for them we would always go all out. Protective? Damn straight. Besides, whatever they did outside of the restaurant was none of our business.

Next on the Mugsymen's resume of fine attributes was that they were never in a hurry, ever. Fine dining service personnel despise any patron in a rush. There was always some ligatory lemur, medical marabou, or congressional bandicoot that had to be somewhere fast. A hurried power-tripper who feels compelled to tell you why he's in such a rush, too stupid to realize that the penguins didn't give a rat's ass. If you want fast, grab a sidewalk dog. Just stay away from the finer confines, we beg you. The Mob was never in a hurry. They did nothing fast and would not be rushed, as it should be.

Table choice was never an issue with the Mob crims, it was always one of three low-profile rounders in King Lear's upper room. Most of our regulars, the majority being Jewish, wanted just the opposite, high-profile tables where they could see and be seen, yak and be yakked at. Oiye. Hebrew ground zero was any of four banqueted tables in the center of the dining room, referred to as "the pit" by the waiters. The penguins hated to be assigned to the pit (called the pit boss) because we were guaranteed to be buried all night long with petty demands, inefficient ordering, and then rewarded with a tip that fell far short, like a seventy-yard uphill field goal into the wind with Lucy holding. If you sat in the pit, you weren't necessarily Jewish, but it was a given you ate cake the day you were circumcised, were the plaintiff in at least three active lawsuits, had never set foot in the Honeybaked Ham store, and wouldn't blink at paying a dime a piece for Streisand tickets. Your dark-haired, early twenties daughter had never worked a day in her life, but did have a secret penchant for Gooden flour, quietly fed by the penguins in exchange for a deep kiss and handful of her ample young bosom, each having something the other one wanted, badly. When a penguin was assigned pit duty, the other waiters would mock the pit boss by singing "Start feedin' the Jews" to the tune of "New York, New York." Unlike teen-targeted magazine clothing ads where the model ensemble always includes the obligatory black dude and China girl, the penguins never cared much about political correctness.

The Mob never complained. Ever. It was amazing. Serving the Mob required that you follow one rule and, if you did, the crime organizers would always be happy. That rule was to always keep their drinks and wine glasses filled. There was no communication involved, only the sight of a half full glass. It was a given they would have wine with the meal, each Mobbie and union head having a favorite grape squash that he and his subordinates drank exclusively, always red, usually American, though a few drank Italian. No tasting ritual was required. We just opened and poured, bringing additional bottles when the one on the table was down to a third. By keeping the tommy gunners knee-deep in firewater, they never complained, even when a complaint seemed warranted.

One of our Mob regs once found a live inchworm in his salad. He jokingly said, "Hey, Johnboy, look what I found." "Uh, sorry Mr. Mancuso, that little guy must have escaped from one of our tequila bottles." He laughed, picked up the squirming inchworm, put it in his mouth, crunched, swallowed, and said, "Hey, that's not too bad." I felt horrible about the incident; the inchworm deserved a better death.

Had any of our pit persons found an inchworm in their salads there would have been federal indictments. The fact that lettuce grows on the ground where spiders, ants, and inchworms abound would not have been an acceptable excuse. Once, I was very loudly reprimanded by an angry woman, but it was croutons, not inchworms, that cracked her second facelift. She said, "This salad has croutons, and it's Passover!" (croutons are leavened bread). I was well aware it was Passover, as were all my fellow penguins. Gavin marked every significant religious/political date in the reservation book, be it Passover, Ramadan, autobahn, Chaka Khan, Shark Week, Black History month, year of the cat, Rosh Hashanah, or Sha-na-na.

I didn't know this woman was Jewish (her last name was Avenal), nor was she wearing an armband labeling her a Jew, nor had she said anything about her dietary or religious restrictions when she ordered. I would have gladly honored her requests had she informed me in a civil tone. Her pairless, poorly-plugged guggenheim of a husband just watched, not objecting to the unwarranted verbal lashing I had just received. But I was smart enough to know that when a customer went mental it was a deflection of hostilities and frustrations culminating from other parts of that person's life, their emotional teakettle whistling with no one listening (known as *transference*, or in severe cases *compensation hysteria*). Nonetheless, I could have done without her obloquy, diatribe, and fulminations. This lady wasn't upset at me or the leavened, crunchy cubes of butter-painted brioche. She was upset that her Barbie Doll-headed husband was banging an associate, that every year she was invited to fewer and fewer cocktail parties, that her daughter had a chronic case of the sniffles and penguin-pawed breasts, that the pool boy had rejected her advances even though she promised to advance him, and that the guilt of treating waiters, maître d's, maids, mechanics, cashiers, dry cleaners, car washers, trashmen, caddies, bellhops, gardeners, postal workers, desk clerks, ticket agents, bank tellers, and flight attendants like shit for thirty years had left her unfulfilled and despising what the looking glass returned. Her physical beauty had been fading since the day she chased three Xanax with two bottles of Moët Chandon White Star, passing out on the ultraviolet shores of Archachon. Her inner beauty had punted long before that.

One of our cherished union regulars, Jackie Eastman, was entertaining a couple of fine fillies when he said, "John, I need an ashtray here, partner." I flipped around and held out my bare palm and Jackie tapped the ashes of his lit Lucky into my hand and said, "You fucking smooth bastard, I knew I liked your style." The ashes didn't burn my hand and the two damsels looked on in sheer amazement, jaws on the floor, one saying, "Damn Jackie, these guys adore you," referring to the over-attentive King Lear staff. Jackie gave me a wink and gracious nod, whereupon I brought him a real ashtray.

Sometimes the waiters acted as shuttle drivers. Since many of the subordinate mobsters didn't have their own personal limos or drivers, the waiters often drove them home when the zooters were having difficulty forming sentences. We wouldn't do this for most of our other regular fishes. We'd stuff them in a cab and say, "Get this man to Tupelo, and step on it!" But there was a different set of rules with our mobsters. The waiters would drive the drunken men to their homes after checkout and cab it to our own homes from there. On a normal evening we weren't completely dry ourselves, but if we were serving any of the big boys that evening, we would ease up a little on our consumption just in case, and if needed throw back a double espresso and wolf down a sandwich just before the ride.

On occasion, the Mob ordered carryout when detained by a meeting, interrogation, negotiation, or political persuasion that kept them from making it in to dine. This wasn't an ordinary to-go box with foiled food and plasticware; it was everything that comprised a meal in King Lear minus the walls, tables, and chairs. We're talking plates, silver, linen, candles, wine opener, glasses, as well as the food and drink, all stuffed into an oversized Igloo cooler that was originally purchased as project housing for homeless lobsters. The next day a young hitter would return the cooler, linens and hardware, plus a hard cash tip for the previous night's packing effort. All the Mob and union heads had King Lear house accounts, so check collection was never an issue. Plus, they weren't about to welsh on dollars due.

King Lear's staff was always delighted to serve the Mob, even when that service was unrelated to fine dining or the subsequent effects of alcohol. Gavin once got a call from Micky Orzabal, a prized underworld regular who was having an emergency at his Georgetown home just off of Wisconsin Avenue. Since our big boys didn't normally call the police when problems arose, Micky called and asked if Gavin could spare a couple penguins to help him deal with a domestic situation. Dying of curiosity and hoping it didn't involve dying literally, Preston and I jumped in a cab for Micky's house, and arrived to find Mrs. Orzabal having an all-out screaming tantrum, throwing her husband's belongings from the top stair of the Mickster's three-story townhome. Micky thanked us for coming, handed us garbage bags, and the three of us dropped to our knees and started gathering whatever his wife had thrown, dodging projectiles, and listening to an insane woman's tirade.

Apparently Micky had faltered in his marital vow of fidelity with a Virginia Tech sophomore, a young honey whose belly was supposedly swelling with his love child. Displeased with his inaction in regards to her and her bambino's future, the hussy Hokey called Mrs. Orzabal, disclosed the affair, and demanded substantial financial remuneration. That one phone call marked the beginning of the end for Micky and his tantrum-throwing spouse, the fork in the road confirmed by the surreal ranting and raucous hailstorm of cufflinks, collar studs, shoes, socks, boxers, ties, toiletries, belts, books, and memorabilia. Preston and I were both thinking the same thing, and without our even asking, Micky answered our question. "Don't worry guys, she already threw down the bedside when she found out it wasn't loaded." The cussfest and haberdasher's rain of ricocheted items continued, as did our frantic gathering and agile dodging. Neither Preston nor I could believe that only one person was doing all this throwing and swearing, and like a furious Ray Lewis, her energy, volume and momentum only seemed to be increasing.

You never realize how much stuff you have until a crazed woman hurls it all down from forty feet above in a marital fall of Saigon. A sizable framed picture of the Mickster and Bride Screamalot careened off a wall and exploded atop the banister rail at the bottom of the stairs, just missing Preston's head with glass shards flying everywhere. Micky bellowed up to his wife "Fuckin' bitch, you're God damned crazy!" Then he looked at Preston and said, "Sorry, buddy, she's just a little upset right now."

After gathering what we could, we pitched the trash bags into the back of Micky's Mercedes, piled in, and peeled away, his wife's screams still audible in the distance. Micky tried to give Preston and myself each a Texas dollar, but we declined, saying we'd rather he buy us a drink. We zipped over to the Jefferson, sat down at the bar, and listened to the distraught Mickster tell his tale. He said he had always worn cellophane when sampling his collegiate side dish and couldn't believe that she was pregnant. But apparently she was, and it would cost him his marriage.

Almost a year later I was serving Micky and a few of his boys and we got to talking about the day Preston and I helped move him out during the hostile barrage, the war zone on Wisconsin. Micky recalled that as one of the worst days of his life, but said that his wife was an excellent housekeeper. I said,

"Really? She got that mess all cleaned up, huh?" He said, "No, she *kept* the house in the divorce settlement."

As it turned out, his Hokie Pokey was never pregnant and he had lost his wife and home on a schoolgirl's bluff—a girl who was playing with a lot more fire than she ever knew.

But tipping is the final call in determining whether or not a customer is great. The tip is the single black-and-white action that separates the men from the boys, the good from the bad, the loved from the hated, the players from the pretenders, the polished from the imposters, the handsome from the ugly.

It's a matter of numbers, like an SAT cut-off score that determines which Alma your child will martyr. There are no excuses, including ignorance. Either you tip properly or you're a niggardly blob of plankton.

If one of your tablemates pays the check and they fall short of the mark, then you're duty bound to bat cleanup. If you're one of those business brohams who claims the corporate guidelines don't allow a one-fifth tip, then muscle it up out of your own pocket.

If you don't tip a fifth, then all those gracious things we said were lies. We're not glad you came in. It was not good to see you. It was not our pleasure to serve you. Your wife does not look beautiful tonight. And we don't give a damn if you did or did not enjoy the meal, though we did enjoy getting our mitts on your daughter's tits, but fine dining decorum prevented us mentioning it. To all those regular customers at any restaurant who haven't been tipping a hard 20 percent—you're nothing more than a duplicitous chicanerous Scrooge to the staff. You could learn a lot from the Mob.

The Mob's generosity went well beyond tipping 20 percent on the check. They gave the valets $20, tipped the coat checker $10, as well as the tenders, busmen, and maître d's. If they spent an excessively long amount of time at their table, they doubled the tip because they had the common sense to know their waiter might have turned it had they left.

And come December, the mobbies and unioneers took their gratitude to the next level. One of our union heads would take a stack of crisp fifties and spend the afternoon walking around the restaurant giving each employee an Ulysses Grant, a grateful handshake, and a thank you for all the hard work. This meant a lot to front housers, immensely more to the men and women in the kitchen who sweat away their years in anonymity. Imagine the gratitude in the eyes of a forgotten pot washer, an unnoticed dot in the chaos of busy Washington, when a powerful union kingpin comes into the kitchen, stands beside his pot sink, shakes the man's hand, and tells him to have a Merry Christmas and that what he does matters. This unioneer also made sure that every employee not present got a thank you and a fifty.

Some of the mobsters forced the waiters to join them for a drink, and we ain't talking Smirnoff Ice. But perhaps one of the most impressive gestures was a Mob man who obtained a roster of all the employees from Gavin, and then signed and hand-delivered over seventy Christmas cards, each with a twenty inside. Each card was accompanied by a handshake and a sincere thank you, gracious to the point we got watery-eyed. Most of the staff wanted to become Mob associates and work for this guy. Such sincerity and graciousness. We couldn't believe these guys were supposedly involved in criminal activity. But it mattered not. To us, these guys were gods, and would always get whatever they wanted, whenever they wanted, inside or outside of the restaurant. Always.

And to those who might argue that the Mob's alleged illicit and unethical activity enables them to produce more income and, thus, spend money more generously, I insist you have no basis for such an argument. Money spent in a restaurant is a percentage of how much money or credit one owns or possesses. The Mob doesn't know how much money you have nor do you know how much money the Mob has, making your feeble-minded argument moot. I recommend

you scrutinize the absence of ethics in your own life before
you endeavor to judge the boys of organized crime.

"An exact death toll and definitive list of names of those killed in the New York City attacks of September 11, 2001 will never be known due to the undeterminable number of homeless people lost that day."

—Vander Braveaux

Chapter 16

A Vagrant's Chafing Dish

(The Lonesome Jubilee)

"But before you come to any conclusions
Try walking in my shoes,
Try walking in my shoes."

Depeche Mode, "Walking in My Shoes,"
Songs of Faith and Inspiration, Warner Brothers, 1993.

To win in this life, you have to connect the dots. Don't connect the dots, and you'll die unfulfilled. Restaurant people see two dots that rarely get connected. The first dot is wasted food. The second dot is hungry people. Many of the hungry live on the streets in the harshest of harsh worlds, losers in the worst possible way. Forgotten souls who are devoured by a different kind of invisible shark, dying unfulfilled because the dots never got connected.

Seeing vast heaps of food thrown away is surely the most disturbing of all the troubling sights in a modern commercial kitchen. Perfectly edible food thrown away like water over a fall. The majority of the waste occurs in two ways. First is the kitchen's excess production of prepared items like sauces, soups, potatoes, vegetables, casseroles, breads, cakes, and even meats. Sauces break or have limited microbiological shelf lives, vegetables lose their texture and color, breads and cakes become stale, and precision cooked meats and roasts become tough and juiceless. Food not recycled or force-fed to the staff is pitched, two and three times a day, every day.

There are thousands of hungry adults and children throughout the city to whom that food, albeit secondhand, would have meant so much. But they never see a crumb. The reason why is liability and the lawyer who would pay off his seven-figure Glen Echo brownstone by representing one sick street person who became ill after eating redirected restaurant food. No restaurateur, no matter how philanthropic, wants to open himself up to more liability. He already has the Dram Shop Law (Alvin Alky drives his Dodge Intrepid into a day care center full of Jerry's kids, and sues his watering hole), and patrons doing premise pratfalls in search of quick cash settlements. If the restaurateur survives the lawyer's wrath, he may not survive the damage done to his restaurant's reputation. Hence, food production excesses never make it to a shelter, soup kitchen, or church basement. All of it is just thrown away. Welcome to America.

The other major form of food toss in restaurants is food served but not eaten, and in this SUV age of power gluttony, many meals go unfinished. This is especially true at steak houses where giant pieces of beef, enough to satiate a lion pride, are thrown away. Food that could have provided nourishment and nutrients for the malnourished is simply discarded. The dots remain unconnected. A conservative estimate on beef wasted is anywhere from one to four ounces of meat per customer, which multiplies out to more than two steers a year per server. For me, that's thirty head of cattle, plus a half-dozen toddler cows compliments of the veal demand. Good company for the twenty-two miles worth of discarded bottles emptied by my customers, all from one waiter over a fifteen year period. This is not even factoring in the uneaten percentage of the 16,000 pounds of lobster I served during that time. Somebody please shoot me.

The only consumable not wasted in a restaurant is alcohol, which the staff drank like staggering cavaliers in large part due to the distress of seeing so much good food get wasted. The waste that clangs the town bell of affirmation that what we do in a restaurant is wrong—feeding the corpulent, pouring stumblers their fixes, monetarily raping the patrons, and then chucking out dump trucks full of perfectly edible food. As John Mellencamp says, *"The ugly truths that freedom brings."*[†] Waste is part of life, but unlike the child's fad toy whose Teletubby antennas will be poking out of a landfill in five month's time, all that discarded food could have lessened someone's pain. But it never happened, at least not with restaurants, and all that food got thrown away in greasy, square-wheeled, roach-covered, rat-rocking dumpsters. The vagrant's chafing dish.

[†]A lyric from John Cougar Mellencamp's song "Jackie Brown," from the album *Big Daddy*, (Mercury) 1989, the follow-up to Mellencamp's incredible 1987 album, *The Lonesome Jubilee*. *"But we keep no check on our appetites, so the green fields turn to brown like paper in fire."*

New Slogans For Las Vegas:

Only jerks trash their hotel rooms

Responsible gaming?, ¿Que es eso?

Where has-been bankrupt pop stars come to die
(Air Supply, everyone's looking at you)

What happened in Vegas will be revealed on
Maury Povich *(And the father of Baby Bellagio is...)*

You've overstayed your welcome
(Like a Friday morning Thanksgiving guest)

TSA will be searching your luggage
for towels and flatware

Give us till noon to clean up the vomit

If you brought your children, you're much
too stupid to win anything in our casinos

What happens in Vegas disgraces your family

A three hour wait and monster cover charge
gets you into our finest nightclubs

The over-Red Bulled rental skank who shows up
at your hotel room will look NOTHING like the
one on the porn pamphlet

Get married here every year ... and divorce in Reno

Where corrupt NFL refs come to collect their
Superbowl winnings *(Offensive pass interference my ass!)*

We support responsible gaming ... in New Hampshire

That tuxedoed dude holding the giant lobster
is actually a midget holding a crayfish

Don't know how to party? Our mayor will show you

Tip the maid or she'll scrub the crapper with
your toothbrush *(Seriously)*

Chapter 17

When Elephants Go Mad

(*Come to Vegas and get destroyed*)

"Watch me tearing myself to pieces
Hunting high and low."

a-ha, "Hunting High and Low,"
Hunting High and Low, Warner Bros., 1985

Penguins don't fly. They just wander about the Antarctic with the weight of the world on their minds, lonely nomads dreaming about being able to fly. Sometimes they dive into the sea and soar under water, but the grip of the icy ocean never lets them forget that penguins don't fly.

Self-assessment, deductive reasoning, and meditation on lessons learned can tell a person a great deal about where they are and where they are going. I pondered my lessons. The most important was that intelligent people look down the road of life to see what lay ahead. For me, it was a cliff into a black oblivion. No happy ending in a restaurant for me, only personal mental calamity. The only person who harbors any possibility of changing your life is yourself. And for me, a change was double-past due.

Leaving King Lear wouldn't be easy, but I couldn't stand to stay. If I didn't escape now, the straight ahead for me was a jump from the top of a tall building. No exaggeration, only the factual scientific equation that uncontented whereabouts divided by sanity times velocity equals acceleration to the square root of madness, solved for the integer self reduces to the fraction that would be one sidewalk-pancaked penguin.

I felt like the circus elephant that went mad. She tried to be a good sport, to please the crowds and do all the tricks that made everyone happy, but she had been pushed too far. Her trainer knew it, too, even pleaded with the circus owners that this elephant just couldn't do it anymore. But no. No one listened or cared. She was just an elephant, a piece of property, a thick-skinned hay-eater. So one day that elephant cracked, going insane and killing her trainer, running down the street screaming. After the authorities gunned her down, the elephant leaned against a car dying with a look in her eyes that said "Why did this happen to me? I tried to be good, to get everyone's approval. I tried my best to get through it, and look what you did to me." Her name was Tyke. She was killed on September 20, 1994 in Hawaii. It took Honolulu police a hundred rounds to bring her down.[†]

I felt like that elephant, and maybe I, too, would have to be gunned down in the street.

I was thirty-three and desperate for my chance to escape, depressed daily by all who surrounded me, people who had stopped trying. The abused faces of people who dragged their feet, pumped themselves full of pollutants, and hammered the nails of fate into their own coffins. People content to stay stuck in the La Brea tar pit of vice.

Intelligent people not only look down the road, but they also accept the blame for their own life's whereabouts. The blame for my own unhappiness fell squarely on me. There was no blame for the lobster, or the elephant, but there was for me. I had accomplished nothing in my thirty-three years, especially my highest desire to become a naval aviator.

Navy fliers my age were lieutenant commanders with Desert Storm ribbons on their blues, logbooks full of high-tech flight time, and mailboxes stuffed full of six-digit airline job offers. They had beautiful wives and well-mannered children named after cities in Texas, and spent their weekends on their boats or at their beach homes in Cape Cod, sipping Opus One and looking out over the Atlantic while musing philosophy, stock

[†] Circus elephant rampages resulted in 74 human fatalities worldwide between 1993 and 2004. Elephant training methods include food, water and sleep deprivation, pen confinement, chained leg constriction, electric shock, and club beatings. The most distressful event for an elephant, however, is the temporary or permanent separation from family members. It's hell to never forget.

picks, and self-worth. When they weren't on their boats or judging the ocean, they were hiking in Europe or skiing in Telluride, laughing fireside, or sitting in a steamy Jacuzzi with a giant mug of hot chocolate cut with Peppermint Schnapps.

Such speculations of Schnapps, Jacuzzis, and idealism about other people's lives held little truth, but such thoughts fueled my desire to escape all the more, particularly when assessing the facts as they pertained to my brief existence on this planet so far. I wasn't enjoying life, not even close, and the highest rank I had ever attained was maître d'— managing drunken waiters, thieving coked-up busmen, and pathetic patrons (the adjectives are interchangeable) who looked at me with disdain and saw only a servant who worked in a restaurant by default, a sad man who was a failure, someone not good enough to marry their daughters. If I had, they would have broken the news to their friends and family with the same solemnity as if saying she was terminally ill. I didn't spend my weekends at the shore. Instead I was working at the same time most other people were relaxing and enjoying themselves. I had never made it to Europe and skiing might have led to a broken leg, leaving me unable to support myself. Time was slipping away fast, life's hourglass having been flipped long ago, its center of gravity lower with each passing day. At the same time F/A-18 Hornet pilots were making night traps on the USS *Carl Vinson,* snagging the three-wire on the cutting edge of life, I was playing car key keepaway with customers who needed three penguins to stand up straight, trying to figure out who puked in the piano, and trying to convince the piano tuner that it was his job to clean it up. I was getting nothing done, only dying in every way possible, listening to the calendar pages flipping away in the back of my mind while achieving a new high in self-loathing.

Drink denied that feeling for temporary periods, but the battering ram of reality always followed, pounding on the door, each additional blow getting harder and louder, letting me know it was time to get moving. That, or jump. I desperately wanted to have honor in my life, to do something noble, to exist for thinking, not fetching. I wanted to marry a woman of worth and have a son or daughter. But all the things I wanted in life were contingent upon my learning to love myself, and that wasn't happening as long as I was rotting away in a restaurant.

The first move to save myself was to leave King Lear, or find that tall building. It was past time to get my ass to flight school. I didn't have enough money, but would have to figure it out along the way. Naval aviators my age were ten years ahead of me in their flight educations, a tormenting thought that so filled my heart with jealousy that I almost felt comforted when I read about military pilots killed. But I couldn't ever take satisfaction in other people dying, reminding myself of the grief of their families left behind, children without daddies, mothers without sons, and fathers without their boys. The scourge of the invisible sharks. But at least such men and women died with honor. If I died as a waiter, if I died in a restaurant, it would be damnation of the cruelest kind. It was time to go.

When I left King Lear, the true colors of those around me came to light. Most were sad to see me leave, many expressing themselves with thoughtful gestures and gifts. Pearl Styles gave me an entire case of Vancluse-Jaxon Reserve Juxtapose, a Bordeaux-inspired dark fruit and cedarish, wicked fine red wine blend from the Cypress Valley. Jody and Gavin took me to dinner at Vidalia and expressed how my departure would be a tremendous blow to the high standards of King Lear. Colonel LaSalle gave me a picture of him standing next to his B-26 taken after his one hundredth mission with an inscription that was a line from Macbeth that read, "To John, Always remember, *If we fail, we fail, but screw your courage to that sticking place, and we'll not fail.* Your Friend, Lawrence." Clay Papandreas and Jackie Eastman each gave me a loan to help pay for flight school and a couple of the Mobbies insisted I join them for an ancient orange snifter of Grand Marnier Cent Cinquatenaire. Micky gave me a hundred dollars and a promise to snuff anyone I wished, which I actually stopped to think about. Several other customers gave me cards and congratulations, even Catherine broke her DAR silence and bid me farewell.

But a couple of my fellow penguins did not wish me well, but instead bid me a black-hearted "get the fuck out." The most

vocal was King Lear's Beatles freak, Tyler Orr, the shortest of
D.C.'s short waiters, now a breakless alcoholic and drug drone.

I had paid my state and federal taxes the same week I left for
Florida, and Ty asked me how much I had declared one morning
while setting up. Thinking nothing of it, I told him the truth,
$45,200 for the year, even though I had made a couple thousand
more than that. The second I quoted the figure, Ty snapped and
began yelling at me, asking why I had declared so much. I told
him that I always declared within five percent of what I made
and that the thought of being beaten and gang raped in a prison
shower made me want to obey the law. The system does work.
Ty had made about the same amount of money I had, as did all
the penguins, but hadn't declared even half of his earnings. He
screamed, "God damn it, Galloway! You're going to get the
entire fucking restaurant audited by over-declaring! None of the
other waiters have declared more than $25,000 and when the IRS
sees the discrepancy, we're fucked!" Ty was incorrect when he
suggested that all the penguins had severely under-declared their
incomes. Most had declared the majority of what they made,
several every cent, but angry Ty and a few others had not.

Tyler Orr, whose drinking, coke blowing, and pill popping
had escalated proportionately with his marital warring, had
declared only $18,400, just over a third of his actual income,
landing him a sizable tax refund check, at a sizable risk, a risk he
had taken in several previous years as I later learned. He was a King
Lear waiter, owned a home and two cars, had a wife who was a
lawyer and together they made upper-middle class money. But
on paper, they almost qualified for food stamps. That morning,
Ty rallied a few other penguins against me and made it a point
to tell everyone what I had declared. Sinclair and Angus, who were
both every-penny claimers, asked me why I had told Ty what I
had declared. I said, "Because Ty asked me," to which Angus said
I should have lied or simply refused to say.

Ty kept on barking and moaning at me all that morning. I
finally returned his hostility saying, "Damn it, Ty, that's enough.
Don't try and instruct me on how to cheat the government. I'm
not in collusion with you or anyone else in this God damn

restaurant. I'll pay what I feel is appropriate and you do the same and if the IRS does audit this place, then deal with it! And why don't you ease up on the fucking breakfast wine? You're out of control!" After firing my last syllable, I knew that I had stepped over the verbal line of fair exchange, but I couldn't stand to listen to his beratings anymore, the words just flowed out of my mouth. When people fight, cruel words often do.

From a customer, I would have to withstand a certain amount of abuse, but not from a snorting coworker. The "breakfast wine" comment struck a painful nerve with Ty, a battering ram bang on his subconscious door, more hurtful than me saying anything about his felonious tax filings. Though now clearly an alcoholic, he was deeply entrenched in the denial phase, hissing and moaning to the point that Gavin suspended him for both shifts that day. Ty was watching his world crumble fast, drunken most of the time and spending his spare cash on cocaine. With his increased chemical usage came arrogance, common among sniffers who think the world is blind to their little sniveling habit. Ty confirmed his air of arrogance when Mitch and Omar advised him to ease up on the euphoria powder. Ty replied, "I know what I'm doing, damn it. How dare people like you accuse me of being arrogant? This place is full of imbeciles!"

During the last four days we worked together, Ty and I spoke only once. It was my last shift at King Lear, an hour before closing on a Saturday night. I still had tables but saw Ty was doing his checkout at the service bar. I walked over, sincerely apologized for my comments, and extended my hand. Ty refused to shake, looking me square in the eye, and saying, "Fuck you, Galloway. I hope you crash and burn."

Preston, who had just finished his own checkout at the service bar, saw my face turn tombstone cold and jumped between me and Ty, though there was no need. Someone here needed intervention but it wasn't me. I wasn't about to ruin seven years of hard work by pummeling Ty, nor let his rage infect me. Instead I repeated myself, still with sincerity, saying, "Like I said, Tyler, I'm sorry for what I said on Tuesday. You take care of yourself." It was my last night at King Lear, and I was able to avoid confrontation just as Constantine had advised me several years before. More furious than ever, Ty gave me the executioner's eye and stormed off.

Preston looked at me and said, "Don't let the tiny man piss you off, John. He's just uptight 'cause he worked waiting tables for eight years putting his wife through college and law school and she's probably gonna divorce his ass."

I said, "All women are whores, huh?"

Preston said, "I've been trying to tell you that for ten years now and here it is your last night and you *finally* got it straight."

I said, "Even . . ." and Presto cut me off saying, "Ahhtt. There are no exceptions. None."

To this day I regret what I said to Tyler Orr. You can never take back cruel words, so your best strategy is to never speak them. But sometimes you feel like you've just been pushed too far. Ty had been picked on all of his life for his vertical measure, something over which he had no control, and which meant nothing in the grand scheme—unless you live in America where looks, strength, and stature mean everything and intelligence, moral fiber, integrity, character, and compassion are just knick-knacks and afterthoughts. Tyler had the same feelings as I did about restaurant work, but as I became depressed and withdrawn, Ty just coked, toked, pilled, and drank as many veteran waiters do. Ty had a lot of great things going for him, but all his positive traits were overshadowed by the depression of working in a restaurant, being ridiculed his entire life for his physical stature, and having a genetic disposition that left him unable to resist the temptations of drugs and alcohol. His lack of resistance would cost him more than just cash for an eightball, money due for a dime bag, or the price of another round. The long and winding road, indeed.

As it turned out Tyler, Preston, and I were all correct in our suspicions of what the morrow would bring. As Preston predicted, Tyler's wife did divorce him and marry a partner in her law firm, and though I still question Preston's whore theory, it proved accurate in regard to the Orr ex.

Ty was correct about the audit. The IRS did audit King

Lear's penguins in 1997, four of whom ended up serving jail time, with five others sentenced to probation and a few months at halfway houses.

And I was right about Dante being trouble and Ty's losing his battle with the bottle. Dante was the worst of King Lear's tax evaders. Though fired after the thwarted assault on a U.S. Marshal in 1996, he continued to work as a waiter at several upscale restaurants throughout the District. Still being paid in cash, he hadn't filed taxes in over a decade and would be in debt to the government for the rest of his life when the IRS caught up to him. The Fed's grip on Dante wouldn't last long. At last word, he had gotten out of prison after two years served, broke parole, and is rumored to be living somewhere in California, dealing drugs and beating on women. If you live in California and know a short, crude, dark-haired man who does drugs, has a bad temper and a propensity toward domestic violence, that's Dante. Please call the local authorities immediately.

The audit cost me $900, which I paid from Florida, and Sir Tyler Orr, a whopping $30,000 and a three-month stay at the Razorwire Resort, released a month early for good behavior. Tyler would only have to pay $15,000 of the debt, his ex-wife was liable for the other half, but Ty increased his debts by another $20,000 by getting two DWIs in three weeks in the summer of 1998. The second offense was a hit-and-run on a suspended license. That cost him his driving privileges for several years and his self-respect permanently. He blamed his ex-wife, his ex-wife blamed him, and I blamed his vocation.

Along with Ty and Dante, Omar, and King Lear's albino-haired custodian of the cannabis, Dustin Vannoy, were the other penguins to serve prison sentences for tax evasion, though Ty was the only one of the cheatin' four who hadn't previously been a jump-suited, rifle-guarded trash-poker of the Commonwealth of Virginia. *Note:* In August of 2005, Preston wrote a book entitled *"Chicken Soup for the Soul Brother."*

I had two more stops left before I could bow out of the restaurant business completely. Augustine's in election-notorious West Palm Beach was second to last. Flight training is an expensive mistress, more costly than a Trump ex. The price of multi-engine instruction in a light twin is approximately one American dollar for every fifteen seconds. Time is counted from the instant the master battery is switched on, which is, by no small coincidence, at the top of the procedures list. Your plane may be roaring on the ground, slated fifteenth for takeoff, vectored out to Tampa for an approach into Orlando, put in a holding pattern for a half hour, or you may simply bust a flight lesson because you said a chart marking was red when the instructor was looking to hear the word "magenta." All that time is money out of your pocket. When you fail a lesson, a remedial flight is required as well as a redo of the original flight itself, making a pink-sheeted lesson about a thousand-dollar affair. Then it was Kraft macaroni and cheese for a month. Other flight school pricy items include textbooks, landing fees, approach plates and maps (all with milk-like expiration dates), simulator time and classroom instruction; as well as food, housing, and uniforms. The drive back and forth to West Palm was tiring, but the job was good, without which I may have not finished my initial flight training.

Ty's wish that I crash almost happened twice. The first time was during a take-off roll on a wet runway in Pahokee. My Piper Commanche blew a tire on runway debris and went into a skid. Fortunately I had attained enough speed to get airborne and avoid the spinout. The subsequent landing back in Vero Beach was rough but without incident.

The second time was in a Beechcraft Duchess BE-76 during a precision instrument approach with severely compromised visibility due to the extensive forest fires in Florida at the time. A low-time solo student in a PA-18 Super Cub in violation of visual flight rules visibility minimums blew across my flight path. Fortunately the instructor sitting next to me caught the Cub just in time to pitch our plane up and avoid a mid-air collision. We missed hitting the student by less than fifty feet, a very short distance for converging aircraft. ATC apologized for dropping the ball. I was just glad I was alive to hear it, however furious.

Living in Florida made me realize how much I missed Washington. There isn't a discernable sense of culture or history in Florida. People go to convenience stores barefoot, and tattoos on women are mandatory (known as "tramp stamps"). But there were a few things I did like about the Sunshine State, in particular the several dozen foxes that lived in the woods on the airport grounds. Some were defiant enough to walk in front of the taxiing aircraft, knowing the pilots would always brake. I also marveled at the space shuttle launches and the sonic booms of their return, Vero Beach being just south of Cape Canaveral. There are also the lightning storms whose ground-striking bolts rattle your windows and bring such fierce rains that it makes the world seem like it's underwater.

But Florida also helped me realize how much I hate insects, especially fire ants. And where there is water and heat, there will be bugs, and brutal, asthma-inducing humidity, and senior citizens who never cared much for sunscreen, and endless strip malls that will someday connect Jacksonville and Marco Island, and heartless compulsives betting on starving greyhounds, and bedroom-darting geckos who are too quick to be caught, and manatees half-mutilated by speed boat propellers, and the smell of salty driftwood and chopped bait shrimp, and road-crossing turtles endeavoring not to get squashed. Usually without success.

Las Vegas was the final bastion in my career of restaurant travail. Despite the tight grip of Philip Morris, I found Vegas is a very pleasant place to live. There's little humidity, some wildlife, no state tax, and the magnificent winter cloud formations shadowing the snow-capped mountains defy description.

Easily described are the many destitute gambling addicts, wandering the casino floors like forlorn lovers, regressing to an integer far less than their means, hanging on by threads. Such chancers believe the phrase "house statistical advantage" to be a shoddy myth or unsubstantiated hypothesis, forever trying to swim upstream against a relentless current that splashes down on them four times faster than their best stroke. They've pawned everything stolen, borrowed or formally owned for a fraction of the value and left it all on the felt tables. But perhaps the best way to describe a pathological gambler is to image a person with a raging hunger. You can give them a sandwich so large it takes a million bites to eat, but the very next day, the sandwich is gone and they're starving again. Just thank God your name isn't Pathy Gambi.

And, of course, in Vegas, there are the bankrupt and bloated tourista slow walkers. They have survived two weeks of bad gambling and sensory-overloading buffets. They wear elastic-waist pants and can barely move, though with melted ATM cards and the buffet lines closed for restocking, they have no destination anyway. Their only remaining task is to somehow squeeze through the airplane door and hope that the jet can still attain lift given the additional human tonnage.

People visit Las Vegas to behave in ways they never would in their own towns, especially in the baboon pens otherwise known as "gentlemen's clubs" where rowdy cowboys from Lubbock howl like wolves beneath the full moon. Vegas life revolves around the Strip, despite the many sights outside of the city that only fools would not run to see. Hoover Dam is an incredible monolithic creation, built at a cost of 500 lives. The Grand Canyon also merits a visitation, and for those willing, you can burro down, fly over, raft-thru, chopper in, or train beside to see Natural Wonder number 3 of 7.

To the west of Vegas is Red Rock Canyon, a national park comprised of undisturbed (for now) mountain ridges. Some of the mountain summits are climbable. My favorite is Turtlehead Peak. Though it took three hours and four liters of water to get to the top, the view from 6,721 feet above sea level proved worth the caloric expenditure. From the top, Turtlehead Peak is devoid of sound, and on a clear day you can see Utah, Arizona, and California. Las Vegas appears as just a small patch on the eastern horizon.

A little further to the west, yet less than a hundred miles from the Strip is Death Valley, a spectacular dry lakebed in the Mojave Desert. It is the size of Manhattan, 282 feet below sea level.

Ironically, Death Valley may save the life of drying, dying Lake Mead. A gravity-flow aqueduct could be constructed to fill Death Valley with nearby Pacific Ocean water, and from there the water could be desalinated and pipelined to Lake Mead.

Every couple months in Las Vegas, a displaced and hungry mountain lion will venture into the suburban sprawl. The residential hens cry foul and invariably the poor creature is destroyed. Perhaps the new city motto should be *"Come to Vegas and get destroyed."*

Although I liked Nevada much more than Florida, I knew with great certainty that I belonged back east. Las Vegas didn't have insects or dog tracks, but it also didn't have trees, and I love tall trees. Seeing trees reminds me of autumn in Washington and long bike rides along the Potomac River where the bike trail is crowded by giant, majestic trees—the natural pillars of this earth. These trees stand tall throughout time. They were there when your dog was just a puppy. There when a blizzard canceled school. There when your mom made your Halloween costume. There when you played football in the rain. There when loved ones lost were still alive. These trees were your noble friends who always listened, always cared. Vegas is a better city than rumors suggest, but I missed the trees too much to stay in the desert forever.

Cosmic cues, symbolic metaphors, and intuition have always played a significant role in my life. In 1975, three months after my mother died, an enormous old tree she had saved from the lot clearer's chainsaw fell over on our driveway after a late season ice storm. It was the day before we were supposed to move out of the house she had designed, built, and died in.

In 1987, I knew, in the middle of the morning, the very moment my sister died, ten minutes before my dad called to tell me. Liz had given me a picture of a Rhode Island gull and on the back she had written "Mervin, my pet seagull." Since her passing, Mervin would visit me at very coincidental times and places.

In 1998, after a ten-hour Mother's Day shift at Augustine's, I was sitting in the accountant's office with a fellow server and good friend, Josephine. It was raining and we were having a glass of wine, talking as I was playing with a penny I had found on the floor. Jo asked me if Mother's Days were bothersome to me because I had lost mine as a boy. While pondering my response, I looked down at the penny I was holding to see that the year it was minted was 1975.

The beginning of the end of my service career began on the final hour of the last day of the first year of the third millennium, and reconciling my restaurant career was like getting a new lease on life. The symbolic metaphors were everywhere. On Christmas Eve of 2000, I had just finished a flight at the North Las Vegas Air Terminal. In the parking lot standing next to my car was Mervin, there to wish me a Merry Christmas. More intriguing than the time was the place. This seagull was well over two hundred miles away from the nearest ocean.†

That New Year's Eve, I drove away from Romeo Charlie's just as the first of 13,000 rockets exploded from ten different hotel roofs welcoming in the new year. On the radio, the song "Faith of the Heart" was playing. *"It's been a long night, trying to find my way. Been through the darkness. Now I finally have my day."* The day after the Purdue Boilermakers played the Washington Huskies in the Rose Bowl. I had spent a third of my life serving Washington huskies. Purdue didn't prevail, but I would.

The number 222, the month and day I was born, was coming up everywhere: time left in a football quarter, a license plate number in front of me in traffic, time remaining on the microwave, or the number of miles on the trip odometer. Even when it was a quarter past midnight, the clock always seemed to read 2:22. My favorite musical group, whose songs had depicted the trials and turmoil of my life (*"and all of us, who are traveling by trap doors, our souls are a myriad of wars, and I'm losing everyone,"* a lyric from their 1987 album *Stay On These Roads*, Warner Bros.), released their first album in seven years. Norwegians Magne Furuholmen, Paul Waaktaar-Savoy, and Morten Harket, better known as the pop trio a-ha, released British Music Presses' twenty-ninth best new album of 2000, *Minor Earth, Major Sky*. The CD cover was a boneyard picture of the detached head of a Boeing 727 with "a-ha" painted on the side. *"Can you hear me when I speak out loud, hear my voice above the crowd. And I try, and I try, and I try, but it never comes out right. Yes I try and I try and I try, but I never get it right. But it's a minor earth, a major sky."* (Minor Earth, Major Sky, *Minor*

---

† The California Gull is not only found in Nevada, but abundantly further east in Utah. The *Larus californious* was credited for saving pioneer settlers in the summer of 1848 by eating swarms of black crickets that were destroying crops. In 1955, the California Gull became Utah's State bird.

Earth, Major Sky, Warner Bros., 2000.)

Yet another cosmic cue came on the third evening of the new year. As I was tuning in the Orange Bowl, I came across the conclusion of *The Shawshank Redemption.* Tim Robbins was standing in the rain after escaping Shawshank by crawling through a sewage pipe. "Andy Dufresne, who crawled through a river of shit and came out clean on the other side." I didn't feel clean, but I would. The process might take the rest of my life, but it would happen.

I would stop drinking like a frat pledge, easily done once away from the places that made me want to numb myself. I would still enjoy a few glasses of wine here and there, but not even close to the hundreds of bottles a year like I had been drinking.

I would become one of those intolerable fitness types, committed to working out, and cognizant of diet, water intake, fat percentages, and cardiovascular rates, trying to undo twenty-two years of abuse. Much of the damage was irreparable, but I had to try.

I would become much more spiritual but not very religious, confident in my conclusion that a few weekly hours of philanthropic activism accomplished more than sitting in a church pew, daydreaming during the sermon and coveting other parishioners' wives.

But most of all, I had to remember how lucky I was to have made it out unbroken. Battered and bruised, but not broken.

It was time to go, to shove off. No more whiskey tango. The sea I would sail wouldn't always be calm. There would be bumps on the road ahead, and invisible sharks for sure, but somehow I had survived to this moment, and had earned my wings along the way. The chocks had been kicked out and an arduous preflight that started at the age of fourteen was finally done. Now it was time to strap in, check the wind, advance the throttles and fly.

That, and to go back to Virginia to the banks of the Potomac and spend some time with the trees.

About the Author

John Galloway is the author of FINE DINING MADNESS, a humorous, autobiographical book about his experiences in fine dining. He says the motivations for writing the book were many, the predominant being his gift for humor, wealth of unbelievable experiences, of which he was "tired of recounting by word of mouth," and the opportunity to school all diners on restaurant world realities. He credits his father as being the primary catalyst in writing his book.

Born in Indianapolis in 1963, and raised in Carmel, Indiana, John graduated from Purdue University in 1985. His vast, hard knocks hospitality education was honed in the private clubs and upscale restaurants of Indianapolis and West Lafayette, Indiana; Cincinnati; Washington, D.C.; Alexandria, Virginia; West Palm Beach, Florida; and Las Vegas.

In 1997, after ten years working in front-house fine dining in Washington, D.C., John moved to Vero Beach, Florida to attend commercial flight training at Flight Safety Academy. He is now a Certified Flight Instructor and Commercial Seaplane Pilot with Multi-Engine Instructor, Instrument Instructor, and Glider ratings.

John enjoys visiting his father in Boston, as well as hiking, mountain biking, skydiving, and flying. His favorite aircraft to pilot are seaplanes, for which "70% of the world is your runway." His interests also include animal welfare, environmental issues, American history and his personal ancestry. On page 178 is the 1864 obituary of his great, great grandfather, Lieutenant Elias Alexander Galloway (Wisconsin 36th Infantry, Company K). Lt. Galloway was mortally wounded in the Union assault on Petersburg, Virginia. John's paternal grandfather, Colonel Clark Hewett Galloway, was a veteran of WWI and WWII, and John's father, John, Sr., is a retired doctor who served as an infantry officer in the Korean War (Third Division, 65th Infantry, Fox Company) before attending medical school in Nebraska.

Currently John is modifying an aircraft he and three other pilots will fly in homage to all who have served in the United States armed forces, and most especially, those killed in Afghanistan and Iraq. The plane is called *The Tribute* and the names of the fallen will be painted on wings and fuselage. For more information about *The Tribute* and its historic mission, log onto: www.TributeFlight.com.

Media representation for all of John Galloway's books
provided by BookPros in Austin, Texas
(www.bookpros.com)

Interior layout by Erich Kocher Design
(e.kocher@sbcglobal.net, kocherdesign.com)

Edited by Dr. Judith Goldberg and the Harvard team.
For editing questions, comments, or to report an
error, contact Leah Sanchez at HarvardUEditor@aol.com
reference number FDM63Q97Z5.

A thirsty Dora. Photograph by Roy Conklin.

"No more whiskey tango."

978-0-595-33777-4
0-595-33777-5

Printed in the United States
122761LV00001B/257/A